The New International Monetary System

THE NEW INTERNATIONAL MONETARY SYSTEM

ROBERT A. MUNDELL

AND

JACQUES J. POLAK

EDITORS

NEW YORK   COLUMBIA UNIVERSITY PRESS   1977

LIBRARY OF CONGRESS CATALOGING IN PUBLICATION DATA

CONFERENCE ON THE NEW INTERNATIONAL MONETARY SYSTEM,
WASHINGTON, D. C., 1976.
THE NEW INTERNATIONAL MONETARY SYSTEM.

CONFERENCE SPONSORED BY THE INTERNATIONAL MONETARY FUND
AND COLUMBIA UNIVERSITY AS A MEMORIAL
TO J. MARCUS FLEMING.
INCLUDES BIBLIOGRAPHICAL REFERENCES.
1. INTERNATIONAL FINANCE—CONGRESSES.   2. FOREIGN
EXCHANGE PROBLEM—CONGRESSES.   3. INTERNATIONAL
LIQUIDITY—CONGRESSES.   I. MUNDELL, ROBERT A.
II. POLAK, JACQUES JACOBUS.   III. FLEMING, JOHN
MARCUS, 1911–1976.   IV. INTERNATIONAL MONETARY FUND.
V. COLUMBIA UNIVERSITY.   VI. TITLE.
HG3881.C663 1976   332.4'5   77-10485
ISBN 0-231-04368-6

COLUMBIA UNIVERSITY PRESS
NEW YORK   GUILDFORD, SURREY
COPYRIGHT © 1977 COLUMBIA UNIVERSITY PRESS
PRINTED IN THE UNITED STATES OF AMERICA

CONTENTS

CONTENTS

Session 4. Techniques to Control International Reserves

Concluding Remarks

PREFACE

THE CONFERENCE on The New International Monetary System, held at the International Monetary Fund (IMF) headquarters in Washington, D.C. on November 11–12, 1976, derived its impetus from the desire for a suitable memorial to the late J. Marcus Fleming and the recent adoption by the Board of Governors of the Second Amendment to the IMF Articles of Agreement, which was then in the process of ratification by IMF member countries.

As Deputy Director of the Research Department, Fleming had played an important role in the shaping of the new international monetary system embodied in the Second Amendment. Earlier in his career he had also served as Professor of Economics at Columbia University; thus the IMF and Columbia University decided to sponsor this conference jointly. The conference represents part of the continuing interaction between academicians and policymakers—a dialogue to which J. Marcus Fleming contributed much in his lifetime. The significance of the crosscurrents between the two spheres is further underscored by participation in the conference of academicians and high officials in national and international institutions.

The international monetary system has undergone profound changes in the last few years. Many of these changes are embodied in the Second Amendment to the IMF Articles of Agreement. The conference was designed to elicit the views of the participants on two sets of problems that will be crucial to the operation of the reformed international monetary system, namely, exchange rates and international liquidity.

The first topic concerns the proper role of national and international authorities in a flexible exchange-rate system. Fundamental to this topic is the relationship between monetary policy and foreign-exchange rates.

Should countries coordinate their monetary policies to attain a reasonable degree of exchange-rate stability? If this is feasible, what operational problems might emerge? Part of the same complex of problems is the proper role of the IMF in discharging its mandate to exercise firm surveillance over the exchange-rate policies of member countries.

The second problem area addressed at the conference relates to the control over international liquidity. Is such control feasible and desirable under a system of widespread floating exchange rates—including those of reserve currencies? What will be the role of the various reserve assets, such as, gold, foreign currencies, and IMF-related assets in the new international monetary system? What is the impact of public and private international credit facilities? And finally, what avenues would be open to the international community to control international liquidity if this should be deemed desirable? All of these are important policy questions that need to be answered if informed policy choices are to be made. It is hoped that the results of this conference will lead to a clearer understanding of the issues and problems involved and contribute to resolving these questions.

Many individuals contributed to the planning and organization of the conference, and we are grateful to all of them. The Managing Director of the Fund, H. Johannes Witteveen, and the Board of Executive Directors took a keen interest in the conference from its inception. We are grateful for the excellent cooperation received from the IMF Administration Department under the direction of Phillip Thorson, and the Secretary's Department under W. Lawrence Hebbard. H. Robert Heller, Chief of the Financial Studies Division of the Research Department, assisted in the planning of the conference and the editing of this volume. The summaries of the discussions were prepared by Malcolm Knight and Joanne Salop of the Research Department. The views expressed are those of the individuals concerned and do not necessarily represent those of the institutions with which they are associated.

R. A. *Mundell*
J. J. *Polak*

viii

PARTICIPANTS

Edward M. Bernstein
EMB Ltd.
Washington, D.C., U.S.A.

Emil-Maria Claassen
Université Paris IX-Dauphine
Paris, France

Richard N. Cooper
Yale University
New Haven, Conn., U.S.A.

Rüdiger Dornbusch
Massachusetts Institute of Technology
Cambridge, Mass., U.S.A.

Otmar Emminger
Deutsche Bundesbank
Frankfurt, Germany

William Fellner
American Enterprise Institute
Washington, D.C., U.S.A.

Ronald Findlay
Columbia University
New York, N.Y., U.S.A.

Herbert Giersch
Institut für Weltwirtschaft
Kiel, Germany

Herbert G. Grubel
Simon Fraser University
Burnaby, Canada

Gottfried Haberler
American Enterprise Institute
Washington, D.C., U.S.A.

Sir Roy Harrod
Oxford University
Oxford, England

Fred Hirsch
University of Warwick
Coventry, England

Samuel I. Katz
Georgetown University
Washington, D.C., U.S.A.

Peter B. Kenen
Princeton University
Princeton, N.J., U.S.A.

Alexandre Lamfalussy
Bank for International Settlements
Basel, Switzerland

Fritz Machlup
New York University
New York, N.Y., U.S.A.

Robert A. Mundell
Columbia University
New York, N.Y., U.S.A.

Rinaldo Ossola
Ministry of Foreign Trade
Rome, Italy

Jacques J. Polak
International Monetary Fund
Washington, D.C., U.S.A.

Walter S. Salant
Brookings Institution
Washington, D.C., U.S.A.

Robert Solomon
Brookings Institution
Washington, D.C., U.S.A.

Robert Triffin
Yale University
New Haven, Conn., U.S.A.

Paul A. Volcker
Federal Reserve Bank of New York
New York, N.Y., U.S.A.

Henry C. Wallich
Board of Governors of the Federal
  Reserve System
Washington, D.C., U.S.A.

Marina v.N. Whitman
University of Pittsburgh
Pittsburgh, Pa., U.S.A.

John Williamson
University of Warwick
Coventry, England

The New International Monetary System

SESSION 1

The Role of Monetary Policy Coordination to Attain Exchange-Rate Stability

OTMAR EMMINGER

DEUTSCHE BUNDESBANK,
FRANKFURT, WEST GERMANY

IN THIS PAPER I briefly discuss whether—and how—better coordination of national monetary policies can contribute to more stable exchange rates.[1]

This problem has not recently arisen with the transition to widespread floating. Coordination of national monetary—and other economic—policies was a watchword already under the Bretton Woods system as an essential condition for balance-of-payments adjustment under fixed parities, and thus for the maintenance of the latter.[2] Now, we have today a mixed exchange-rate system. A large majority of countries have either pegged their currency to another currency—or Special Drawing Rights (SDRs)—or float jointly as a group with fixed but adjustable parities among themselves. Only nineteen countries adhere at present to a system of independent floating, but they comprise important currencies and are responsible for over 50 percent of the total foreign trade of IMF member states.

The problem is, therefore, twofold: what can coordination of monetary policies contribute toward more stability among floating currencies and what can it contribute toward maintaining a more or less fixed exchange-rate relationship between groups of countries?

I illustrate the second problem by referring to the recent discussion on monetary coordination among the member countries of the European Economic Community (EEC), and to the experiences of the member countries of the "snake" currency arrangement.

[1] I do not deal here with monetary coordination in the sense of coordination of interventions in the foreign-exchange markets.

[2] "Monetary policy is the traditional instrument for dealing with difficulties in the balance of payments" (Earl Hicks, in *The Revival of Monetary Policy*, edited by the IMF for the Eighth Annual Meeting of the Board of Governors, September 11, 1953, Washington, D.C.).

OTMAR EMMINGER

Monetary Policy in a Regime of Floating

I start with the assumption that in the foreseeable future the chances for a return of the major currencies to a general par value system are very slim, for reasons on which I do not need to elaborate (e.g., insuperable inflation differentials and the possibility of large destabilizing money and capital flows). Even in the EEC, with its much greater commitment to and formal opportunities of policy coordination, we still have three independently floating currencies (the pound sterling, the French franc, and the Italian lira), and a recent proposal to establish at least target zones—adjustable or variable zones (!)—for the exchange rates of these three currencies has had to be shelved.

Why should the balance of payments not be left "to look after itself" in a regime of floating, at most with the support of occasional smoothing interventions in the foreign-exchange market, so as to avoid disorderly conditions? Why should monetary policy be oriented toward an external goal at all? Is it not one of the essential advantages of floating that in such a system monetary policy can concentrate on its domestic tasks, that is, of maintaining—or restoring—domestic equilibrium?

I hasten to emphasize that the best contribution that monetary policy can make toward stable exchange rates, is, of course, precisely by maintaining domestic equilibrium.[3] Any deflection of monetary policy from this primary goal, such as by large-scale money creation of the central bank for the financing of external surpluses, will in the longer run render a disservice also to international monetary stability.

How far does floating really provide countries with freedom to pursue their domestic monetary goals? For countries like Germany and Switzerland, the main—or even only—reason why they went over to floating in the spring of 1973 was the necessity to *regain control over their own money supply* by ending the obligation to purchase dollars at a fixed price. After the transition to floating they could leave the defense against destabilizing money inflows from abroad largely to the flexible exchange

---

[3] See, for comparison, Annual Report 1975 of the Federal Reserve Bank of New York, p. 21; "Stability in exchange markets cannot be sought except on the basis of adequate domestic stability."

4

rate.[4] Thus they gained new freedom to pursue their antiinflation policies.

On the other hand, deficit countries that are living persistently beyond their means have not gained full freedom over their domestic monetary policies through floating. For if they refuse to effectuate necessary adjustments in real terms—real wages, public borrowing, and so on—their exchange rate will continue to remain under pressure. This may result in the notorious vicious circle of exchange-rate depreciation and inflation. Thus external adjustment through a more flexible exchange rate *does not render domestic adjustment superfluous.* On the contrary, floating may bring out the external constraints to domestic mismanagement more powerfully and more quickly than a fixed exchange rate where the impact of domestic inflation is at first taken on the reserves or on reserve credit.

In the necessary domestic adjustment, monetary policy will usually have to play its role. The vicious circle of exchange depreciation and inflation can only be broken if the central bank ceases to finance inflation. Furthermore, monetary policy is apt to make a positive contribution also by its effect on external capital flows. It is sometimes claimed that a country with a persistently higher inflation rate than its partners can engineer a gradual fall in its exchange rate exactly in line with the inflation differential by maintaining—on a permanent basis—correspondingly higher interest rates so as to balance the downward exchange-rate expectations. According to my experience, the real world is unlikely to be so "rational," especially in its expectations. And a true dilemma may arise if monetary policy, for external reasons, is required to compensate by extreme tightness for lax fiscal policies for too long.

In the recent past we have witnessed temporary excessive fluctuations and overreactions in exchange rates, partly because of the rather long time lag between exchange-rate shifts and their positive effects on trade, and partly in connection with confidence-induced capital movements. Such experiences of "erratic" or "excessive" movements in exchange rates have strengthened the widespread feeling that floating exchange rates

---

[4] Germany was also able to dismantle, after 1973, all other defense measures, such as capital import controls, while Switzerland has not yet been in a position to rely on the flexible exchange rate alone.

have somehow to be "managed." "Managed floating" can imply a number of things. It can mean intervention in the foreign-exchange markets in accordance with certain rules—such as the rules agreed at the Rambouillet Summit Conference of November 1975[5] or the "Guidelines for the Management of Floating Exchange Rates" adopted by the IMF in June 1974. It can also mean an attempt to influence the exchange rate indirectly through official or officially induced borrowing abroad,[6] or through applying trade and payments controls, and so forth. It can also mean pursuing a monetary policy oriented toward the external balance and the exchange rate. This may raise the question as to how far the term "to avoid manipulating exchange rates" in the revised Article IV of the IMF Agreement should be extended into these various fields. And why stop at monetary policy? On this line of reasoning, in the end *all* policies having an impact on the external balance will have to come under the "surveillance" of the IMF.

The Special Role of Monetary Policy

For various reasons, increasing emphasis has been placed on monetary policies and international monetary coordination to influence exchange rates. In a statement at the Annual Meeting in Manila, one governor pointedly termed monetary policy "an instrument for exchange rate management."[7]

Why is monetary policy so often singled out as the main tool for achieving such a goal? There are other economic policies, such as fiscal and incomes policies, which also exert a powerful influence on the external balance and the exchange rate. There are, however, some good grounds for paying special attention to monetary policy in this respect.

First, the exchange rate represents the price relationship between na-

---

[5] To counteract erratic movements but to let underlying trends work themselves out.

[6] I leave aside here the problem as to how far the existence of an inevitable global oil deficit of the oil-importing countries may make a deliberate policy of borrowing abroad unavoidable.

[7] Compare with the statement by Dr. W. Duisenberg, Minister of Finance of the Netherlands.

tional moneys. It is natural to assume that this price relationship is influenced by the relative supply of these moneys and that monetary policy has something to do with it. There are even those who believe that, by simply agreeing on "common norms"[8] for their respective money supplies, a group of countries can stabilize their mutual exchange rates.

Second, monetary policy, either directly or by influencing demand pressures and costs, has a strong impact on price movements, and relative cost and price movements can, of course, be important determinants of the exchange rate (though not the sole nor ultimate ones).

Third, monetary policy can have a very direct effect on the external balance through its influence on external capital flows.

Fourth, the effect of monetary conditions on exchange rates is simply an observed empirical fact; or to quote the 1975 Annual Report of the IMF, p. 19, "A noteworthy feature of exchange rate experience in the last two years has been the powerful effect of changes in relative monetary conditions on exchange rates."

Fifth, monetary policy is, in the eyes of many, the preferred instrument for coordination because it is considered to be much more flexible and more easily manageable than, for instance, budgetary or incomes policies, and can be more easily coordinated internationally.[9]

The Unmanageable Aspect of Monetary Policy

Yet is this really true? We cannot overlook the fact that in many countries monetary conditions are largely influenced—or even determined— by *the size of budget deficits and the way they are financed.* Excessive public sector deficits that cannot be financed out of genuine savings in the private sector, or from abroad, will lead directly or indirectly (through

[8] "Common" in the sense of commonly agreed and coordinated.

[9] See the statement by Guido Carli, former governor of the Banca d'Italia in a lecture delivered at the 24th International Banking Summer School, May 1971, "International cooperation is easier in the case of monetary policy because appropriate institutions exist (the IMF and the BIS), the monetary and credit structures in the various countries show a greater degree of uniformity, and community of interest is more apparent in the monetary field."

7

bank financing) to an expansion of the money supply. Even a fairly independent central bank will, in such circumstances, no longer be a free agent; its monetary policy will at least in part be captive to budget policy.[10] I would, however, not go as far as Mr. E. Hoffmeyer, the Governor of the National Bank of Denmark, who stated in a recent speech, "It is not very fruitful to ask the central bank to control the money supply if no one can control the public deficit."[11] In my view it may be useful or even necessary, by trying to control the money supply, to bring the fact into the open that an excessive public deficit is incompatible both with stability and the needs of the private sector for capital.

Money creation through the budget not only has a great effect on demand and prices in general. As recent events have shown, it can also exert a direct influence on external capital movements. Thus in Italy during the second half of 1975 liquidity creation through oversized budget deficits initiated and facilitated large capital outflows even before political events since the beginning of 1976 exacerbated the pressure on the lira. Similar cases could be quoted from other countries.

The problems involved in money creation via the public sector are reflected in a recent report of the EEC Central Bank Governors. They agreed that in their periodic examinations they should discuss in particular:

—the development of the public sector financing requirement and the differences between member countries in this respect;
—the methods of financing envisaged and their impact, together with that of domestic credit, on the money supply and interest rates;
—the probable effects of the policies pursued on the exchange rate and the balance of payments.

I don't think we can escape the conclusion that *there will not be effective coordination of monetary policies that does not also encompass money creation through the budget.*

[10] A confirmed monetarist such as Professor D. Laidler recently wrote, "The key to maintaining a reasonable monetary expansion rate in Britain must be a reduction of public-sector borrowing. It is inconceivable that this can continue to run at the rate of 12 per cent of GNP without thereby generating a renewed acceleration in the rate of money creation." D. Laidler, "Inflation in Britain," *The American Economic Review* (September 1976), 66:499.

[11] See Bank for International Settlements, Press Review No. 221 of November 12, 1976, p. 3.

This makes monetary policies much less amenable to international coordination. For the rest, it has also turned out that the monetary institutions and structures of the various countries are much more diverse than had previously appeared to the casual observer.

What Does Coordination of Monetary Policies Mean?

1. *Coordination does not necessarily mean parallel (or "harmonized")* *monetary policies.* In the pursuit of a common goal—for example, domestic and external equilibrium—very different policies may be required in the various countries. Their starting positions may differ: some may start from large internal and external imbalances, others not. In some countries monetary policy may have to make up for a persistently lax budget policy. Each country's economic "environment" and ability to cope with difficulties will differ: the responsiveness of wages and of foreign trade to demand pressures, the responsiveness of external capital flows to interest rate and liquidity differentials, and so on.

2. Monetary coordination cannot be limited to interest-rate policy, but must comprise all of the elements influencing monetary conditions, including bank liquidity and monetary creation via the budget.

3. Money-supply targets can play an important part as intermediate goals in international monetary coordination. But their effects on exchange rates are not so clearcut as is sometimes assumed in theoretical models, partly due to the diversities mentioned above in starting positions and the "environment" of monetary policies. From this I would draw the conclusion that it is *impossible to forecast,* with any degree of precision, *from an announced monetary policy goal, or an observed rate of money* *growth, the resultant future exchange-rate movement.* [12] Thus it is also impossible to *guarantee* by commonly agreed "monetary norms" stable

---

[12] The Citibank (formerly First National City Bank of New York), in its "Money International" letter of April 1976, forecast on the basis of relative money growth rates that by the end of 1976 the DM would be "at best . . . at DM 2.57–2.60 per dollar or at worst . . . fall to 2.75 DM/$ by the end of 1976." On present indications it looks as if this shot at forecasting is going to be a miss by at best 5 percent and at worst, 12 percent (and what is more: the *direction* of the actual exchange-rate movement has been forecast erroneously).

exchange-rate relationships among the participating countries with any degree of probability. It can, however, be said that "monetary norms" that are likely to contribute to better domestic stability are also likely to lead to less instability in exchange rates.

4. *Coordination does not necessarily imply formal agreement, but a de facto similar or complementary orientation of monetary policy.* We have a good example of such de facto similarity in monetary developments—without any formal agreement—in the case of the U.S. and Germany between 1975 and 1976 (see chart 1.1 and table 1.1 of the annex at the end of this chapter). There has been a surprising parallelism since the beginning of 1975 in cyclical developments, in monetary aggregates (in relation to GNP),[13] long-term interest rates, and—to some extent—in prices in the two countries.

This resulted in a remarkably stable exchange-rate relationship between the DM and the dollar from mid-1975 to mid-1976. Short-term movements in the exchange rate between the dollar and the DM were influenced by changes in relative short-term interest rates (see chart 1.2). It appears, however, that short-term equilibrium usually required a somewhat higher level of short-term interest rates in the United States (by 1–1.5 percentage points).[14]

However, the de facto stability of the dollar–DM relationship between August 1975 and August 1976 cannot be taken as proof that the time is ripe for any formal setting of a rate or a target zone between the dollar and the DM. Past experience has taught us that fixing a firm exchange rate band for intervention would only invite destabilizing speculative flows.

5. We have not quite had the same de facto parallelism in monetary and price developments inside the *"snake" currency area*, although here quite formal commitments to coordinate monetary and other policies do exist (see chart 1.3). Therefore, tensions in the exchange markets and

---

[13] M3 has been used for the comparison as M1 and M2 are not comparable between the two countries.

[14] The most recent weakening of the dollar against the DM since mid-September 1976 can be explained by the decline of the interest-rate differential in favor of the U.S., by the unexpectedly large deterioration of the U.S. trade balance, and perhaps also by election uncertainties.

widening discrepancies in interest rates (table 1.2) arose, until the recent realignment of intervention rates inside the "snake" removed the tensions for the time being.

Possibilities and Prospects

1. The orientation of monetary policy has undergone great changes since the time of the Gold Standard when it was entirely, or at least predominantly, directed toward maintaining external equilibrium at fixed parities. The recent tidal wave of inflation has strengthened the tendency to use monetary policy primarily for the purpose of fighting inflation, or, depending on the situation, for dealing with stagflation, but at any rate for domestic purposes. The spreading of national money growth targets is a symptom that priority is being given to fighting inflation.

Countries that have advanced further on the path toward stability, and are in a stronger balance of payments position, will find additional support in a flexible exchange rate, not only because it can shield them from destabilizing external money flows, but because it can also insulate them to some extent from inflationary price movements abroad (provided the stronger country lets its exchange rate appreciate freely). Countries in a weaker payments position have also increasingly begun to use money supply targets. Their restrictive monetary policy is aimed simultaneously towards domestic and external goals—fighting inflation and strengthening the balance of payments.

As long as inflationary trends still predominate and restoration of better price stability is of paramount importance also internationally, coordination of monetary policies must necessarily be asymmetric. In such a situation a member country cannot be asked to inflate in order to contribute to a coordinated policy. The question of sharing the "burden of adjustment" will have to be merged with the question as to what is contributing most to international stability. The more inflationary (deficit) countries will have to move toward the common goal by a cautious monetary and fiscal policy, while the more stable countries (in strong payments positions) "should ensure an adequate recovery in domestic demand, but

11

should not be pressed beyond limits that would frustrate anti-inflationary policies. The main instrument of adjustment in their case may therefore have to be an appreciation of the exchange rate."[15] In the longer run, success in reducing inflation all around will also mean reducing inflation differentials among member countries, and this is the most important precondition for more stable exchange rates.

2. Apart from this longer-run strategy of stabilizing exchange rates by moving toward more price stability all around, there may be also short-term occasions for monetary coordination in a floating system, such as to attenuate unduly rapid or obviously excessive trend movements of major currencies as well as to smooth out unnecessarily large ("erratic") short-term swings around the trend movements. Occasionally an important part of such coordination may consist of avoiding abrupt swings in monetary policy in a major country that have a disturbing effect on the exchange markets.

How far are individual countries prepared to let their monetary policies be guided not only by domestic targets but also by such external considerations? Here we have to distinguish between various categories of countries.

a. Countries with a great degree of "openness," that is, with a relatively *large external sector*, have often found it necessary to orient their monetary policy, and in particular their interest-rate policy, largely toward external goals, for example, in order to forestall wide exchange-rate fluctuations or to support a desired level of their own exchange rate. Some smaller countries have let it appear that such an external orientation is of primary importance for their monetary policy, while they would leave the domestic field to fiscal and other economic policies.[16]

b. It is natural that the *United States*, as the largest economy in the world with a foreign-trade sector that is small relative to its domestic economy, is at the other end of the spectrum. It is sometimes maintained that interest rates in the United States are entirely dominated by develop-

---

[15] Quoted from a note submitted by the Managing Director of the IMF to the Interim Committee in Manila on October 2, 1976.

[16] Compare, for instance, with the statement of the Banque Nationale de Belgique in "Bulletin de la Banque Nationale de Belgique," September 1976, pp. 3–14.

ments in the domestic economy, while interest rates in Europe (and else-where) are supposed to be predominantly governed by developments in the foreign-exchange markets.

This black-and-white picture does not quite correspond to reality. It is, of course, true that U.S. monetary policy is predominantly determined by domestic considerations.[17] But in some situations even U.S. monetary policy has taken external effects into consideration. One such case was "operation twist" in the years 1961–64, under the system of rigid parities. Another case was the measures taken by the U.S. Treasury and the Federal Reserve at the time of the large dollar outflows in March/April 1971 when domestic short-term rates were boosted and the U.S. Treasury and the Export–Import Bank issued $3 billion worth of treasury bills and notes on the Eurodollar market in order to mop up excess dollar holdings abroad. But also since 1973, that is, under the system of floating, there may have been cases where interest rate policy was marginally influenced by the external situation of the dollar on the exchange markets.[18]

c. A number of industrial countries are somewhere in the middle of this spectrum. For Germany and Switzerland, for instance, one of the main reasons why they were forced to go over to floating in 1973 was precisely the necessity to free their monetary policy from the inflationary constraints arising from disequilibrating inflows of volatile funds. Orienting their monetary policies largely toward external goals would be dif-

---

[17] See the statement by William Simon, Secretary of the Treasury, before the Senate Foreign Relations Committee on October 23, 1975. In speaking on the mutual repercussions of monetary policies in the U.S. and in Europe, he went on to say, "Neither they nor we can allow our domestic monetary policy to be determined by the other." And even a professed advocate of international monetary coordination, Alfred Hayes, then President of the Federal Reserve Bank of New York, said in a speech in January 1973, "When we talk of better coordination of national monetary policies to help achieve a more stable international financial system, this means some degree of willingness to let comparative levels of interest rates among industrial nations have some influence on national monetary policy *when domestic considerations permit*" [sic].

[18] See also Sherman J. Maisel (former member of the Federal Reserve Board) "Managing the Dollar," New York, 1973, p. 221, "The dollar is managed primarily to achieve domestic, not international, objectives; few conflicts arise between policy determined entirely on domestic grounds and that which would be adopted for the purpose of affecting the international monetary situation." Doubts cannot be suppressed, however, as concerns the second part of Mr. Maisel's statement; it is still fresh in the present writer's memory how disturbing the sudden swings in American monetary policy in both 1970 and 1972 were for the international payments equilibrium and ultimately also for the external position of the dollar.

13

ficult for these countries whenever it would imply a return to inflation imposed from abroad. This does not mean that they would not, in their monetary policy and, in particular, their interest-rate policy, pay attention to their external impact; but this would clearly be subordinated to the primary objective of domestic stability. These countries would, as a rule, prefer to let their currencies appreciate rather than allow their economies to be exposed to an inflationary push. Switzerland has adjusted its interest-rate level to its external position (with its discount rate at a record low of 2 percent since June 1976), but at the same time it has pursued a domestic money-supply target and has successfully reduced its inflation rate to nearly zero.

d. The member countries of the *European joint float* ("snake")—which maintain an adjustable peg among themselves—represent a special case. They are under a commitment to coordinate their domestic—including monetary—policies with a view to supporting their mutual parities. This external commitment can come into conflict with domestic money-supply targets, especially in surplus countries that are obliged to intervene in the exchange markets at fixed intervention points, thus involuntarily increasing their domestic monetary base. They are not free to escape this involuntary reserve accumulation by an appreciation of their exchange rate vis-à-vis other members of the "snake," as this can be done only by mutual agreement (which, as events have shown, is sometimes difficult to achieve). However, there now appears to exist a tacit understanding among the "snake" members that the exchange-rate arrangement should be managed in such a way as not to become *a vehicle* of inflation.[19]

Some Special Cases

1. During the European currency turbulences of 1976 we have seen that a number of countries that suffered acute external pressures put up interest rates and tightened credit in other ways. In such situations of acute ex-

[19] Nevertheless, Germany had to take in nearly DM 14 billion (net) in foreign exchange from other "snake" countries in the first ten months of 1976.

ternal pressure, a country will have to choose between taking the pressure, (partly or wholly) on the exchange rate, supporting its currency through foreign-exchange intervention and/or adopting restrictive monetary measures. Very often a country will adopt a policy mixture—as did a number of European countries during the recent currency turbulences. The kind of mixture chosen will very much depend both on the strength of the external pressure and on the underlying position of the country as concerns economic activity, its rate of inflation, and its basic balance of payments—not to mention the magnitude of available reserves and reserve credit. It is interesting that at the beginning of May 1976 the Secretariat of the OECD noted that countries under acute external pressure "have been reluctant to allow domestic monetary policies to be dominated by speculative pressures in the foreign exchange markets." But a few months later, most of the countries concerned turned to monetary measures as their main defense (see table 1.2). These measures thus became a direct instrument for "managing the exchange rate" in the short run. It may well be that in such cases high interest rates were also the right prescription to combat an existing domestic imbalance so that external and internal considerations did not conflict with each other.

Should we call such a defensive reaction of monetary policy to outside pressures a kind of "coordinated monetary policy"? I hesitate to do so—although the result may be just what should have been done voluntarily (and perhaps earlier) if a proper coordination of monetary policies had existed.

2. In the EEC there has been for years a formal obligation of member countries to "coordinate their monetary policies." [20] This was a natural concomitant of the intention to maintain a parity system and work toward a monetary and economic union. Up to now, however, these resolutions have proved to be more in the nature of vague declarations of intent than of actual policies.

At the end of 1972—a few months before the transition of the "snake" countries to joint floating—the Ministerial Council of the EEC laid down common norms for the growth of the money supply in member

[20] See Council Decision of the EEC of March 22,1971 on the strengthening of cooperation between the central banks of the member states of the EEC.

15

countries for the two years 1973 and 1974.[21] However, this ambitious attempt was swept away by the monetary turbulences of 1973 and 1974 and passed into oblivion.

Now, as part of a general effort to achieve greater external stability, monetary coordination in the EEC has again become a topical issue. In its recently submitted Economic Report for 1977, the European Commission suggested:

For each Member State the following common criteria for the expansion of the money supply in 1977 should be adopted, taking into account any expected changes in the velocity of circulation:
 —a real rate of growth, consistent with the medium-term target, that would allow an appreciable increase in the utilisation of capacity;
 —a rate of price increase that would allow the rate of inflation to be progressively reduced to an annual rate of change of between [within] 4–5% by 1980 at the latest.
As the initial situation in each country is different these quantitative guidelines will necessarily also differ and should be defined in relation to the various instruments of monetary policy that are available in the various Member States (central bank money, M2 or M3, or total credit).

On November 8, 1976, the Ministerial Council, at the proposal of the EEC Monetary Committee, came to the following conclusion:

The Council considers that it would be appropriate to make pragmatic use of any opportunity of aligning monetary policy objectives without encroaching upon national powers and areas of responsibility. The Council thus concludes that internally established national monetary objectives which vary from one Member State to another should be discussed from time to time in the Monetary Committee, which should compare the outturn with the objectives, examine and account for any deviations and discuss possible remedies. The theoretical and technical studies of ways and means of gradually aligning intermediate monetary objectives should be pursued.

[21] Member countries should progressively reduce, over the two years 1973 and 1974, "the rate of expansion of the money supply (M2) to that of the GNP in real terms, plus a normative rate of increase as regards prices, fixed in accordance with the aims of general economic policy, account also being taken of the relation of money supply to the national product." The "normative rate of price increase", though not laid down officially, was intended to be around 4 percent for 1974.

16

This cautious approach can be explained by the fact that the member countries of the EEC do not all have the same kind of monetary goals. As a matter of fact, only a few have already embarked on a preannounced money supply target, whereas others aim at a certain target for bank credit, and still others lean toward interest rates or the external balance as their main indicators. However modest, this may at least be the beginning of a realistic approach toward some monetary coordination by monitoring national goals for monetary policy in a regular, institutionalized procedure.

Summary

Let me conclude with a brief summary. First of all, the real trouble in the exchange-rate field is persistent high inflation differentials among major countries. They not only make an early return to "stable but adjustable rates" impossible, but also contribute to the destabilizing anticipation of changes in, and overreactions of, the exchange rate. *The best way in which monetary policy can contribute to exchange stability in the longer run is by aiming at the greatest possible domestic stability;* the more countries pursue this objective, the greater is the prospect for stability in the exchange markets.

Second, monetary policy cannot achieve this in isolation. It has to be supported by adequate fiscal and other policies. This is the more necessary as budget deficits can become themselves a major source of money creation with a direct impact on the balance of payments and the exchange rate.

Third, for the many countries that have either pegged their currency to another currency or float jointly as a group ("snake"), the problems of monetary coordination are in essence similar to those of the former parity system.

Fourth, in a system of floating, coordinated money-supply targets can play an important role as a means of reducing inflation differentials among countries. There is, however, no such direct connection between money-supply targets and exchange rates as to render the latter predict-

17

able on the basis of the former (nor is it so easy to comply precisely with preannounced money-supply targets). National money–supply targets, by making interest rates a dependent variable, may lead to short-term fluctuations in external money flows.

Fifth, coordination does not mean parallel or harmonized money targets but complementary policies to reach common goals, nor does coordination necessarily imply formal agreement, but a de facto similar orientation of monetary policy. The short-term objective of monetary coordination in a regime of floating should be to attenuate abrupt or obviously excessive movements as well as unnecessarily large swings around the trend movements of exchange rates ("erratic" movements).

Finally, it is difficult to see how a formal multinational coordination of monetary policies can be instituted–except in regional organizations such as the EEC where coordinating bodies already exist. What can be expected is that countries recognize the external impact of their national monetary policies, and that in pursuing their domestic policies they take this impact on other countries into consideration.

Chart 1.1

Development of money stock, and real GNP in Germany and the United States
(Indices, first quarter 1974 = 100; seasonally adjusted)

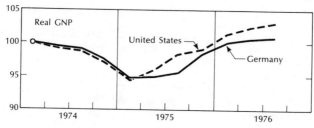

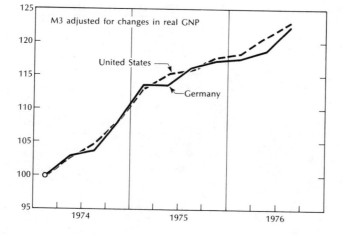

Table 1.1
Monetary Key Data of the United States and Germany
(Quarterly averages or quarterly data)

Item	Standard	1975				1976		
		I	II	III	IV	I	II	III
1. Exchange rates								
U.S.$:DM	D-Mark per US-$ 1	2.34	2.35	2.55	2.60	2.57	2.56	2.53
Effective exchange rates [a]	Indices, 1974 = 100							
U.S. dollar		98	99	103	104	104	105	104
DM		103	102	99	99	103	107	109
2. Money stock and GNP [b]	Indices, 1974 = 100							
Money stock M3								
United States		104	108	111	114	117	120	124
Germany		105	105	108	112	114	116	120
Nominal GNP								
United States		102	105	110	112	116	118	121
Germany		101	103	105	109	111	113	115
Real GNP								
United States		96	97	100	100	103	104	105
Germany		96	96	96	99	101	102	102
Income velocity of M3 (ratio of nominal GNP to M3)								
United States		98	97	99	98	99	98	98
Germany		96	98	97	97	97	97	96
M3 adjusted for changes in real GNP (ratio of M3 to real GNP)								
United States		108	111	111	114	114	116	118
Germany		109	109	113	113	113	114	118

20

Item	Standard	1975				1976		
		I	II	III	IV	I	II	III
3. *Interest rates*	Percent per annum							
One-month loans								
United States (CD's)		6.2	5.3	6.1	5.4	4.8	5.1	5.1
Germany (interbank loans)		6.2	4.8	3.9	3.8	3.6	3.7	4.4
Public authority bonds								
United States[c]		7.6	8.0	8.1	8.1	7.8	7.8	7.8
Germany		8.9	8.4	8.3	8.4	7.9	7.8	8.0
4. *Balance on current account*[b d]								
United States	U.S.$ billion	+1.4	+3.9	+3.2	+3.1	−0.1	+0.7	
Germany	DM billion	+5.4	+2.5	+1.1	+0.6	+3.3	+2.5	+1.4
5. *Indicators of price competitiveness*	Indices, 1974 = 100							
Consumer prices								
United States		106	108	110	112	113	115	116
Germany		104	106	107	108	109	111	111
Relative consumer prices[e]								
United States		99	97	97	96	95	94	94
Germany		96	95	94	92	92	90	89
Export unit values								
United States		113	112	112	112	114	115	116
Germany		107	107	108	107	108	108	111
Relative export unit values[e]								
United States		104	103	102	102	102	101	.
Germany		99	99	99	98	96	93	.

[a] Trade-weighted external value against the 16 currencies officially quoted in Frankfurt/Main.
[b] Seasonally adjusted.
[c] Government bonds excluding issues with special tax privileges.
[d] Including official transfers.
[e] Ratio of price movement in the country in question to the trade-weighted average of price movements in national currencies in other industrial countries. A decrease in the index indicates a price differential in favor of the country concerned.

21

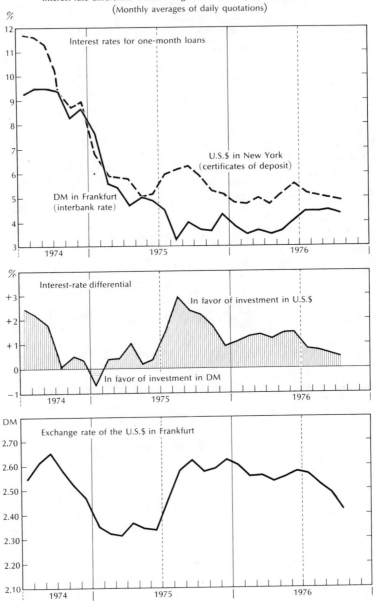

Chart 1.2

Interest-rate differential and exchange rate: Germany and the United States

(Monthly averages of daily quotations)

Interest rates for one-month loans

U.S.$ in New York
(certificates of deposit)

DM in Frankfurt
(interbank rate)

Interest-rate differential

In favor of investment in U.S.$

In favor of investment in DM

Exchange rate of the U.S.$ in Frankfurt

22

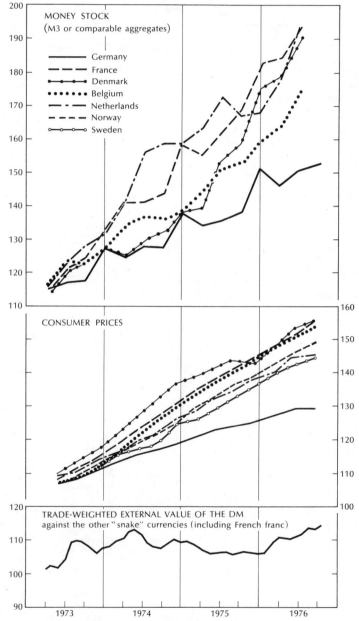

Chart 1.3

**Development of money stock, inflation, and exchange rates:
"snake" countries, including France**
(Indices: March 1972 = 100[a])

MONEY STOCK
(M3 or comparable aggregates)

——— Germany
– – – France
●—●—● Denmark
●●●●● Belgium
–·–·– Netherlands
- - - Norway
○—○—○ Sweden

CONSUMER PRICES

TRADE-WEIGHTED EXTERNAL VALUE OF THE DM
against the other "snake" currencies (including French franc)

1973   1974   1975   1976

[a] In April 1972 the arrangement between EEC central banks provided for
narrower margins for exchange-rate fluctuations entered into force.

Table 1.2
Recent Development of Money Market Rates in Selected Countries
(Percent per annum)

Country	Beginning of 1976[a]	Mid-October 1976[b]	Change in percentage points
Germany	4.0	4.7[c]	+ 0.7
Switzerland	1.5	1.0	− 0.5
United States	5.0	5.0	—
Netherlands	4.6	8.8	+ 4.2
Belgium	6.1	13.5	+ 7.4
Denmark	5.0	20.5	+15.5
Sweden	4.8	6.4	+ 1.6
Norway	8.0[d]	8.0[d]	—
France	6.4	10.5	+ 4.1
United Kingdom	10.1	14.7	+ 4.6
Italy	7.3	17.4	+10.1

NOTE: Three-month loans or treasury bills.

[a] Average of rates in the second full week of January (12–16th), immediately before the Italian lira began depreciating strongly.

[b] Average of rates in the second full week of October (11–15th), immediately before the realignment of exchange rates between the "snake" currencies.

[c] Last week of October.

[d] Maximum rate for interbank loans as fixed by the Norwegian central bank.

PAUL A. VOLCKER

FEDERAL RESERVE BANK OF NEW YORK,
NEW YORK, N.Y.

I AM VERY grateful to be able to participate in this conference because I can't think of a more appropriate kind of tribute to J. Marcus Fleming, who spent so much time dealing with precisely the kinds of issues that we have on the table. I think that they are important issues. I think they are in large part unresolved issues, and it is too much to expect that we are going to resolve around this table in two days what Marcus didn't resolve in his lifetime. But I think we can respect the intellectual integrity and analytic mind that he brought to this work in our own conversations here.

I note that I am on the other side of the table from Otmar Emminger. I hope that does not mean my views must be dramatically opposed. In any event, both of us are treading upon areas that practicing politicians and even central bankers don't like to discuss too much in public. Questions of monetary policy, and particularly international coordination of monetary policy, are naturally sensitive. Nevertheless, I do not think they can be escaped in the kind of world in which we live, with real economic and financial markets so closely linked.

In approaching this problem of monetary policy and exchange-rate stability, our experience in moving from fixed rates to floating rates, and our earlier experience in the 1920s and 1930s should have provided an enormous amount of empirical evidence to help us resolve the issues. But even with all that wealth of observation and the high-powered analytic and econometric techniques we have at our disposal, I don't find the record exactly crystal clear. For that reason, I am not going to spend a lot

25

of time on trying to provide statistical support for my argument, rather relying on what, I hope, is a reasoned analytic approach. In so doing, and in focusing on the problems of differential monetary policies and their potential effects on exchange-rate instability, I don't want to overlook the fact that we need not look to monetary policies to explain much of the recent instability. We have had a great many virtually unprecedented disturbances in the world economy that have affected the performance of exchange rates—inflation and recession, the oil shock, and, indeed, the mere fact that we have had to learn how to live with floating rates after a long period of being on a par value system.

Nevertheless, in the course of these remarks I defend the general proposition that monetary policy coordination is one important element in achieving an effective functioning of the exchange-rate system, and I do think too little attention has been paid to that issue in considering the management of floating rates. The difficulties are immediately apparent, because monetary policy is a prime domestic issue as Dr. Emminger has already emphasized.

By "effective functioning"—the term I just used to describe the objective for the exchange-rate system—I don't mean to imply stability, in the sense of no or very little change in exchange rates. I take it for granted that when economies move divergently as structural or other real factors change, or as a result of differential inflation rates, the exchange rate should, and will need to, move as well. If the divergencies are large, the movement in the exchange rate will also be large.

Certainly, when we talk about differentials in inflation rates, we can presumably trace these to differential monetary policies in the broadest and most general sense. But if the exchange rate in fact adjusted relatively smoothly to a persistent differential in inflation rates and related monetary policies, we could not complain. In that circumstance—and it could be important—I do not think there would be any compelling need to achieve coordination; it may not be the best of all conceivable worlds, but it doesn't strike me as a terribly pressing problem.

The trouble is that observation does suggest that there have been important changes in exchange rates that don't seem to reflect in any very obvious way changes of comparable magnitude in differential rates of

26

inflation, or shifts in real factors at work in different economies (of course, we can often rationalize what has happened in the exchange market in terms of expectations, and I return to the role of expectations later). If I can just make a very brief reference to this historical record, the most obvious case in point seems to be the substantial fluctuations in the "snake"–dollar relationships that were apparent in the first years of floating. Specifically, we saw the German deutsche mark (DM)–U.S. dollar rate moving up and down in a range of something like 15 percent in the course of a year or less on several occasions, prior to that period of stability to which Dr. Emminger referred beginning in mid-1975. That stability has been impaired a bit in recent months, as he also suggested, so the future remains open as to whether that seemingly greater sense of stability can persist. We have had other very large changes in exchange rates during this more recent period. Those changes for sterling and for the lira, in particular, have tended to move in one direction, a direction that, of course, does seem broadly appropriate in terms of purchasing power parity and other considerations of general equilibrium. But even in those cases, I don't find that purchasing power or other identifiable considerations (apart from expectations) can satisfactorily explain the size and timing of the movements. We are left with some concern as to whether substantial "overshoots" or "undershoots" may have complicated problems of economic management. In the context of the subject this morning, we have the question of whether better coordination of monetary policy could perhaps have done something about avoiding these apparent "overshoots" or "undershoots."

One other preliminary comment seems relevant. It is basic to my thinking that instability in exchange rates, in the sense of sizable deviations from levels or changes that seem explicable in terms of differential inflation rates and the real factors, will in time prove harmful to economic efficiency and international integration. Sooner or later, we would end up with less trade and less investment and, therefore, less effective international competition than otherwise. That is not necessarily the end of the world; it is a matter of degree. If, in fact, we achieved something worthwhile in return—presumably in terms of domestic autonomy and stability—we could examine the trade-off. In other words, the degree of

27

international integration and levels of trade are not the only dimension to be considered. Assessing that trade-off—how much domestic stability and autonomy are we getting in return for some international disintegration and inefficiency—seems to me the essence of the problem. More specifically, the issue posed is whether better coordination of monetary policy internationally can improve the terms of the trade-off.

I would also note again a point to which Emminger already alluded in a slightly different way. One of the main difficulties in reaching agreement on that trade-off, and in managing a floating-rate system generally, is precisely that different national authorities may view the same set of circumstances quite differently, depending on their external exposure and economic structures. It is pleasant to say that in this new world everyone should be free to choose the exchange-rate system and the approach that suits him best. In some degree, by regional and other groupings, we can indeed try to have it both ways, or at least strike more satisfactory compromises. But the essence of the problem is always that exchange-rate relationships are multisided in a multilateral world—our trading partners have to live with the same arrangements we live with.

I don't do justice to all the theorizing about flexible exchange rates when I say that proponents of floating left the impression that a system of floating rates would in itself permit and enhance national economic self-determination in a manner consistent with the integration of world markets. Independence for national monetary policy was one aspect of that general point. Whether I do the theorists justice or not, I do think that was the impression that came through in the nonprofessional mind.

Much of the popularized analysis focused most particularly on one aspect of independence. The observation was made that different countries would want, or at least tolerate, different rates of inflation (presumably accompanied by different rates of monetary growth). Under those circumstances, floating rates were presented as a device for accomplishing the inevitable exchange-rate adjustments relatively smoothly, compensating for changes in price levels and competitive position without substantially disturbing real variables in either the depreciating or the appreciating countries. Nor were floating rates viewed as transmitting inflationary (or deflationary) impulses from abroad, although they would, of course,

28

limit the possibility of "exporting" inflationary impulses originating at home.

That is one aspect of what was meant by autonomy, but I think there is another aspect perhaps more clearly related to cyclical concerns. Consider a situation where there are no substantial secular differences in inflation rates, but where differences in interest rates between countries do exist. Such interest-rate differences, by any theory I think, would affect exchange rates. But the suggestion has been made that shifts in the interest-rate differential, if not expected to persist, should not drastically change a floating exchange rate over time. Presumably the market would appraise the longer-term equilibrium exchange-rate level, and relatively modest appreciations or depreciations above or below that longer term equilibrium would encourage stabilizing or "benign" speculation, and offset the impact on the exchange markets of the opportunity for interest arbitrage.

Now I would like to examine each of those cases—the differences in inflation rate and the more cyclical problem—in turn, looking first at the second, the question of potentially temporary shifts in interest rates as a source of disturbance to the exchange-rate system. The proposition I just described seems to be valid, provided two assumptions are met: first, that reasonably firm expectations about the equilibrium rate do exist and, second, there is an institutional setting permitting and encouraging equilibrating speculation. My doubts arise from wondering whether, in many practical situations, either or both assumptions are valid.

I recognize that in the early period of floating, circumstances were particularly unfavorable for exchange-rate stability. We had had a series of devaluations (and revaluations) that upset long held market assumptions about appropriate relationships in exchange rates—assumptions that had been ingrained over the years. Then we had the oil-price increase. We had massive inflation. We had a deep recession. All of that together contributed to an absence of firmly held views about what exchange rates were, and would be, appropriate in the course of time. Those circumstances were exceptional, but they also give us some taste of what does happen when expectations are unsettled.

Whether or not expectations are firmly held, a shift in an existing pat-

29

tern of relative interest rates will presumably move the exchange rates as borrowers and lenders adjust to the new interest-rate situation. The difference is that, provided that substantial uncertainty exists about the appropriate or the likely exchange rate in the future, there will be no early and strong resistance to continued movements in the exchange rate as the interest rate differential, and the incentive to transfer funds, persists. Indeed, the cluster of expectations as to the future exchange rate may for a considerable time tend to move up or down along with the observed present market rates on the simple premise that, in the absence of other evidence, the best guess is that "tomorrow" will look like "today." Indeed, in some situations, the traders may assume that it is the *direction* of movement, rather than the *level*, that may persist for a time, giving an incentive for "bandwagon" effects.

In circumstances of weak and shifting expectations, as long as the interest rate differential persists, the potential then arises, it seems to me, for a fairly large swing in the exchange rate. Ultimately, if nothing else comes along, the process should be brought to a halt by a change in the current account, in incentives for profitable direct investment, and in other factors providing feed back on economic activity, and eventually on interest rates themselves. But I don't find that thought terribly comforting. Changes in current account and direct investment are notoriously slow, and are subject to *J* curve perversities. Provided the changes in interest-rate differentials ultimately prove cyclical or otherwise temporary, the danger is that a considerable wrench is implied for domestic economy, as well as for trade, by the shifting exchange rate and competitive position.

The point is often made that a change in the exchange rate resulting from a shift in interest-rate differentials might typically be associated with different phasings of the business cycle. Consequently, the resultant exchange-rate changes—appreciating or depreciating—should broadly support the objectives of the domestic monetary authorities—the *differing* objectives that gave rise to the potential "problem" in the first place. Up to a point, that seems to me a valid observation. But I doubt we can count on the association to be benign for all or even most trading partners when the changes in exchange rates are large. The lags and potential structural distortions to which I just alluded are relevant. To the extent that exchange-rate changes tend to be transmitted rather fully and quickly to the price structure—a point still at some issue, I recognize—problems of domestic economic management will as likely be aggravated as eased.

Conceptually that kind of problem—and I don't think it is entirely a bogey man—can be dealt with by stabilizing expectations. On the hopeful side, perhaps that was what we saw emerging quite naturally in the more stable dollar–DM relationship from mid-1975 to mid-1976. That exchange rate stabilized without substantial intervention, and I should add without anybody breathing any word about any official "target" or "reference" rate. But I must say I think the jury is still undecided as to whether this period really demonstrates that expectations are stabilizing. That was also a period, as Dr. Emminger emphasized, during which relative interest rates between the two countries changed very little and when monetary policies were pretty steady in both countries. So the stability of the exchange-rate relationship has not really been tested in the face of significant shifts in monetary policies. Indeed, since the summer, the appreciation of the DM relative to the dollar has broadly paralleled a shifting in the interest-rate differential. While the move in the exchange rate and interest differential has not gone terribly far, their apparent mutual sensitivity may suggest the danger of renewed instability.

Another interesting and often cited case in point is the Canadian–U.S. dollar relationship, which has remained relatively stable at times in the face of significant shifts in interest-rate differentials. The exchange rate changes but not drastically or continuously; it seems to behave more as the theorizers hoped and expected. But in this case we probably do have a special factor at work—a kind of unstated mutual target range—in the notion that, for two countries so closely linked, a dollar should be worth about a dollar. Moreover, if I read the record right, the Canadian authorities have typically kept an eye on interest-rate differentials in shaping their monetary policies, taking care to limit the differential. In that sense, they seem to accept the proposition that floating rates do not give them anything like full internal monetary autonomy.

Now let me turn to the other case, where differential rates of monetary growth and inflation persist over a substantial period of time. Lurking in

31

the background in a consideration of this problem are complicated issues about whether different rates of monetary growth can really affect real employment, real growth, or real interest rates over time, and whether, therefore, monetary autonomy in that sense serves a real purpose. I don't want to go deeply into that issue; let me assume initially that different rates of monetary growth will affect the economy in a real way, as well as in rates of price increase.

In that case, exchange rates can certainly be expected to adjust to the different trend in national price levels and monetary growth. But as I suggested earlier, they often seem to do more—to overadjust, with the exchange-rate change outpacing purchasing-power parity. Part of the explanation of that phenomenon may run in terms of a simple bandwagon psychology. But we need not revert entirely to that explanation. We could also explain the tendency if the relative performance of prices (and the relative performance of the money stock) is expected to persist, and if the differences in price performance are not matched by similar differentials in nominal interest rates. In other words, if real interest rates are different in the two countries, pressures on the exchange rate should arise, just as in the case I discussed earlier.

Jack Polak has just distributed a little paper that examines this point a bit empirically. The numbers do suggest that real interest rates are lower, or tend to be lower, in inflating countries. I think it might even be said that some of them want it that way—lowering interest rates is presumably the object of the monetary expansion, to get more stimulus (or perhaps to redistribute income) in the domestic economy. If lower real interest rates are part of the essence of an inflationary monetary policy, then rapid depreciation in the exchange rate of the inflationary country, outrunning current changes in competitive relationships, should not be surprising. The tendency would be to produce some chronic under- and overvaluations in terms of current price levels. In this context, concern that exchange-rate changes may reinforce an already existing inflationary movement in particular countries seems real enough.

Certainly, the idea of achieving and reinforcing monetary autonomy is attractive. And the idea is not new. But my concern is that the possibilities of achieving a high degree of autonomy—a really meaningful degree of autonomy—over time by means of floating exchange rates have been substantially overstated, if not in carefully developed economic analysis, then in the public and political mind.

For one thing, autonomy achieved at the expense of large volatility in exchange rates or chronic over- or undervaluation is likely to exact substantial costs. Perhaps more fundamentally, I wonder how long a high degree of monetary autonomy could be sustained over time under those circumstances. If the exchange-rate trend exaggerates the inflationary impact of an autonomous expansionary policy, the real effects will be dampened. A country will, to be sure, have autonomy of some sort—the ability to inflate—but it becomes increasingly doubtful that expansionary monetary policies will effectively and consistently work to expand activity if exchange depreciation speeds up the adjustment in nominal values to the monetary expansion. If, on the other hand, real interest rates are maintained, the exchange depreciation may be controlled, but the expansionary thrust will be lost.

Now it is substantially easier to express these concerns than to suggest how in practical ways, and in an imperfect world, the danger can be curtailed and limited. In a sense, it seems to me that we are dealing with something of a paradox. Floating rates provide some new degrees of freedom for domestic policy in the short run provided that expectations about the future are reasonably firm. But those expectations will not be firm unless monetary-policy harmonization or coordination is taken seriously. In other words, we can get along with temporary policy divergencies (and floating rates should help substantially here), but only when they are seen to be indeed temporary. I suppose this argument might be carried to the point that the greatest autonomy for monetary policy can be achieved today by fixing the exchange rate at some point in the future! Thoughts of this sort lie behind some of the thinking about "zones" or "targets" or "reference" rates. But I would remind you that I am only dealing with one variable here, namely, monetary policy. One of the difficulties with target rates is to adjust them to cope with other factors that render exchange-rate change necessary and desirable over time, bringing new and undesirable rigidities back into the system.

Everything I have said does seem to me to support the conventional wisdom that stability in domestic economies is a prerequisite for stability in exchange rates. That is true not just in the obvious sense that, without large inflation, one of the main reasons for observed exchange-rate changes will disappear. Beyond that, stability domestically will certainly assist in the formation of better market judgments about what the appropriate exchange rate might be over time.

However, I still wonder if that is the whole story. The danger to the stability of the floating-rate system seems to me to lie in the presumption that it promises more autonomy than it can really deliver in an integrated world. Even in circumstances where inflation rates were to be more generally stabilized, attempts to exercise a high degree of monetary autonomy, and failure to consider what others are doing at the same time, would tend to produce a record of instability and give the new system a bad name. Eventually, the effort at full autonomy would prove an illusion. Stated another way, I fear as potentially dangerous the symbolism, or lack of symbolism, that implies that in domestic policy "anything goes" in a floating-rate system.

The question does arise, and I alluded to it earlier, as to whether the governments can shape expectations more directly by setting ranges or targets for exchange rates backed, presumably, by intervention. This raises a number of political, as well as economic issues—questions of who sets the target as well as where and how it is set. I don't want to leave any impression that I think a simple notion of ranges aggressively supported by intervention is what I am talking about. The ranges themselves would only be credible if they were backed by some broader coordination of policy. I don't think they can be made credible by intervention alone. Credibility would depend on those much tougher decisions about monetary and other economic policies. I think decisions about targets or zones is one which, certainly for the time being, governments generally are not willing to make with any precision or openness, perhaps quite wisely, given all the uncertainties in the world, apart from monetary policy proper. I think we have to pursue this approach—and here I find myself very much in alignment with what Dr. Emminger had to say—slowly, tentatively, and informally. Selected countries may indeed find it useful over time if they arrive at some mutual judgment as to an appropriate range of exchange rates, provided that they accept the corollary that there are implications for coordination. In an extreme form, I think this is what the European "snake" is all about.

I am not left with any magic in this area, but bankers often like to conclude their remarks talking about the "three C's" of lending: collateral, capacity, and character. It strikes me that three different C's may be appropriate in this area.

The first one seems to me simple *comprehension*—understanding that floating rates do not really mean we can achieve autonomy and that the old problems of cooperation and coordination have not disappeared, in monetary policy as in other areas.

Once we have the comprehension, *consultation* will be seen as an indispensable element in working with monetary policy to achieve greater stability. For as far ahead as I can see, I suspect we will have to rely more on consultation than more formal agreement, a point that has been made.

The final C that occurred to me, and certainly the most important of all, I can sum up in the word *courage*. It is not easy for any domestic policymaker, particularly in the larger countries with relatively smaller external sectors, to make a lot of allowance for the external effects of its policy and to work with other countries toward achieving some consistency and compatibility in the interests of a broader stability.

In some circumstances, the necessary and requisite courage can be assisted by incentives and penalties. I raise that point because it does seem obvious that this institution, where we are meeting, has the capacity, actual and potential, to provide such assistance in particular situations. How to apply incentives and penalties in practice to promote greater stability in the mutual interest is part of the problem with which we are grappling. However difficult the process, progress in this area offers one of the more promising approaches toward achieving, in particular cases, a greater degree of policy coordination. In all of this the problems will be obvious, and strong support will be necessary from the member countries. But I do think that it is wrong to think that nothing can be done—to, in effect, give up. Even in circumstances where the question of sizable IMF lending operations may not be relevant, there is some room for action. Questions of the policy mix and timing are not rigid and preor-dained in any of our countries. I would like to think the time has come to be a little more open in putting those kinds of issues on this and other ta-bles as part of the processes of comprehension and consultation. It seems to me a necessary part of running the floating-rate system as effectively as I think it can be—and should be—run.

COMMENTS

RINALDO OSSOLA

MINISTRY OF FOREIGN TRADE, ROME, ITALY

I AM PARTICULARLY glad to participate in this seminar honoring the memory of my dear friend J. Marcus Fleming. I am the author of a report in 1964 that bears my name; but more appropriately, it should have borne the name of J. Marcus Fleming. As a matter of fact, the contribution of J. Marcus Fleming was outstanding in this context. He was very good-humored, endowed with a high degree of professionalism, and patient but firm in his arguments and discussions. He was one of the most important members not only of this group but of others in which his personality was familiar, such as the Bellagio gathering and Santa Colomba.

Theory and experience teach us that monetary policy, via its impact on capital flows, can have substantial impacts on exchange rates in the short run. Monetary policy should, therefore, be conducted not only in view of domestic objectives, but also of external objectives and constraints. Clearly, a dilemma can arise in the conduct of monetary policy if domestic and external objectives conflict. The openness of an economy, and its current account position, determine the strength of the external constraints operating on monetary policy. I distinguish three cases: countries with a current account deficit; countries with a current account surplus; and countries with a relatively closed economy.

I start with the case of deficit countries. During the recent period of severe balance-of-payment difficulties and financing problems, countries

37

such as Italy, for instance, had no choice but to pursue a tight monetary policy in order to influence capital movements. In 1974, when we needed to deflate the economy in order to contain our current account deficit, this policy did not conflict with our domestic objectives. Thus from mid-1974 our short-term interest rates were above 16 percent. In 1975—in the midst of our worst postwar recession—we tried to stimulate the economy, and we eased monetary policy to support this domestic objective. However, balance-of-payments difficulties at the beginning of 1976 forced us to tighten monetary policy again, and to subordinate its conduct to external objectives. Of course, had we been prepared to let our exchange rate depreciate freely, we could have conducted monetary policy without worrying about external objectives. In theory it is well known that floating exchange rates allow national monetary policy to be independent of external constraints. However, in the present world, where inflationary biases exist in most countries due to factors such as—for example—the structure of the labor market, the choice of depreciating the exchange rate until external equilibrium is reached does not exist in practice. Continued depreciation of the lira would only have aggravated our inflation, worsened our terms of trade, and postponed the stabilization of our economy. *Thus in our case capital outflows had to be stemmed through a tight monetary policy. This is generally the case for countries in weak balance-of-payments positions.*

Countries in strong balance-of-payments positions clearly have more choice in the conduct of monetary policy. Since appreciation of a currency in an inflationary environment is less painful than depreciation, countries with a current account surplus could run a tight monetary policy if they so wished. However, this would obviously conflict with their responsibility to adjust their balance of payments, and would be damaging to the stability of exchange rates. *In fact, symmetric responsibility in the adjustment process requires that deficit and surplus countries alike promote stabilizing capital movements, the former by maintaining relatively high interest-rate levels and the latter, by holding rates down.* It would be inappropriate to place constraints only on the monetary policies of deficit countries.

A third case is of a relatively closed economy such as the United States, where exchange-rate movements have only a small effect on domestic activity and price developments. In principle, monetary policy in such a country could be directed toward domestic objectives only. The experience of these last years clearly indicates that this has been the case. However, if such a large country, with large financial markets and the potential for large capital movements, conducts its monetary policy only in function of domestic objectives, there is the possibility that serious instability of exchange rates will arise. This is what happened in 1974 and 1975 when the dollar–DM relationship fluctuated frequently, partly in response to expectations regarding the effect of the oil crisis, but also as a consequence of movements in interest-rate differentials. *Since we all agree that exchange-rate stability is necessary to a smoothly operating monetary system, it follows that countries whose overall balance of payments are close to equilibrium, or that do not have problems financing a deficit because their currency is a reserve asset, should manage their monetary policy in a way that prevents the occurrence of large capital movements.*

From these considerations it follows that not only countries with a deficit or a surplus in their current account, but also those in balance-of-payments equilibrium have an international responsibility to conduct monetary policy with external factors in mind. In the case of deficit or surplus countries, monetary policy should contribute to adjustment by inducing compensating capital movements; in the case of countries in current account equilibrium, monetary policy should avoid inducing capital movements that destabilize exchange rates. These conclusions indicate that international coordination of monetary policy is needed.

The countries in the European "snake" already coordinate their monetary policies to a large extent. In fact, monetary actions are the main instruments that these countries use to maintain their parities. Important European countries outside the "snake" also conduct monetary policy with the aim of promoting external equilibrium. Given the openness of their economies and the inflationary dangers of excessive depreciation, they do not, in fact, have any other choice. On the other hand, coor-

39

dination appears to be relatively lacking between both sides of the Atlantic. Improvements in this regard should be high on the international agenda.

Let me now turn briefly to three specific observations in the two papers. First, Dr. Emminger said that monetary policies are heavily influenced by the budget deficit and he cited in this context, as in others, the case of Italy. I want to emphasize that the necessity for coordination exists not only *between* countries but also between the treasury and the central bank of a particular country. This is the case in my country, where a large deficit on the part of the treasury seriously hampers the conduct of any meaningful monetary policy. In fact, the huge cash deficit of the treasury leaves little room for maneuver in this regard. We have been compelled to introduce many constraints on both the banking and exchange-rate systems; we have done so unwillingly, but our margin of maneuver has become very narrow. Thus there is much room for improved coordination at the national level, and I feel this need especially in my own country. Secondly, Volcker noted that movements in the exchange rate might have an immediate effect on internal prices, causing feedback on the exchange rate, and a downward spiral. Again, the case of my country is typical. We have the mechanism of a "sliding scale" in Italy that adjusts with a very short time lag (three months) and operates in a way that is virtually automatic (because indexation is very generalized). As a result, any depreciation of the exchange rate, instead of being conducive to the adjustment of the balance of payments, merely accelerates the inflation, forcing the rate down still further. Finally, I believe that Mr. Volcker's comment about movements in the real interest rate is very interesting and deserves much further study. He indicated that countries with strong inflationary trends experience negative rates that are larger than those in other countries. This is also typical of my own country, where the negative interest rate is probably the highest in the industrial world.

ALEXANDRE LAMFALUSSY

BANK FOR INTERNATIONAL SETTLEMENTS,
BASLE, SWITZERLAND

MR. CHAIRMAN, I am so much in agreement with what Dr. Emminger and Paul Volcker said (and perhaps also with what they did not say) that I have found some difficulty in inventing critical observations in the short time available for writing down a few notes. But I will try to do my best. Instead of discussing in the abstract the desirability and the feasibility of monetary policy coordination for the sake of stabilizing exchange rates, I prefer, to be more practical, to center my remarks around two very different cases.

First of all, I would take the one that can be defined as the dollar–DM case. Here we have two countries in which economic fundamentals seem to be basically similar. This had not always been so, but there is some degree of agreement that today fundamentals no longer differ in these two countries. Policy preferences in the fields of both monetary and fiscal policies, rates of growth in monetary aggregates, and the actual success in fighting inflation—in all of these areas there is strong resemblance between the United States and Germany. Assuming that this similarity continues to prevail, the question then is whether monetary policies could (and should) be coordinated with a view to stabilizing the exchange rate.

Let us return for a moment to history. It was pointed out that between 1973 and mid-1975 there had been three complete cycles in the dollar–DM relationship. Then from September 1975 until June 1976 we had a period or relative stability. More recently we have experienced a decline of several percentage points in the value of the dollar against the DM. Is this the beginning of a new cycle? I certainly do not venture to make forecasts! But it seems possible to draw some conclusions from the experience of the last three years on the following lines. The cycles had been produced by a number of external shocks of which the two most important were the oil-price increase (or more precisely, its expected differential

41

impact on the German and the U.S. economies) and the reversal of the U.S. policy regarding capital exports. When shocks of this magnitude occur, interest-rate differentials of a moderate size are probably ineffective to counteract their impact on exchange rates. In contrast, when there are not external shocks and when fundamentals of the kind referred to above become similar, uncovered interest differentials *do* begin to matter. Chart 1.2 suggests for the most recent period a certain correlation between changes in interest differentials and movements in exchange rates. This points to a potential impact of monetary policies, and therefore of their coordination, on exchange rates.

But assuming feasibility, *should* one aim at coordination? I would certainly advance a very strong plea in favor of a minimum coordination of German and U.S. interest-rate policies; I do not think we can expect relative peace or even a semblance of order in the international monetary scene so long as there are strong fluctuations in the dollar–DM relationship. I would like, therefore, to first address a question to our academic colleagues as to whether they believe that I am correct in assuming that once the fundamentals are reasonably similar between two countries, and in the absence of major external shocks, small interest-rate differentials could influence the exchange rate. Do they also think, as I do, that it would be a good idea to implement a policy of interest-rate coordination for that purpose? And then I turn to the policymakers. Does my analysis make any sense? Are my recommendations completely unrealistic?

Let us now envisage the effects of monetary policy on exchange rates between countries where fundamentals are basically different. Take, for instance, for the sake of example, the cases of: (a) the United Kingdom and Italy and (b) Germany and Switzerland. Here "fine tuning" of interest-rate coordination seems to be an unrealistic weapon. Of course, interest rates in both sterling and lira should be much higher than those in DMs and Swiss francs. Of course, there is an interest-rate differential that would stabilize exchange rates even in these cases. But is it possible to know in advance what these differentials are? Is it really possible for policymakers to detect the differentials one would need to stabilize the exchange rate between, let us say, the DM and the pound sterling?

Should the short-term interest rates in the United Kingdom exceed the current 15–16 percent? To 20? To 25? I do not think that it is possible to give any rational answer to the question because we lack the necessary information needed in order to establish the required differentials. The main difficulty lies in the problems related to a proper definition of real interest rates. These could be defined correctly only if we know about expectations, and these latter cannot be detected simply by looking at current or past inflation rates. My own conclusion, therefore, is that coordination of monetary policies of the "fine-tuning" type, which I recommend for the United States and Germany, would be unrealistic in these cases. Here policy should address itself to correcting the basic imbalances, and such correction will have to take place through the simultaneous use of fiscal, monetary and, perhaps, incomes policies as well.

DISCUSSION

THE DISCUSSION dealt with five points: (a) the meaning of monetary coordination, (b) the Phillips trade-off and its relevance for monetary coordination, (c) the nature of monetary independence afforded by floating rates, (d) the relationship between government budget deficits and money growth; and (e) the adequacy of forward markets.

On the issue of *monetary coordination* there was general agreement that policy should become more predictable, and that mutual understanding of each other's policies was crucial. Beyond this, however, there was substantial disagreement on the meaning and desirability of coordination. Wallich indicated that in a world characterized by varying rates of inflation, coordination of policies could only refer to a stabilization of the rates of change of exchange rates, and not their levels. He noted that, because of the shift in attention away from interest rates toward monetary aggregates, any coordination would presumably involve monetary growth rates. Such coordination should not entail their equalization, however, but simply the announcement of targets. He argued that, in the interests of price stability, virtually all money growth rates should be reduced. He pointed out that coordination *qua* equalization of monetary growth rates would imply increases for some countries, which, in his view, would be contrary to their domestic interests.

This view was supported by Emminger, who indicated that Germany was prepared to alter its policies for the sake of coordination, by way of choice of monetary instruments, for example, as long as such action did not pose a threat to domestic stability. He referred to the resolution of the EEC Ministerial Council cited in his paper, which called for the monitoring and discussion of internally established monetary objectives, and

44

repeated his appraisal that this was a more modest but perhaps more realistic approach to the question of monetary coordination than had been entertained in the past.

Volcker reiterated the position enunciated in his paper, namely, that an attempt to achieve surface coordination of monetary policy was bound to be self-defeating, since it would upset expectations and the stability of the domestic economy. If priority were given to the target of domestic stability, international coordination might suffer, and some instability in exchange rates might ensue. Nevertheless, he argued that the attainment of domestic stability would, in the long run, lend stability to the international sphere.

Solomon provided a more activist interpretation of coordination, concerned largely with the employment consequences of policy coordination. He argued that the industrial countries should be prepared to adopt policies that minimize movements in combined aggregate demand. In his view, the recent cyclical synchronization was a failure of coordination, since world aggregate demand was not maintained. Furthermore, he proposed that respective monetary and fiscal policies be coordinated to allocate the $50 billion current deficits implied by the corresponding OPEC surpluses.

Similar sentiments were voiced by Katz, who found the stability of the dollar–DM relationship in 1975 and 1976 (raised initially in this session by Lamfalussy) highly undesirable, in that it was obtained at too high a cost in terms of U.S. employment. At the same time, however, Katz strongly supported the notion of greater predictability of monetary policy which, he acknowledged, would imply severe limitations on its use for stabilizing short-term variations in aggregate demand.

Mundell's view of coordination differed from these, however. Elaborating on a point raised by Wallich, who emphasized the difficulty of coordinating monetary policy in a world of uncertainty, Mundell noted the possibility of successive reverberations between policymakers who are uncertain as to speculative behavior and speculators who are uncertain about policy. As a way to break out of this circle, Mundell supported Lamfalussy's proposal that U.S. and German monetary policy be coordinated to fix the dollar–DM exchange rate. With that rate established, he argued, concern could be narrowed to only one important inflation rate, and a considerable degree of the uncertainty in the system would be thereby eliminated. He further noted that the common inflation rate in such a scenario would depend on how liberal the reserve system was.

On the stability of the dollar–DM exchange rate, Emminger noted that it had lasted about 13 months and had helped to stabilize expectations about the relative values of these currencies. Nevertheless, he observed that some sources of uncertainty, such as due to pending national elections, are inevitable and that central banks can neither remove nor counter these by intervention.

Kenen's response to a point raised by Lamfalussy elucidates another aspect of this issue. Lamfalussy had suggested that "fine tuning" of interest-rate differentials between countries whose fundamental situations were similar, such as the United States and Germany, would have a greater impact on their exchange rate than comparable operations between dissimilar countries, such as the United Kingdom and Germany. Kenen, while agreeing in principle, objected to the particular examples cited. Scrutinizing the importance of exchange-rate stability from a currency union vantage point, he argued that since both the dollar and DM areas are rather "closed" to each other, stability of the dollar–DM relationship is less important than stability of the exchange rate between the pound sterling and the DM. Kenen further noted that it might be preferable to intervene directly in the foreign exchange market rather than to manipulate short-term interest rates to stabilize exchange rates. The latter, he suggested, could destabilize expectations about the medium-term evolution of monetary policy and exchange rates.

Addressing this question of methods for stabilizing expectations, Emminger disputed Kenen's suggestion that direct intervention in the foreign-exchange market would be preferable to the coordination of interest rates. He argued, instead, that such intervention, for a country of Germany's size, would destabilize domestic monetary policy. Moreover, he referred to a BIS report that indicated that even massive intervention by central banks could not succeed in stabilizing the exchange rate against large underlying forces. He called for an improvement in the monetary and general economic policies of the countries concerned,

46

which would be credible to both policymakers and the exchange markets.

In assessing the significance of monetary coordination, Fellner distinguished between countries who have rejected the idea of a *trade-off between inflation and other economic objectives*, such as the unemployment rate, and those who have not. He argued that if all countries were in the former group, we could return to fixed exchange rates, and monetary coordination would be very promising. However, with the world split as it is, the issue is political rather than economic. Countries in the latter group, he contended, get themselves into situations of accelerating inflations accompanied by accelerating exchange-rate depreciations. Other countries must then extend financing so as to prevent those economies from collapsing. He added that these conflicts among nations will be resolved only by bilateral bargaining and not by economic theorizing.

Giersch noted that those countries who rely on money illusion to attain full employment are losing "customers" for their currency and assets. Hence, their currency areas are shrinking as currencies from countries with low, stable inflation rates tend to replace the ones of countries with high inflation rates.

Solomon challenged the view that "if you just adopt the right monetary policy you can put an end to wage–price spirals." He argued that this argument fails to take account of deepseated political and social realities, which seriously limit the freedom of monetary policy regardless of the exchange-rate regime. This point was amplified by Harrod, who contended that the primary cause of inflation was to be found in the practice of trade unions pushing up wages in excess of productivity increases. Thus he favored the introduction of an incomes policy.

The disagreement as to the causes of wage–price spirals was also reflected in Giersch's observation that low, stable inflation-rate countries are characterized by a degree of social consensus lacking in the countries with inflation problems. He argued that in some countries there is an implicit social consensus that holds the monetary authorities responsible for price stability, and the trade unions responsible for full employment if the rate of monetary expansion is known in advance.

In reply to Volcker, who implied that academicians had led policymakers to expect from floating *a greater measure of independence for monetary policy*, Machlup differentiated between monetary policy and effective monetary policy. He took the position, which Volcker subsequently acknowledged, that floating allows monetary policy to be independent in terms of setting the inflation rate, but that it does not necessarily enable a nation to attain all of its objectives. He indicated that he had, in the past, only warned that exchange-rate flexibility was required if countries were to persist in pursuing divergent inflation rates.

The kind of policy independence afforded by floating was evident in Emminger's response to Ossola's recommendation that symmetry of the adjustment process be achieved through greater expansions on the part of surplus countries. Rather, Emminger argued that it was the EEC position that, because of the continuing problem of inflation, surplus countries should appreciate rather than expand. Moreover, he indicated that the other "snake" countries wanted to benefit from German discipline. Finally, he quoted the IMF Managing Director's words to the Interim Committee in Manila to the effect that surplus countries should act to achieve an adequate recovery in domestic demand without abandoning their antiinflationary policy.

Wallich drew an analogy between the freedom of monetary policy under floating and the evolution of the Phillips curve, in that both offer fewer options than initially supposed. In particular, he noted that the exercise of the apparent autonomy conferred by floating tends to destabilize expectations in such a way that responses become less predictable and policy loses much of its effectiveness. Fellner and Wallich agreed with Lamfalussy's point that it is unclear whether interest-rate differentials are sufficient to stabilize the exchange rate of a country in such a situation.

As a sidepoint, but with some relevance to this discussion, Hirsch provided an explanation for the observation that real interest rates tend to be lower in high-inflation-rate countries. He argued that since the real value of principal plus interest payments declines to a relatively greater extent over time in high-inflation-rate countries, the lender is compensated by higher real and nominal payments during the early periods of payback. This creates a cash-flow problem for borrowers and tends to decrease the demand for such funds. He further noted that in high-inflation-rate countries there may be a considerable risk that the rate of infla-

48

tion will be reduced, with costly results for borrowers at high nominal interest rates, which also diminishes the demand for credit.

Machlup took issue with Emminger's assertion that monetary coordination requires *coordination of budget policy.* He argued that the deficits could be financed through security sales, and, since the treasury cannot print money, monetary independence is secure. Cooper pointed out that Machlup was correct to the extent that international capital markets are well developed and a country's credit rating is good. He noted that a country's central bank may, out of habit, convert foreign currency borrowed abroad into domestic money. Alternatively, Cooper proffered that the domestic currency could be obtained from the foreign-exchange market, without affecting the domestic money supply. He added that this would tend to appreciate the exchange rate and relieve inflationary pressures induced by the fiscal expansion.

Solomon agreed with Cooper's emphasis on the role of capital markets in breaking the link between monetary and fiscal expansions, but he stressed the difficulty of developing these markets where none exist. He further noted that, along with the OPEC surpluses and trade-union power, the inadequacy of financial markets is the most pressing structural problem confronting the world today.

In rebuttal to the argument that monetary growth could be independent of the budget deficit, Emminger cited the Italian situation. He noted a time in the recent past when the entire budget deficit had to be financed by recourse to central bank money, and other times when 50 percent had to be financed in that manner. He argued that it was not so much a problem of underdeveloped capital markets, but rather an excess of the budget deficit over real savings in the economy. Hence he maintained his position that coordination of monetary policies must take into account the possibility of money creation through excessive budget deficits.

Cooper noted that very few new *forward markets* had developed in response to generalized floating. He noted that advocates of flexible exchange rates had assumed that markets with the required "maturities" and "resilience" would follow the move to floating. Instead, he saw little progress and some evidence of deterioration. Specifically, he noted that

49

the American banks are not willing to broker transactions for any but their "legitimate customers," which effectively bars speculative transactions.

Volcker responded by saying that the relationship between spot and forward exchange rates has been largely consistent with interest-parity considerations, which is the true test of the efficiency of the forward market. On that basis he would argue that forward markets may have been working more effectively than in the past. Emminger, on the other hand, expressed skepticism about the possibility of their playing a significant role in stabilizing foreign-exchange markets. He maintained that forward markets have occasionally imparted a stabilizing influence, but that in speculative situations they have contributed to speculative sentiment. He further argued that it is illusory to think that central banks could provide stabilization by intervention in forward markets. Finally, Emminger and Volcker agreed that the important task in stabilizing either forward or spot exchange rates was to stabilize expectations.

SESSION 2

IMF Surveillance Over Exchange Rates

HERBERT GIERSCH

INSTITUT FÜR WELTWIRTSCHAFT,
KIEL, WEST GERMANY

1. EXCHANGE-RATE surveillance is regarded as necessary for two reasons, which are expressed in the following quotations:

> 1a. Each IMF-member shall ". . . avoid manipulating exchange rates or the international monetary system in order to prevent effective balance of payments adjustment or to gain an unfair competitive advantage over other members." [1]
>
> 1b. "Sound economic policy calls for a greater brake on movements in exchange rates than private speculators can always be expected to provide." [2]

The first argument implies that government or central-bank intervention might be harmful in special cases, while the second one states that interventions are necessary to stabilize the market. Both together call for a controlled and coordinated intervention in foreign-exchange markets.

2. This view may be contrasted to an alternative policy system, which is characterized by the following three "commandments":

> 2a. Governments and central banks should proceed toward full convertibility for short-term as well as long-term capital movements.
>
> 2b. Central banks should announce and thus commit themselves to a money supply strategy for the foreseeable future.
>
> 2c. Central banks should refrain from intervening in foreign-exchange markets.

In preparing the paper, the author has greatly benefitted from constructive cooperation and many suggestions by Harmen Lehment, who, however, should not be debited with any of the remaining shortcomings.

[1] Section one of the proposed new Article IV of the IMF Articles of Agreement.

[2] Richard N. Cooper, "Prolegomena to the Choice of an International Monetary System," Center Paper No. 239, Economic Growth Center, Yale University, 1976, p. 96.

The first two points of this package, which aim at the improvement of free exchange markets, may be acceptable also to proponents of surveillance, while the last one is generally not—except if surveillance over exchange rates is interpreted as "surveillance over nonintervention," but this does not seem to be what the proponents of surveillance have in mind.

Commandment 2a, which goes beyond guideline 5 of the present IMF guidelines for the management of floating rates, is a precondition for a well-functioning foreign-exchange market.[3]

Commandment 2b pays tribute to the fact that exchange rates are closely connected to monetary policy. As the exchange rate is the relative price of two monies, it is extremely difficult to make any forecast about exchange-rate changes in the absence of reliable information about the future money supplies. A more predictable money-supply policy would therefore render exchange rates more predictable and reduce uncertainties and transaction costs in a multicurrency world.

Commandment 2c rests on the assumption that once central banks have disclosed their money-supply strategies, they cease to have better information and hence a basis for a better judgement than private market participants. It can also be taken to imply that central banks might rather irritate private stabilizing speculation, which can be expected to be even more effective under conditions of full convertibility and preannounced money-supply policies.

3. Several objections may be raised against this position. I first deal with two major objections against a preannounced monetary policy, and then turn to the arguments against nonintervention.

4. The first objection against preannounced monetary growth rates is that monetary policy can no longer be used as an instrument of discretionary demand management. This argument does not convince me, as I believe to observe forces that have largely destroyed the effectiveness of discretionary monetary policies as a tool of demand management.

4a. Inflation has reduced the available stock of money illusion so that monetary policy has become less potent as a means of raising

[3] Full convertibility would especially help many developing countries to become more attractive to foreign capital.

the level of employment and capacity utilization above its sustainable trend value. In the same way, inflation and the destruction of money illusion have shortened the time lag between monetary growth and its impact on the price level (more rational expectations).

4b. Flexibility of exchange rates further shortens this time lag. If monetary authorities expand the money stock for employment reasons, they immediately induce a depreciation of the exchange rate, so that at least import prices will rise more quickly than under fixed exchange rates. The acceleration of monetary growth thus transforms itself earlier into price rises. The destruction of exchange-rate illusion adds to the decline of money illusion mentioned above.

4c. The price of attempts to restore money illusion by engineering a recession or foreign-exchange illusion by selling foreign exchange (including borrowed exchange) seems to be rising. This price is, of course, to be expressed in opportunity costs, that is, in the costs of alternative strategies. The best alternative strategy, at least in advanced countries, appears to be one that anticipates rational expectations and fully incorporates them as part of a new economic policy.

4d. In a world of declining money illusion and foreign-exchange illusion, governments and central banks are increasingly forced to recognize and to concede quite openly that monetary policy is price-level policy and that the level of employment and capacity utilization in any one area (firm, region, or national economy) is being determined by those who conclude wage contracts binding others (collective wage bargaining with minimum-wage effects) or who fix product prices. This entails a shift of responsibility from governments to markets and from (short-term) demand management to (long-term) supply policies, including policies to maintain and strengthen competition and the flexibility of relative prices and wages.

4e. The announcement of money growth targets in the United States, Germany, Switzerland, and other countries and the emphasis on steadier policies are illustrations of the fact that the required change in economic policies has already begun.

Thus I envisage a transition toward forms of economic policy in which steadiness and predictability play a greater role than discretion and policy uncertainty. This transition should help to improve the functioning of

55

decentralized planning in domestic and international markets and should facilitate the international *ex ante* coordination of policies.

5. The second objection against a preannounced monetary policy is that unexpected shifts in the demand for money may lead to deflationary or inflationary results. A monetarist's answer to this objection would be that the demand for money (or the income velocity) is rather stable over the longer run, although it is not constant over the cycle. He would add that the time lags tend to vary and thus to be fairly unpredictable; monetary acceleration or deceleration in order to neutralize changes of demand originating from the real sector may, therefore, even turn out to be procyclical. He would thus recommend a stable monetary expansion.

6. In my opinion the most important aspect of monetary policy is that monetary growth rates are predictable—they need not be constant. In the present circumstances monetary growth rates still must be different from the long-term trend, because we still have to cope with the cyclical disturbances resulting from past errors of monetary policy (fast monetary acceleration followed by unanticipated monetary deceleration). If, despite preannounced money growth rates, there are still marked shifts in demand arising from the real sector, they might (hopefully) be met by fiscal policy within the constraints of the preannounced monetary targets.

7. Thus far the discussion has mainly concentrated on the relation between money held by domestic residents in the country of origin and domestic expenditures. But should we not take a wider view to include changes in the international demand for money, that is, shifts in currency areas? In the international competition of currencies, a good currency will be preferred to a bad currency as an asset by official as well as by private holders. Foreigners can thus "immigrate" into a country's currency area or enlarge it. If this additional demand is not accommodated, the domestic economy will experience an unintended and unanticipated deflation combined with an equally unforeseen appreciation of the exchange rate. On the other hand, the country whose currency has become less attractive will suffer from inflationary pressures combined with a devaluation of its currency. A stabilizing strategy would therefore involve an immediate reduction of the money-supply target in the latter country

and an additional monetary expansion in the former country, in other words, in both cases a deviation from the preannounced rate.

8. The immediate correction of the target is mainly a problem of information. As to changes of demand by foreign central banks, the problem can be solved rather easily: all that is required are notifications once foreign central banks have decided to hold larger (or smaller) amounts of the currency in their reserves. The matter can then be settled between the central banks outside the exchange market. In this case, the monetary authorities can still follow the concept of preannounced targets, if the money-supply target is defined in a way that it does not include foreign official holdings.

9. A more difficult question relates to what can and should be done if there is little or no such instant information about demand from private foreign-exchange holders. One answer is that central banks will have to watch what is going on in the market and accommodate after the event. This strategy has three important drawbacks:

9a. Reliable indicators for a sustained shift in the international demand for money may not be readily available.

9b. If monetary accommodation takes place with a time lag, it may be a source of cyclical disturbances.

9c. Deviations from, or unanticipated revisions of, money-supply targets, although accommodating, may create uncertainties in foreign-exchange markets.

10. A second answer is to regard changes in the international demand for money as similar to changes in domestic demand for money, and stick to the preannounced rates for the sake of credibility. This solution seems to have a special appeal to large countries, where changes in the international demand for money can be expected to be fairly small in relation to its stock of money.

11. A third answer is to replace the money-supply target by an exchange-rate target with an endogenous money supply. The exchange-rate target has to be announced *vis-à-vis* another currency area (single currency or basket of currencies). In this case, the country can still

57

choose its own rate of inflation, if the monetary expansion in the reference currency area is known.[4] If the desired rate of inflation in the dependent country is lower than in the reference currency area, the exchange-rate target would have to be formulated as a preannounced upward crawl. The advantage of this solution is that unexpected movements in the international demand for domestic money ("immigration" or "emigration") will be endogenously compensated, and negative effects on the demand for domestic goods or services can be avoided. This solution appears to be especially favorable to small countries with a small stock of money, where changes in the international demand for money have a strong influence on the domestic economy.

12. On the other hand, a preannounced exchange-rate target means that the country cannot rely on the exchange rate as a protection against foreign fluctuations in the demand for domestic goods, which is especially important for small countries with a large foreign-trade sector. This can be demonstrated by a brief example: Country X chooses the same rate of inflation, which is to be expected for the reference currency area and announces as its target to maintain the present exchange rate[5]; in other words, the country has decided in favor of a fixed exchange rate. Consider now two symmetrical cases of foreign disturbances:

> 12a. Foreign demand for domestic products *falls* unexpectedly because of a foreign recession due to an insufficient monetary expansion compared with the announced rate or to changes in the real sector. In order to prevent a devaluation of its currency, country X has to use contractive policies, that is, to import deflation.
>
> 12b. Foreign demand for domestic products *rises* unexpectedly. In order to prevent an appreciation of its currency, country X has to increase its money supply, that is, to import (additional) inflation.

To prevent the import of such disturbances I have advocated flexible exchange rates even for small countries, where the foreign trade sector tends to be relatively large.[6]

---

[4] This implies that at least one country must have a money-supply target.

[5] This abstracts from expected changes in the real sector.

[6] See Herbert Giersch, "Enterpreneurial Risk under Flexible Exchange Rates," in *Approaches to Greater Flexibility of Exchange Rates. The Bürgenstock Papers*, George N. Halm, ed. (Princeton, N.J.: Princeton University Press, 1970), p. 149.

13. The choice to be made here is between protection against foreign disturbances in the demand for domestic currency (preannounced exchange-rate changes and endogenous monetary expansion) and protection against foreign disturbances in the demand for goods and services (preannounced monetary expansion and endogenous exchange-rate changes). The decision will depend on: the reliability of monetary policy in the reference currency area; probability of strong shocks arising from the foreign real sector; capability of the domestic government sector to compensate for cyclical disturbances arising from abroad (fiscal policy); and the flexibility of domestic wages and prices in response to changes in foreign demand.

14. My personal view is that as long as there is no clear evidence for a dominating influence of unforeseen shifts in currency areas, not only larger but also small countries should announce money-supply targets and leave the exchange rate to the market. The risk of unexpected changes in the international demand for money can be reduced by choosing a rather short announcement period. On the other hand, the period must be sufficiently long to represent at least a reasonable short-term planning period for firms and trade unions. Both points, aggregately seem to recommend an announcement period of about one year.[7] If, as a result of this policy, the present heavy shifts in international portfolios will have slowed down, a somewhat longer announcement period may be advisable, especially for larger countries.

15. Having discussed the role of central banks as producers of currencies via their monetary policy, we can now turn to the influence that official authorities can or should exert on the demand side by selling or buying foreign currencies; this relates to commandment 2c which states that the exchange market should be left to private market participants and that official authorities should not intervene.

16. The first possible objection to this commandment is that official interventions are necessary, because private speculators, if left alone, will cause heavy and costly fluctuations of the exchange rate. There are two points in this objection:

[7] This is in agreement with the present policy of the Deutsche Bundesbank.

16a. Private speculators cannot do the job of stabilization.
16b. Official intervention (speculation) can do it better.

17. The debate about the quality of private speculation (point 16a) has been a long one; let me briefly summarize two ideas that I regard as especially important in this connection:

17a. Sharp fluctuations in the exchange rate are generally the result of heavy changes in the underlying economic conditions. There is much reason to assume that these changes have in most cases not been caused by a highly unstable private sector but rather by government policies, for example, by unforeseen stop-and-go monetary policies or massive short-term interventions in the exchange market. Preannounced government policies will greatly reduce insecurity and improve the efficiency of stabilizing speculation.
17b. Private speculators have an interest in stabilizing the exchange rate, as they gain when they buy at a low rate and sell at a high rate. There is a possibility that some speculators might try to push the rate above its equilibrium value in the hope, that unexperienced speculators will take this as a signal to buy and cause an even further rise of the rate. However, this is not only a very risky strategy, but also requires a strong market position, a high degree of insecurity and considerable differences in information. Whether any private speculator has a dominating position in the exchange market must be doubted regarding the large number of banks and other companies acting in the market.

Yet, even with more comprehensive information about government policies it is not to be expected that private speculation will smooth all fluctuations in the exchange rate; the adjustment process may be too slow or there may be overshooting of equilibrium rates.[8] However, even if overshooting exists, this is not yet an argument for government or central-bank interventions. To effect stabilization, official authorities must know *when* the rate is overshooting.

18. The only convincing reason why an official authority should be a

---

[8] It should, however, be noted, that in a world with imperfect information and thresholds in the adjustment process "overshooting" may even play a useful role, if it speeds up necessary economic changes, which would otherwise be delayed.

better speculator than private market participants (point 16b) is that it has better information. In respect to a central bank, this essentially means better information about its own monetary policy. If monetary growth rates are preannounced, the information gap disappears and with it the argument for official interventions: private and official agents having the same level of information can only differ in interpreting the data. Under these conditions it is doubtful whether official authorities will make better forecasts than private agents. As Milton Friedman has pointed out, the latter, after all, "are risking their own money."

19. A second source of better central-bank information may stem from consulting the IMF, but IMF information is to be regarded as a public good and should therefore be freely disseminated; in this case, the information argument disappears.

20. If we look at the exchange-rate system during the last three to four years, three points have to be stressed:

20a. It is increasingly admitted that flexible exchange rates have generally worked rather well.
20b. There have been marked fluctuations in some exchange rates.
20c. There have been large-scale official interventions between currencies with fixed rates and those with floating rates.

The question of interest, which those in favor of official interventions will have to face, is whether central banks made a gain or a loss from their exchange-market operations. My impression is that official interventions have to a great deal delayed rather than expedited the necessary exchange-rate adjustments by leaning against the wind.

21. The second possible objection against commandment 2c is that international institutions should leave the choice as to which assets a central bank elects to hold in its portfolio to the bank itself and not prevent it from buying or selling foreign currency.

22. Exchange-rate interventions would not pose a great problem if central banks were entrusted with the task of stabilizing speculation. Under flexible exchange rates their mandate could then be defined as follows: maximize profits from exchange-rate dealings and other open-market operations under the constraint that the money supply is increased

at the preannounced rate. The question as to whether it is advisable to let official agents speculate with taxpayers' money in this narrow sense is not of international concern.

23. A problem arises, however, as to whether a central bank has a strong position in the exchange market, for instance, because of large foreign exchange holdings. Under these circumstances, it cannot be completely excluded, that the central bank in pursuing a profit-maximizing policy might attempt to gain from starting a destabilizing speculation. In this case a second constraint has to be added: any official speculator should behave like a competitor in a polypolistic market; otherwise, exchange-rate interventions would have to be ruled out completely as under commandment 2c.

24. At this point it seems appropriate to discuss briefly whether foreign currency can be an attractive asset for a central bank. In so doing, it appears legitimate to apply the Keynesian motives for holding money to central banks.

> 24a. Under flexible exchange rates the transaction demand and the precautionary demand for money play no role, as the central bank has extremely long-term liabilities (its own money), so that there is no need to hold liquid assets.[9]
> 24b. The speculative motive can apply to central banks, which expect that a foreign currency will appreciate at least as much as is necessary to compensate for the foregone interest earnings.

Apart from these motives, a central bank may wish to acquire liquid foreign reserves in order to make use of external economies for example, of the benefits from confidence which the country gains in international financial markets.

25. In the following we shall consider different cases of interventions that might be expected to take place, if commandment 2c does not (yet) apply. We shall first discuss interventions under short-term asset-return aspects and long-range development aspects and then consider interven-

---

[9] Even under fixed exchange rates, foreign reserves are not absolutely necessary, as a country can prevent a devaluation not only by selling foreign exchange, but also by selling domestic securities.

tions as an instrument of demand management, including "beggar-my-neighbor" policies.

26. A country may regard its holdings of foreign currency as being too large and wish to sell its excess reserves against other assets with a higher return. For the foreign central bank this amounts to an additional fall in the demand for its money. If the latter has fixed a monetary target net of foreign official exchange holdings the decline in demand has to be neutralized. The easiest way of doing so is to offer the foreign central-bank assets with a higher rate of interest to replace the low-interest debt (money).

The adjustment process will work rather smoothly if notification between central banks about their foreign-exchange operations, as mentioned above, is made compulsory.

27. In the opposite case, a central bank may wish to increase its foreign reserves. Apart from speculative demand, the reason may be to increase international confidence into the country's economy. This argument, which is especially important for less developed countries, is closely connected to the convertibility postulate (commandment 2a). Foreign investors are inclined to regard a high level of foreign-exchange reserves as an index of the country's ability to resist pressure toward restricting convertibility on balance-of-payments grounds. Countries with a low standing in international capital markets may thus be justified to increase their liquid reserves in an effort to show that they are likely to be good debtors. The investment in international liquidity may then pay off in terms of lower interest rates for foreign funds. Once the country has gained sufficient standing in international financial markets, a process that can be promoted most effectively by accepting and adhering to commandment 2a, liquid reserves may be less necessary. Reserves can then be transformed into other assets urgently needed for producing goods and services.

28. As to exchange-rate interventions in connection with demand management policies, we may distinguish four cases:

28a. Expansionary monetary policy plus acquiring foreign reserves.
28b. Expansionary monetary policy plus selling foreign reserves.

28c. Contractive monetary policy plus acquiring foreign reserves.

28d. Contractive monetary policy plus selling foreign reserves.

29. Case 28a, which can be described as the strategy for an "export-led upswing," corresponds to the classical "beggar-my-neighbor" policy of "exporting" unemployment. Four points have to be made here:

29a. The extent to which employment rises depends on the prevailing degree of money illusion and exchange-rate illusion. An "export-led-upswing" can be expected to take place only in connection with an especially high degree of exchange-rate illusion, since the exchange rate will depreciate more, and import prices will rise faster than in the alternative case of an expansionary monetary policy via domestic open-market operations. Thus, the more rational the expectations, the smaller will be the increase in employment.

29b. Whether employment abroad actually falls will essentially depend on whether the additional demand for money can be accommodated, for the deflationary effect will come about because the foreign official demand for *money* rises unexpectedly. (Nobody would complain about "beggar-my-neighbor" policies if goods were purchased instead of currency.)

The solution to the problem of accommodation is notification. Any additional demand for money by foreign central banks could then be met by automatically expanding the money supply, so that the additional demand for foreign exchange is neutralized.

29c. Moreover, one has to remind oneself that the purchase of foreign exchange is not without cost; the official authorities must either spend less on domestic goods or borrow at high rates of interest or impose a tax on the public. In our case, where the purchase is financed by monetary expansion, the cost consists of an inflation tax on money, the proceeds of which are going to the foreign central bank.[10] This means that the foreign country will even benefit from the attempted "beggar-my-neighbor" policy.

29d. Finally, it can be shown that in general it would be less expensive for society to achieve the mercantilistic goal of promoting export and import-substitution industries by means of a direct subsidy rather than by an undervaluation of the currency.

[10] This implies that the foreign central bank does not increase its currency holdings but spends the money it acquired in the accommodation process.

Taking these points together, it appears that in a system of preannounced money-supply targets and an agreed notification on interventions, there would not be much reason to worry about "beggar-my-neighbor" policies.

30. The same applies for 'interventions on cross purposes." The problem of internationally inconsistent policies seems to be most relevant for the duopoly case, when two countries intervene because they consider their respective currencies to be overvalued. The danger in this case is that A may be successful in appreciating B's currency until B discovers it and launches a counterattack. Exchange rates would then fluctuate in a seesaw fashion. This, however, could be prevented very easily if the intervening authorities would have to notify each other; B would learn immediately what A is doing and could react without a time lag. The efforts would neutralize each other and would, therefore, probably not be undertaken.

31. The second case represents a "domestic upswing" strategy. The idea behind this policy is to prevent a fast decline of the exchange rate and a corresponding rise in import prices, which would otherwise come about because of the expansionary monetary policy. It is a strategy to make use of exchange-rate illusion, so that employment effects from increasing the money supply are not too weak and not too short-lived. In this case, foreign exchange is sold in order "to buy time," which, however, cannot be purchased in unlimited amounts.

32. The "domestic-upswing" strategy can be described as follows: The central bank buys domestic securities against its own money (expansionary open-market policy). This will induce a fall of the interest rate and a depreciation of the domestic currency. In order to prevent the latter, the central bank has to sell foreign exchange (including borrowed reserves) against its own money. The monetary expansion due to the open-market policy must be stronger than the monetary contraction due to the exchange-market operation, so that there is a net increase in the money supply. This result is achieved if the central bank sells enough currency to cause the foreign interest rate to fall; the lower domestic interest rate is then compatible with the original exchange rate. Or to state it another way, as the exchange rate is the relative price of two monies, monetary expansion can be achieved without altering the exchange rate, if the

65

supply of the foreign currency rises correspondingly—or if the demand for foreign currency falls, which amounts to the same.

33. A "domestic-upswing" policy thus implies an expansion of both the domestic and the foreign money supplies relative to demand. This means that the foreign country is faced with an inflationary pressure. But if there is notification, the foreign central bank can neutralize this effect by a contractionary monetary policy. Under these circumstances, the expansionary country cannot prevent a depreciation of its exchange rate and a "domestic upswing" policy is no longer possible. (Apart from this, a policy based on the exploitation of illusion is hardly effective, once monetary expansion is preannounced.)

34. Cases 28c and 28d are symmetrical to cases 28a and 28b. A contractive policy as under case 28c will place the main burden on the domestic sector while the export- and import-substitution industries benefit from the prevented exchange-rate appreciation. Case 28d, on the other hand, implies a rather rapid and pronounced appreciation. This might help to break inflationary expectations in the export- and import-substitution industries and to alleviate cost pressures arising from the import side. However, it also depresses profits in the export- and import-substitution sector.

35. Again, in a system where interventions are duly notified, foreign central banks can neutralize the inflationary (case 28d) or deflationary (case 28c) impact on their economics by accommodating the additional fall–rise in the demand for their currencies. Thus any country would be free to protect itself against monetary effects of exchange-rate interventions by foreign authorites.

36. In conclusion, the following remarks are presented:

36a. The most promising international economic policy reforms, in my opinion, are those that help to improve the system of free markets. This essentially requires a reduction of government restrictions and regulations, which interfere with the efficient working of the market mechanism. In respect to the exchange market, this means to prevent new impediments to international transactions and to take progressive steps to abolish existing restrictions, as is implied in commandment 2a above.

36b. Markets will work better when more information is provided about future economic policies. Thus governments should announce their intentions well in advance. Once overall government behavior has become more predictable, markets can be expected to show more stability. Regarding exchange markets, it is of special importance to know which monetary strategy a government or central bank will pursue. In this paper it is argued that generally the information problem can be solved best, if the monetary authorities commit themselves to a preannounced money-supply target, as it is implied by commandment 2b. Difficulties may arise from unexpected fluctuations in the private demand for money, especially shifts in currency areas, and may call for a shorter announcement period, especially for smaller countries. On these grounds, an announcement period of about one year has been regarded advisable under the present circumstances. Once fluctuations have dampened, a somewhat longer announcement period should be considered, especially for larger countries.

36c. If unforeseen shifts in the foreign demand for money are regarded to be more important than unforeseen shifts in the foreign demand for goods and services, a country may decide to have an exchange-rate target with an endogenous money supply. The term "money supply" in commandment 2b would then have to be replaced by the term "exchange rate."

36d. Strategies with either a money-supply target or an exchange-rate target are preferable to policies where targets are kept secret, are internally inconsistent, or are inconsistent over time (target switching). Unforeseen or inconsistent policies, especially if they appear in a stop-and-go fashion, will exert damaging real effects not only on their own economy, but on other countries as well and can, therefore, be regarded as harmful also from an international standpoint. Thus the transition to foreseeable government policies should be considered a matter of international concern.

36e. As to official exchange-rate intervention, one possibility is to accept commandment 2c, that is, to permit no interventions. This, however, seems to be a rather long-term solution. If central banks still want to use the instrument of exchange-rate interventions, which may be even necessary in the period of transition, when past errors have to be corrected, it seems to be appropriate to replace

67

commandment 2c by another commandment that can be briefly stated as, "No intervention without notification!" As has been shown above, notification enables a country to protect itself against the monetary effects of exchange-rate intervention by foreign authorities and is thus an efficient means to prevent competitive devaluations.

37. The role of the IMF in this system can be conceived as follows:

37a. The IMF will be an international center of information.

37b. The IMF should use all of its influence to reduce restrictions that affect international transactions and to prevent governments from introducing new restrictions—an aspect that seems to be of special importance in the present situation.

37c. The IMF may encourage its members to lay open their longer-term economic strategies and prevent them from making inconsistent promises, from pursuing inconsistent policies, and from losing credibility as a result of both.

37d. The IMF can support the efficient working of the exchange market by encouraging the announcement of money-supply targets (or possibly exchange-rate targets); this may include surveillance over announced targets.

37e. Since official exchange-rate intervention cannot realistically be prohibited (surveillance over nonintervention) on a short-term basis, the IMF may establish a system of immediate notification on interventions. Exchange-rate surveillance in the narrow sense will then consist of surveillance over notifications.

RICHARD N. COOPER

YALE UNIVERSITY, NEW HAVEN, CONN.

UNDER THE amended IMF Articles of Agreement, to take formal effect sometime in 1977, countries are free to adopt any of a variety of arrangements for the exchange rates of their currencies; but whatever arrangements they adopt, they undertake to "avoid manipulating exchange rates or the international monetary system in order to prevent effective balance of payments adjustments or to gain an unfair competitive advantage over other members." (Article IV as revised.) The IMF is charged with exercising surveillance with respect to these (as well as other) commitments by member countries. This paper is addressed to the stance that the IMF might take with respect to this new, or rather revised, assignment.

The injunctions themselves raise certain questions. First, is a member country enjoined from exchange-rate action that gives it an unfair competitive advantage against each and every other country? "Unfair" is a weasel-word that permits an affirmative answer to the question, but if that is left aside, the answer must surely be negative; an equilibrium exchange rate may well leave a country with an overwhelming competitive advantage over *some* other countries, which advantage is offset by the position of this rate with respect to other countries. Thus the prohibition must refer to some *average* exchange rate with respect to all other countries. But which average? Different methods of calculation may give quite different results, and no one method seems obviously superior to others.[1] Thus any calculation must of necessity be only rough.

[1] For an illustration of the differences between several different averages, see Rudolf R. Rhomberg, "Indices of Effective Exchange Rates," *IMF Staff Papers* 23 (March 1976), 88–112. Rhomberg argues that for focusing on the effects on a country's trade balance the various exchange rates between the country's currency and those of other countries must be weighted by response elasticities, as is done by the IMF's multilateral exchange-rate model

69

Second, what is the "effective balance-of-payments adjustment" that is not to be prevented? The difficulties with various concepts of the balance of payments are well known, especially for countries with extensive capital and banking transactions with the rest of the world.[2] The most straightforward interpretation of the injunction is that it requires no change in a country's international reserves, net of changes in the valuation of reserves, or net of official compensatory financing (e.g., activation of swap arrangements or transactions with the IMF) in a stationary world, or no deviation from some targeted growth in reserves in a growing world. This formulation, if it is to allow official intervention in exchange markets, obviously involves some time dimension. For example, there should be no deviation from some targeted growth in reserves over a twelve- to eighteen-month period, or over a three- to five-year period. It also obviously (in a growing world) presupposes that there be some targeted growth in reserves, and that in turn suggests (for global consistency of targets and of exchange-market intervention) that the target be an internationally accepted one and that the total supply of new international reserves be adequate to meet the targeted demand for them, either through a decision to create reserves or through a reserve-creating mechanism that is sufficiently elastic to satisfy the aggregate total of nationally determined demand for reserves. Other chapters in this volume address that ticklish problem. Finally, this formulation of adjustment in payments leaves open a number of questions about the countries whose currencies are held as international reserves by other countries. One feasible approach to this last problem is to treat reserve-currency countries like other countries as far as criteria for payments adjustment are concerned,

---

(MERM). Although MERM is concerned with *changes* in exchange rates, it could in principle be adapted to generate equilibrium exchange rates. However, its underlying assumptions, especially with respect to the responses of production to price changes, are too crude to provide persuasive estimates; and in any case it focuses exclusively on trade and makes no attempt to incorporate other important components to a country's balance of payments, such as services and movements of capital.

[2] A recent summary can be found in the Report of the Advisory Committee on the Presentation of Balance of Payments Statistics for the United States, *Statistical Reporter*, No. 76-12, June 1976, Office of Management and Budget, U.S. Government. Because of the difficulties, this report advocated eliminating publication of any overall balance-of-payments statistic for the United States.

and to make allowance in their targeted growth in reserves, or in other credit facilities, for the fact that they have highly liquid liabilities to other countries.

A third question about the injunctions concerning exchange-rate manipulation is whether the second one includes the first. Can a country have effective balance-of-payments adjustment and still have an unfair competitive advantage? Are these meant to be two separate injunctions, or only one? Is it permissible for a country to intervene in exchange markets (by selling its own currency) so as to achieve a large trade surplus, for instance, and then restore overall payments balance through official credits to foreigners? In short, does the new IMF Article IV stipulate implicit trade-balance targets as well as the requirement for overall balance in international payments? Is this provision, to push the point further, designed to block the use of expansionary monetary policy under a regime of floating exchange rates, where the channel by which monetary policy influences the demand for domestic output is via a depreciated exchange rate, and if so, why? Other countries not wishing the deflation in demand for their products arising from an appreciating exchange rate can also engage in monetary expansion, restoring the previous rate. Or is the term "manipulation" meant to apply exclusively to intervention in foreign-exchange markets, and not to other actions that may influence exchange rates? The context suggests a broader interpretation.

The guiding principle, it seems to me, should be that in their actions countries should not impose costs on other nations except when that is unavoidable from the nature of the problem being addressed. Dampening of a domestic boom, for example, will lead to a fall in imports from other nations, a fall that may be unwelcome. But if the boom had produced a payments deficit, the fall would be unavoidable. Any remaining corrective action, for example, with respect to their own domestic demand, is up to other nations.

71

Reasons for Intervention in Exchange Markets

Each individual country would like its exchange rate to move in such a way as to maximize its national welfare, somehow defined. To a first approximation, we can take this to mean some combination of net national output and price stability, where the "netting" of national output is taken to mean not merely net of investment for replacement but also net of all frictional costs associated with the reallocation of resources. On this standard, the welfare-maximizing exchange rate will not in general be the momentary equilibrium rate, that is, the rate that would clear the exchange market at each moment of time, exclusive of speculative positions in the currency. The welfare-maximizing rate will generally show less variability than the momentary equilibrium rate. Perfectly foresighted speculation will bring the two rates together, provided that (a) all frictional social costs are reflected in the price signals to those who decide on the allocation of production and consumption and (b) capital markets are perfect in the sense that risk-adjusted borrowing rates are equated at the margin for all potential speculators as well as investors. Condition (a) will not be met to the extent that labor can be dismissed and will remain unemployed because of downward stickiness in wages or because rational individual search behavior in a world of imperfect information leads to a period of frictional unemployment.

That these two conditions are not in fact met will produce a case in principle for official intervention in exchange markets, even if speculators were accurate in their foresight, exclusive of the official intervention. The monetary authorities should intervene to keep the exchange rate at its welfare-maximizing rate.

It is impossible to make this injunction operational, even if the set of welfare-maximizing rates for all countries taken together were consistent (which is unlikely). Our ignorance of economic structure (including its dynamic properties), of market imperfections, and of disturbances to national economies is simply too vast. As Murray Kemp has pointed out in connection with optimal reserve holdings, they depend on all other aspects of the world economic system, including the economic policies

72

and the reserve holdings of other countries.[3] The same is true of the closely related question of optimal exchange-rate policy. Therefore, any guidelines to exchange-rate policy are necessarily in the realm of second-best, or, as Kemp observes, qth best, where q is a number much larger than two. Many other actions should be involved in framing an optimal economic policy. Exchange-rate guidelines can at best be designed to avoid the obviously undesirable or troublesome outcomes, necessarily admitting many possible deviations as compared with the optimal policy sketched above.

For most countries, the exchange rate represents the single most important price after the wage rate, and "the" wage rate is even more elusive than "the" exchange rate. Modern governments are held responsible for management of their national economies, and it is thus neither possible nor desirable that governments be indifferent to movements in the exchange rate. They can influence it indirectly through their other economic policies, but for reasons given above they will also find it appropriate from time to time to intervene directly in the foreign-exchange market.

Governments may intervene in exchange markets with a variety of objectives:

1. to smooth out short-term fluctuations in the exchange rate, which may be disturbing both to businesses and to consumers (the possibility of transacting in the forward market does not solve the problem in itself, since the forward rate may also fluctuate disturbingly);

2. to avoid mistaken signals to reallocate resources, for example, over a cycle in economic activity, and thus to avoid costly but unnecessary resource reallocations;

3. to avoid external impetus to domestic-factor price increases, and especially wage increases, through one-way escalation in the cost of living or some other price index;

4. to alter the level of international reserves held by the country;

[3] Murray C. Kemp, "World Reserve Supplementation: Long-run Needs for Short-run Purposes," in *International Reserves: Needs and Availability* (Washington, D.C.: International Monetary Fund, 1970), pp. 3–11.

5. to generate domestic employment by increasing exports and reducing imports;

6. to dampen domestic inflation by making foreign goods cheaper in the home market;

7. to keep profits from falling in the export- or import-competing sectors of the economy, and no doubt for other reasons as well.

It is the task of any guidance laid down by the IMF to discourage or prohibit exchange-market intervention for reasons that are inimical to the interests of other countries and to the continued smooth functioning of the world economy, while permitting or encouraging intervention for other reasons. Speaking generally, the first three reasons for intervention given on the foregoing list can be viewed as "legitimate" by the international community, the fouth may be legitimate under certain circumstances but will otherwise be suspect, and the remaining three can be viewed as illegitimate reasons for intervening in exchange markets. But even this is too simplistic, for occasions will arise in which an apparently illegitimate action also serves the interests of other countries. So any guidelines can be presumptive only, and must be applied with judgment.

Strategies for Exchange-market Intervention

With managed flexibility, countries need a principle concerning when to intervene. The 1974 IMF Guidelines for the Management of Floating Exchange Rates envisages as possible two quite different strategies, which could be called the "tracking strategy" and the "smoothing and braking strategy." The tracking strategy involves taking a view on what the exchange rate should be, while the smoothing and braking strategy involves taking a view on what maximum rates of change in the exchange rate should be. The former is closer to a system of parities, while the latter is closer to full flexibility of exchange rates.

The Tracking Strategy. A clear exposition of the tracking strategy is offered by John Williamson.[4] He calls it the "reference rate" proposal, and

[4] John Williamson, "The Future Exchange Rate Regime," Banca Nazionale del Lavoro *Quarterly Review* (June 1975), pp. 3–20.

74

attributes its central features to Ethier and Bloomfield. In essence, it involves the establishment for all countries of a system of consistent "reference" exchange rates, which would be subject to periodic review. Countries would then be permitted (but not obliged) to intervene in the exchange market so as to move the market exchange rate toward the reference rate, but would be prohibited from intervention that would push the market rate away from the reference rate. That is, intervention would track the reference rate. (The 1974 guidelines speak of a "medium-term norm" for each exchange rate and a "target zone" around that medium-term norm, outside of which a country would be permitted to intervene "aggressively," i.e., to reinforce market pressures tending to push the market rate toward the target zone.)

Williamson sees two powerful arguments in support of reference-rate system. First, a rule for compulsory reserve asset settlement could be introduced into a system of floating rates. Without something like a reference rate, it would be difficult to require a country to convert into primary reserve assets its currency that had been acquired through market intervention at the volition of some other country and without any coordination with the reserve-currency country. Presumably by agreeing on a pattern of reference rates, the reserve-currency country would also agree that any of its currency acquired in conformity with the rules of intervention would be convertible into primary reserve assets. Second, organized multicurrency intervention would be possible, thus avoiding the asymmetries for the reserve-currency country attendant on the use of a single intervention currency, for example, the U.S. dollar. An inspection of the pattern of deviaitons of market from reference rates would indicate the choice of currency that any intervening country should buy or sell against its own currency, so that a number of currencies could be potential candidates for intervention, thus eliminating the asymmetrical position of the United States. Both of these considerations were important in the discussions of the Committee of Twenty on Reform of the Monetary System, and Williamson would like to see any exchange-rate system incorporate them.

A further argument in favor of the reference-rate proposal is that currency speculation would reinforce official action as long as the reference

75

rates are credible, while at the same time there is enough flexibility so that speculators are not presented with the one-way option they frequently encountered under a system of fixed but changeable parities.

A key prerequisite to this tracking strategy is obviously to obtain agreement on the system of reference rates and their changes over time. Some of the literature on gliding parities would be helpful in offering guidance to changes in reference rates over time—changes could be linked to movements in market rates, for instance, or to some combination of market rates and movements in reserves[5]—but that would not help in discovering a set of plausible reference rates from which to initiate the process.

The problem of finding and then changing adequately a system of reference rates is especially difficult in a period of rapid economic change, such as has been brought about recently by world inflation, by the sharp increase in oil prices, and by the ensuing world recession. It is also difficult when there are wide variations in the behavior of important national economies, such as can now be observed, for example, between West Germany and the United States on the one hand, and Britain and Italy on the other. Even when the problem involves mainly divergent rates of inflation, purchasing-power-parity comparisons offer only a general guide, not adequately refined for the setting of exchange rate norms. Absolute purchasing-power-parity comparisons are notoriously unreliable as a guide to appropriate exchange rates, and relative purchasing-power-parity comparisons are only a moderately adequate guide, even when a satisfactory base period can be found.[6] Yet what would be an appropriate base period for the present—late 1971, 1968, or 1965? None of these years would be satisfactory without substantial adjustment. Nor are gen-

[5] See Peter B. Kenen, "Floats, Glides, and Indicators: A Comparison of Methods for Changing Exchange Rates," *Journal of International Economics* (May 1975), 5:107–51. Kenen finds, through a series of simulations, that changes in gliding parities based on changes in reserves generally lead to less error in a variety of situations than do other rules, although changes based on movements in market exchange rates do almost as well.

[6] For a recent comprehensive review of purchasing-power-parity theories and evidence, with a conclusion that is sympathetic to the theory but skeptical of its practical application without much further testing and refinement, see Lawrence H. Officer, "The Purchasing-Power-Parity Theory of Exchange Rates: A Review Article," *IMF Staff Papers* (March 1976), 23:1–60.

eral equilibrium analytical models nearly adequate in their present state of development to determine reference rates.[7]

A key problem all along has been our ignorance about the equilibrium exchange rates, and this difficulty would also plague the setting of reference rates. One could, of course, begin with a rough-and-ready set of reference rates and allow for a gradual approach to the "true" set of reference rates, which would itself be changing. But that possibility raises a second difficulty with reference rates, which is their too close resembalnce to exchange-rate parities. Although the differences between a set of reference rates as outlined by Williamson and a set of exchange-rate parities are in fact substantial, they are also subtle and might well be missed by government officials and the interested publics, especially in those countries (e.g., France or Japan) where a hankering after fixed exchange rates is still strong. Governments are too likely to treat reference rates, like parities, as offering no line of retreat without surrender, and therefore are likely to intervene too strongly to maintain market rates close to the reference rates. We perhaps need to allow exchange rates to float for a considerable period without any clear point of reference.

The *Smoothing and Braking Strategy*. For the possibly long interval during which governments are becoming accustomed to exchange-rate flexibility, an alternative strategy for intervention is smoothing and braking. This strategy implicitly acknowledges that we do not know what the equilibrium exchange rate over any time period is, but it allows for the likelihood that the "market" does not know either. The monetary authorities, therefore, intervene to prevent rapid movements in exchange rates except when those are clearly justified by the underlying economic conditions. If the market has been wrong in its collective judgment about the movement of an exchange rate, the monetary authority will have made a profit (capital gain) on its smoothing interventions. If, however, the market has been right, the monetary authorities will lose money by braking a cumulative movement in the exchange rate, for instance, by buying a depreciating currency or selling an appreciating one. But central banks are not endowed with their special legal powers for the purpose of

[7] See footnote 1.

making money. If they lose some money in the pursuit of broader social objectives, the loss may be amply repaid through the attainment of those social objectives.

It is possible to be more concrete. These days wages and other factor costs seem to be quite sensitive to movements, especially upward movements, in the cost of living. In some countries formal indexation of wages to the cost of living is widespread. Under these circumstances, a rapid depreciation of the exchange rate at a time when wage adjustments are scheduled to take place may trigger higher wages than would otherwise obtain, and thus over a period of time justify the expected depreciation of the currency. Prevention of self-justifying speculation against a currency might be one of those social purposes for which, if necessary, some loss of reserves is worthwhile.

Intervention at the wrong time can make matters worse, of course. If a country experiences a sharp deterioration in its terms of trade due to shortages abroad and the currency begins to depreciate, then intervention in the exchange market to prevent the depreciation will involve domestic monetary contraction, and if domestic prices do not fall readily this intervention may lead to prolonged unemployment. Here a choice must be made between allowing the price-increasing effect or the demand-contracting effect of the external disturbance to dominate.[8]

In general, it will be deisrable to counteract the impact effects of purely financial disturbances through exchange-rate intervention, whereas the appropriate action in response to real disturbances involves more complex alternatives among competing objectives. Of course, in a world of uncertainty the monetary authorities will not always be correct in their assessment of the nature of the underlying disturbances. But they must continually weigh the costs and benefits between (a) being wrong in braking the movement in an exchange rate when underlying factors call for such a movement and (b) being wrong in not intervening to brake the move-

---

[8] The OPEC price increase of 1974 represented a major supply "shortage," but it was against virtually the entire world economy, and currency depreciations by each individual oil-importing country, even in unison, would not have represented a helpful response, since a rise in the market value of the Saudi Arabian riyal could not have played a key role in mitigating the impact effects. Appropriate exchange-rate policy thus depends on all the surrounding circumstances.

ment in a rate depreciating under monetary market pressures when underlying factors do not call for a movement in the rate.

A method of correction is possible against excessive intervention. Direct intervention in spot-exchange markets implies a gain or a loss of international reserves, and the cumulative gain or loss in reserves indicates the degree of one-sidedness in intervention over the corresponding period. Each country could be asked to target a gain (or a loss, or possibly no change) in reserves over some stipulated period. If in the course of market intervention it acquires reserves that along with other factors (such as SDR allocations) lead to increases in reserves above the targeted increase, the country would be required under intervention guidelines to sell the excess reserves whenever it could without causing disorder in the exchange market. Thus over a period of time changes in reserves would correspond to targeted changes in reserves, and a monetary authority that had braked a movement in exchange rates during one period would find itself in some subsequent period pushing the exchange rate in the direction that the market had earlier moved it. In this respect exchange-market intervention would be similar to domestic monetary policy in several leading countries today; monetary actions are governed by short-run price targets combined with long-run quantity targets.

As with any international guidelines, one may ask what incentive countries have to adhere to them, especially, in this case, countries that have intervened to hold their exchange rates down and hence have accumulated international reserves. Ultimately, some system of "pressures" such as those discussed by the Committee of Twenty might have to be introduced, including the possibility of internationally sanctioned discrimination against the goods of a country that had persistently undervalued its currency (as evidenced by its excessive accumulation of reserves). But agreement on the injunctions and on the implementing guidelines should be sufficient to assure adherence to them.

Several questions arise in connection with a braking and smoothing strategy. First, why focus on reserve *changes* rather than on reserve *levels?* Especially since the latter target, rather than the former, seems to follow from the application of the theory of portfolio management. The first answer to this question is that it is inappropriate, without substantial adapta-

79

tion, to transfer to nations a theory designed for household asset management. (With adaptation we might, however, still find that reserve levels are a more appropriate target than changes in reserves.) The second answer to the question is that both theoretical and simulation results suggest that targeting reserve levels, because of the response lags of changes in trade and other international transactions to changes in exchange rates, would lead to substantial overshooting of targets and hence might increase rather than reduce the variability of exchange rates. Targeting changes in reserves is more stable.[9]

A second question concerns which countries should engage in braking and smoothing interventions, since every exchange rate is intrinsicially two-sided; especially when all relevant countries may not take the same view on when smoothing should take place or on how hard the brakes should be applied. One possible answer is that each country would be free to take a view on changes in the value of its currency with respect to some appropriate average of other currencies and could intervene in the one or several currencies that are most relevant to it. Examples can be constructed where such intervention may complicate the position of the country whose currency is used for intervention, but these will be relatively rare when the principal currency is used, and they can, if necessary, be compensated by intervention in exchange markets by the country whose currency is first used, that country in turn using currencies that are most relevant to it. The possibility of inconsistent interventions can be avoided by a requirement that all countries report their interventions immediately to some common information center, such as the IMF, and the center would immediately notify countries that were intervening at cross purposes.

A third question concerns the time period over which smoothing should take place—or, to state the same point another way, the time period over which reserve changes should be on target. Here there are important differences of view. Some emphasize the desirability of limiting smoothing interventions to strictly short periods of time, several weeks

[9] Kenen, "Floats, Glides, and Indicators: A Comparison of Methods for Changing Exchange Rates"; see also A. W. Phillips, "Stabilization Policy in a Closed Economy," *The Economic Journal* (June 1954), 64:290–323.

at the outside, to prevent disorderly markets. Others envisage smoothing over a longer priod, three to four years, covering an economic cycle. The longer the period, the greater the risk of being wrong, of intervening systematically against changes in equilibrium rates. This consideration suggests adopting the shorter period of time. On the other hand, it is easy enough to imagine a period of prolonged speculative pressure against a currency, for example, for six months, which the monetary authorities might well feel justified in resisting.

Moreover, consider a country that wants to ride out a world cycle in demand for its products, confident that it is a cycle, but because of price inelasticity of demand for its products and its concern about domestic inflation it does not want a temporary depreciation in its currency. Suppose further that international borrowing is costly compared to the alternative of running down its own international reserves temporarily, building them up again when export demand strengthens. Should the world financial community object to this strategy? The country's actions in this instance help to stabilize world demand.

It has been proposed that intervention in exchange markets should take place primarily or exclusively in *forward* exchange markets rather than spot markets.[10] This would have several advantages, notably that forward rates would provide a reference point to speculators in the spot market, that it would help develop forward markets, that arbitrage flows of capital would reinforce rather than work against the intentions of the authorities, and that the central bank could intervene in exchange markets without immediately also affecting the nation's money supply, as spot interventions do. That is, forward market intervention would permit short-term separation between monetary policy and exchange-rate policy. A limitation on this practice is that it would fail to deal with the direct influence of exchange rates on domestic prices and hence on wages, except insofar as importers and exporters buy or sell their foreign exchange in the forward rather than the spot market. Nonetheless, the proposal has merit.

---

[10] See Egon Sohmen, *Flexible Exchange Rates* (Chicago: University of Chicago Press, 1961); Stanley Black, *International Money Markets and Flexible Exchange Rates*, Princeton Studies in International Finance No 32, 1973; and William Day, "The Advantages of Exclusive Forward Exchange Rate Support," *IMF Staff Papers* (March 1976), 23:137–163.

While the operating decisions would be up to individual countries, the IMF might nudge them in the direction of greater use of forward markets.

General Observations

Exchange-rate policy cannot be logically separated from other aspects of macroeconomic policy. In principle, any view of the exchange rate and of intervention policy to achieve that exchange rate should take all other aspects of policy into account. The distinctive role of the IMF is not to oversee all aspects of macroeconomic policy in all of its member countries, but to serve as the guardian for the interests of other countries, and of the international financial system generally, with respect to the macroeconomic actions of each of its members—to ensure that the total package of policies does not impose avoidable costs on other countries or otherwise impair the smooth functioning of the world economy. The IMF's assessment cannot focus on exchange-rate intervention alone. There will be occasions when the deliberate or inadvertent undervaluation of a currency will impose a burden on other countries. But there will be other occasions when similar actions by a country will be beneficial to the rest of the world—for example, when world demand is exceptionally high and any source of "hoarding" is welcome. No detailed set of guidelines is likely to apply satisfactorily general injunctions to the manifold and diverse circumstances that may be encountered.

It will be difficult to improve on the guidelines adopted in 1974, short of movement to a full-fledged reference-rate system of the type proposed by Williamson. The 1974 guidelines provide a useful framework for the exercise of judgment, both by individual countries and by the IMF in its consultations with individual countries. They also will occasionally provide grounds for dispute about what is allowed and what is not. But since sensible use of guidelines will always depend on the circumstances, and evaluation of the circumstances will not always be fully accepted, this is inevitable. The IMF should enter discussions on exchange-rate practices with its members early, before complete guidelines are fully worked out,

82

because they never will be. Delay will provide precedent for nonconcern and nonintervention by the IMF.

At the operational level, can the IMF maintain the confidentiality necessary for frank discussion of exchange-rate policies? For example, is it possible in 1976 to have a full discussion in the IMF Executive Board regarding Japan's extensive intervention in exchange markets? Was Japan violating the new Article IV or not? The IMF needs some method and procedure for holding forthright discussions on such matters, and for holding them soon, for it is in the early period that the expectations of member countries will be established with regard to IMF surveillance under the new article.

COMMENTS

WALTER S. SALANT

THE BROOKINGS INSTITUTION, WASHINGTON, D. C.

BOTH OF THE PAPERS assigned to me for comment are very thoughtful and stimulating discussions of a difficult subject. The problem of how to exercise surveillance over exchange-rate policies is generally recognized, even at first sight, to be a complicated, one. It appears to me to become still more complicated the more one thinks about it, involving as it does all of the unsettled theoretical macroeconomic problems of closed economies and, in addition, the interrelationships of open economies, the uncertainties about international effects in the real world, and the policy problem of reconciling differences in trade-offs and other conflicts of national goals, including differences in the valuations that different countries attach to short-, medium-, and long-term effects.

Let me begin with the point that must be basic for the IMF, namely, the marching orders that Section 1 of the new Article IV give it. Richard Cooper has pointed out at the beginning of his paper several questions as to the very meaning of those marching orders and has provided answers with which I agree. One other point about the injunctions of Article IV appears relevant to surveillance. The IMF is required to oversee the compliance of members with two constraints on their exchange-rate policies, specifically, that they permit effective balance-of-payments adjustments and avoid gaining "an unfair competitive advantage over other members." Although these constraints are worded in terms of "manipulation,"

84

which implies motivations, an interpretation based on motives is both unenforceable and irrelevant, and I therefore interpret them as injunctions to avoid doing things that have these effects, irrespective of motivation. On that interpretation, these injunctions imply—inescapably, as it seems to me—that there is some exchange value of a currency that is so low as to give the issuing member country an "unfair competitive advantage over other members" and that there is also some rate too high to permit appropriate adjustment on the part of a deficit country or too low to permit appropriate adjustment of a surplus country that is unwilling to adjust by inflation. From this it follows that the IMF, in overseeing exchange-rate policies of members, cannot avoid formulating some idea of what constitutes an exchange rate that is inconsistent with the obligations of a member under Article IV, although this must, of course, be done in conjunction with specified domestic macroeconomic policies. In other words, the IMF, even though it may not be able to determine equilibrium rates, can hardly escape the obligation to determine for each member country a number of *zones*, each associated with a specified monetary and perhaps fiscal policy, outside of which an exchange rate would be inappropriate. Of course, this obligation is difficult to carry out, but the obligation itself is clearly implied in the marching orders of Article IV.

The Giersch Proposal

I now turn to a consideration of the policies that Professor Giersch proposes for member countries, which is the source of the role that he would assign to the IMF. The central proposal is that monetary authorities should announce and commit themselves to a target for the rate of growth of the money supplies of their countries. This rule applies, at least, when the authorities expect that unforeseen shifts in the foreign demand for goods and services are likely to be more important than unforeseen shifts in the foreign demand for domestic money, which the paper seems to imply is the normal case. Second, controls over short as well as long-term capital movements should be minimized. If these two

85

principles are followed, the framework is created for the third principle, which is that, in this case where the growth of the money supply is the target, central banks should not intervene in foreign exchange markets.

If, contrary to the assumption of this normal case, unforeseen shifts in foreign demand for money are expected to be more important than unforeseen shifts in the foreign demand for goods and services, Giersch would allow the country to preannounce and adhere to an exchange-rate target instead of a money-supply target, but then the money stock must be allowed to change endogenously.

Giersch also provides an alternative to the commandment against official intervention in the foreign-exchange market. He recognizes that central banks may still want to intervene and even says that intervention may be necessary during a transitional period in which past errors have to be corrected. In that case, he changes the commandment against intervention to a requirement that the central bank proposing to intervene notify the central bank of the country whose currency it proposes to buy or sell, so that it may take offsetting action if that appears appropriate.

The Underlying Theory

What is the theory underlying the Giersch proposal? First, why is so much emphasis placed on preannouncement of the money supply when the stock of money is an intermediate, and not an ultimate, target of economic policy? The more ultimate targets are the level of employment output, stability of the price level, efficiency in the allocation of resources, and the like. Giersch does not ignore this distinction, but he apparently believes that discretionary monetary policy is no longer an effective tool for influencing real demand and output. In effect, his paper embraces the rational-expectations hypothesis, according to which the money supply affects only the price level, except perhaps for periods of time that he apparently regards as having become too short to be a determinant of policy.

The proposition that foreseen changes in the money stock influence only the price level, leaving output and employment unaffected, could be true only if all nominal variables moved with the expected changes. As long as the real value of even one variable significantly affecting real demand is affected by changes in the price level, the proposition is incorrect. It is true that more widespread use of both indexation for prices set by contract (including wages) and more widespread influence of inflationary expectations on market-determined prices have brought the real world closer to the one envisaged in that model, but the world is still full of variables whose real values are affected by changes in the price level, even in periods of several years. For that reason, the proposition that monetary policy is only price-level policy and has no effect on real variables, while perhaps not as far from the truth as it once was, is still, in my opinion, too far from the truth in short periods to constitute an acceptable basis for policy.

If one does accept the view that monetary policy affects real variables only when it is unforeseen, preannouncement of targets for the money supply and adherence to them would diminish the effect of monetary policy on real variables still further. That raises the question as to whether this is what we want to do. The answer might be "yes" if we had enough other tools or if pursuit of the proposed policy enabled us to rely on an informed market to maintain high employment, so that no other policy tools were needed. But I doubt that either of these conditions is met in the real world.

I might add, how facetiously I have not decided, that if we want to make monetary policy a *more* effective tool of demand management, perhaps it would be best to accept half of his monetary commandment, namely, to have the authorities preannounce their target for monetary growth and then *not* adhere to it!

Second, not only is the money supply an intermediate rather than an ultimate target of policy; it is only one of several intermediate targets. One might mention, among others, interest rates and the exchange rate itself. Giersch focuses on the money supply and leaves these other intermediate targets to be determined in the market. I think that he here assumes that the money supply determines interest rates and the exchange rate, which implies that the demand-for-money function, although not

87

necessarily constant, is foreseen by the authorities, who can, therefore, set their monetary targets to accommodate such foreseen shifts.

As to the reasons for this view, a great deal is concealed in paragraph 6 of his paper. As I understand that paragraph, it assumes that shifts in the domestic demand for money will sooner or later be eliminated if growth rates for the money stock are preannounced and predictable. This view seems to be based on the assumption that shifts in the domestic demand for money are caused mainly by cyclical disturbances. Furthermore, Giersch seems to attribute cyclical disturbances only to past errors of monetary policy. Both of these points may be questioned.

But Giersch can certainly not be accused of having ignored possibilities that he thinks less likely to occur. He recognizes that, despite preannouncement of rates of money growth, marked shifts in domestic demand for domestic money may arise from the real sector. In that case, he suggests, they might be dealt with by fiscal policy, although "within the constraints of the preannounced monetary targets." I wonder whether that restriction would not render fiscal policy ineffective.

Giersch also recognizes that foreign demand for domestic money may shift. If such shifts occur, he would allow a deviation from the preannounced rate of growth of the money stock or, where information about such shifts comes promptly, an immediate (and, presumably, immediately announced) revision of the money-supply target. Where information about them is expected not to be available promptly, he would allow the money-supply target to be replaced by an exchange-rate target "with an endogenous money supply." (I understand "endogenous money supply" to mean "no sterilization," so that the intervention required to meet the exchange-rate target would affect the stock of money held by the public and, therefore, unexpected shifts in foreign demand for domestic money would be matched by shifts in the supply of domestic money and be prevented from adversely affecting the domestic demand for goods and services.)

Under these rules, the IMF would be relieved of concern about which exchange rates are unfairly low or which prevent adjustment. Any rate established by the market presumably would observe the constraints of Article IV, since it would not involve manipulating exchange rates—or manipulating the international monetary system, on any definition of that mysterious latter phrase that I can think of.

The Nonintervention Commandment

I should now like to consider whether this stricture against intervention in the foreign exchange market is desirable from the point of view of two more ultimate targets of economic policy, namely, efficiency of resource allocation and the maintenance of high employment.

First, as to efficiency of resource allocation. There is, of course, a vast literature analyzing the operation of goods and services and factor markets from that point of view and enumerating circumstances under which intervention might increase national welfare. Presumably some forms of such intervention would increase national welfare at the expense of other nations. In the context of international arrangements, presumably a more international view should be taken. Cooper suggests as a guiding principle that countries "should not impose costs on other nations except when that is unavoidable and in the nature of the problem which the country taking the actions is addressing." That seems to me an acceptable principle.

But, as Cooper further points out, the exchange rate that maximizes even national welfare will not be the one established in the market because speculators do not have perfect foresight. Even if they did, the price signals may induce changes in the allocation of resources that do not reflect the social costs of such changes. Furthermore, Cooper notes, capital markets are imperfect. For any of these reasons, a free-exchange market may set an exchange rate that induces changes in the allocation of resources that involve social costs exceeding social benefits. For example, it may induce shifts between industries producing tradable goods and those producing nontradable goods in response to temporary changes in market demand. Thus, there is a case *in principle* for intervention to keep the exchange rate at a level that maximizes national welfare, and in the international context there is also one for intervening to increase the welfare of a larger number of countries. It is true, as Cooper says, that his in-

89

junction is not operational. The broader one that I suggest, which includes taking into account the welfare of other countries, is, if anything, still less so. The argument against intervention then has to be—not that all intervention is bad in principle—but that interventions are more likely than not to be badly conceived or executed, so that nonintervention is likely on the whole to produce better results. This may well be so, but I doubt that objective analysis can establish either that it is or that it is not.

In any event, I do not agree that the preannouncement of monetary targets alone gives the private sector of an economy enough information to put it on a par with the government. The reason is that I do not accept the proposition that "the only convincing reason why an official authority should be a better speculator than private market participants is that it has better information" or that "if money growth rates are preannounced, the information gap disappears and with it the argument for official interventions."

In the first place, preannouncement only of the growth in the money supply would not enable the market to know everything that in my opinion is relevant to the exchange rate and payment adjustment that the government knows, except over periods longer than are relevant to surveillance. While relative rates of growth in money supplies may be the dominant influences on exchange rates over periods of several years, many other variables affect them in the periods that I take to be relevant to surveillance. The government would have to preannounce and adhere to targets for all of these other variables before the market would know as much as the government does about policy plans. I suppose the answer to my point is that on the theory underlying Giersch's proposal these other variables are not relevant to the exchange rate because that is determined by the money stock (in conjunction with the demand for money). Therefore, if the demand for money is not affected, adherence to the monetary target will prevent the exchange rate from being affected, except for a period too short to be of concern. I recognize the logic of this answer, but do not accept its underlying theory as valid, except, perhaps, in a substantially longer run.

Furthermore, information is not all that is necessary. Analysis of effects, including complicated feedbacks, is also necessary. While there

90

are now in some countries several organizations large enough to engage in such analysis, governments can still command larger resources than any private organizations in nearly all countries. Giersch recognizes that information needs to be interpreted, but he thinks it doubtful that official authorities will make "better" (more accurate?) forecasts than private agents in interpreting the data when they have the same level of information. He notes that private agents are risking their own money. That does not appear to me a convincing reason. Even if they do make more money, the argument that this is a good test of the social desirability of their activities appears to me to be based on mistaking equilibrium in the sense of market-clearing, an analytical concept, for a norm of policy. If it is argued that the market will do "as well" as the government from the point of view of social policy, the reasons for thinking so must be other than that private speculators are risking their own money while the government is not.

I would now like to consider whether advance information about the growth of the money stock combined with nonintervention in the foreign-exchange market would in fact lead to desirable results for aggregate output and employment. I can think of a number of situations in which it would lead to changes that are undesirable.

Consider first a situation in which the world is generally in depression and where one or two important countries with slack domestic demand have strong balance-of-payments or reserve positions. In this situation the ideal prescription, admittedly, may be coordinated national policies of demand expansion which, if successful, may leave exchange rates so little affected that no harm would result from nonintervention. But if coordination of either planning or execution fails, it will still be desirable for either or both countries to pursue expansionary policies. Such policies will tend to force their currencies down, and they will in fact go down if there is no intervention. Since it is in the general world interest, however, that the values of their currencies be maintained, it appears to me desirable that they support their currencies. If they do not, the response of the foreign-exchange market will be immediate, but the effects on their domestic demand, including their demand for foreign goods, will be delayed. In the interim they will gain what would be regarded as "an un-

91

fair competitive advantage" and thus be in violation of IMF Article IV. Here I think nonintervention would be both harmful and contrary to Article IV.

The Giersch response to this argument would be, as I read his paper, that with preannounced rates of growth of the money stock in all countries, the cyclical situation that I have envisaged would not occur because business cycles result only from unforeseen monetary policies. I can only say that I doubt that preannouncement of rates of monetary growth would eliminate the cycle.

If one believes, as I am inclined to do, that in its surveillance the IMF must have at least some general view of what exchange-rate policies violate Article IV, that view must be formulated in the context of high-employment levels of income in the world. A rate determined in the market at low income levels might not violate the constraints, but the same rate might violate them if incomes were high. Similarly, a rate affected by intervention that violates the constraints in a low-income situation might not do so in one of high-income levels. In other words, the exchange rate both influences the variables that constitute more ultimate targets (the balance of payments and national output) and is influenced by them. To use it as an intermediate target, one needs to know the zone in which it should lie to be consistent with the ultimate target. This requires excluding from the estimates of the exchange rate any effects of deviations from the ultimate target. The situation is analogous to the use of the high-employment budget in assessing fiscal policies. When one wants to form a judgment about which changes in the government budget are needed to produce a given effect on demand, one must represent the existing budget by a figure that eliminates the effect on it of differences in other determinants of demand. That is why in comparing an actual budget with a proposed alternative, one should estimate the value of its components not at their actual levels but at the same levels of non-budgetary variables as are assumed in estimating the alternative budget. (These levels, incidentally, need not be high-employment levels; any fixed level will do.) Correspondingly, to judge the appropriateness of an exchange rate, one must form a judgment as to the zone that would be appropriate to income levels regarded as desirable and feasible. In this

92

context it is not only the income level in the country whose currency value is being appraised, but in other countries whose income levels substantially affect that currency. To state the point in another way, there are some values of the currency that promote an adjustment that would be undesirable because they are not consistent with a desired position of the more ultimate variables. Adjustment to a depressed income level is undesirable adjustment, and it should not be regarded as a violation of Article IV for a country to intervene to prevent such adjustment.

An answer to this view is that the IMF, instead of tolerating or even encouraging intervention in such a situation, should be sure that its surveillance is not confined to the country with the deficit but includes surveillance of others, and should treat as the culprits those whose depressions create the situation. That would indeed be preferable, but it may not always be possible. When it is not, a country should not be discouraged from maintaining an exchange rate that would appear to be overvalued if judged by market criteria under depressed conditions.

Another case in which the overseers of exchange-rate policies must form some idea of what constitutes appropriate adjustment is provided by the large current-account deficits of the oil-importing countries, taken in the aggregate. Of course, the inevitability of current-account imbalances does not imply that they must have an overall deficit. But the question remains how their aggregate current-account deficit is to be shared. The Interim Committee of the Board of Governors on the International Monetary System, in its communiqué from Manila on October 2, 1976, said that deficit countries should "restrain domestic demand and . . . permit the shift of resources to the external sector to the extent necessary to bring the deficit on current account in line with a sustainable flow of capital imports and aid." The qualification relating to sustainable flows of capital and aid makes macroeconomic sense, but authorities cannot know what flow of capital import and aid is sustainable. If member countries follow this advice conscientiously, in the sense of preferring the risk of too small a current-account deficit to one that is too large, they would add a depressing force to the world economy. This injunction can be made practical only if it is supplemented by some guarantee that a specified sum of capital and aid to each major country with a current-account deficit (or from each one with a current-account surplus) will be forthcoming. That would require underwriting any deficiency in the total of what the private market plus assured official lending provides, this deficiency being appraised in relation to a preannounced target. In short, to avoid interfering with appropriate adjustment, a member must have some idea of what adjustment is appropriate, and to have that idea he must know what flow of capital and aid can be expected from all sources. That means that somebody must be willing to make up, through official international funds, any deficiencies of private and official national sources below targets. Otherwise there is no way of distinguishing between desirable and undesirable adjustments and, therefore, no way of knowing when the adjustment provisions of Article IV are being flouted.

Consider, finally, "bandwagon" effects on exchange-rate movements. I have already noted that the speed of exchange-rate movements combined with lags in other economic adjustments may cause depreciations to give at least a temporary competitive advantage that will be regarded as "unfair." That applies to the case where the exchange-rate movement is not excessive in amount but simply occurs before the other adjustments that it is anticipating. The bandwagon effect refers to exchange-rate movements that are excessive in amount. They, too, are likely to be temporary, but they do give an unfair competitive advantage while they last, and they may also give incentives for excessive reallocation of some resources, or at least to introduce uncertainty about allocation. Intervention to slow up very rapid movements of exchange rates seems to me desirable.

To deal with such cases I think the suggestion of Eddie Bernstein is a promising one; namely, that if an exchange rate changes by no more than 6 to 8 percent in two months, intervention should be withheld, except to prevent disorderly markets. If, after a rise or fall of more than that amount, an exchange rate continues to move in the same direction, the authorities should intervene to limit the movement to a further 1 or 2 percent per month. If the movement is reversed, the authorities should follow the same rule. He proposes that even this rule should be flexible.

Adherence to this rule would limit movements of rates that may turn out to be excessive in relation to changes in fundamental conditions, and

94

it would also prevent authorities from adhering to wrong rates. Besides achieving those purposes, it is a very practical and operational rule of thumb. It could be used as a presumptive rule, to be violated only when it was inconsistent with the basic idea I have suggested of target zones estimated under high-income conditions. I should expect it to be inconsistent with them only rarely. Calculations of such zones may not be feasible for some time to come. In the meantime, the Bernstein rule might be a good rule standing alone. The extent to which its results would differ from those of the Giersch proposal if money supply targets were preannounced and believed is a question I have not had time to consider adequately. Taking into account some of the alternatives to nonintervention and to money-supply targets that Giersch allows for, perhaps the results would not be greatly different.

FRED HIRSCH

UNIVERSITY OF WARWICK, COVENTRY, ENGLAND

I FIND MYSELF a good deal closer to Cooper's approach than to that of Giersch, though perhaps recklessly I don't have the caution in following through the implications of Cooper's analysis (at least as I interpret it), that he has been impelled to himself.

Cooper has made the fundamental point that the conditions required for a perfectly foresighted private speculation to produce a welfare-maximizing exchange rate cannot presumably be met in practice; this is so because (a) the market will not normally take account of the cost of real adjustment in the economy through reallocation of production and consumption and (b) capital markets are not perfect. I would like to elaborate more specifically on this second consideration, and here I think I parallel and perhaps supplement some of the points that Walter Salant just made.

We know on general theoretical grounds, which have been developed

95

in particular by Kenneth Arrow, that private markets cannot be expected to make provision for uncertainty—uncertainty in the sense of contingencies for which no probabilistic estimate can be made as distinct from calculable risk. It is this inability to anticipate uncertainty, and not simply mere institutional underdevelopment, that explains the absence of markets in future contingencies, including forward exchange markets in maturities beyond very short time periods. I am continually amazed that this general point, which is well known even in simple theoretical literature, never seems to be applied by monetary economists to the institutional position in foreign-exchange markets. Instead, at conference after conference, people sit around waiting for the forward market; it's going to happen by the next time we meet. Yet if we paid attention to these theoretical considerations, we would know that we can no more expect private speculators to commit their own money against these uncertainties than we can expect them to sell us a cost-of-living bond, and for fundamentally the same reason; namely, that this will involve uncertainty of a kind for which private money cannot conceivably be staked.

Now it is true that this is not the end of the matter, and Giersch very fairly raised the question as to whether we can expect officials to make better judgments about future uncertainties than private speculators. I want to suggest that in at least one important set of cases, a *prima facie* answer can be affirmative, that we can expect officials to make better judgments. This set of cases includes those where uncertainty relates to some major area of future governmental action or nonaction, for example, the threat of an adverse political upheaval or a complete loss of financial control. The crucial point is that neither of these contingencies—political upheaval or complete financial collapse—is independent of the exchange rate itself. Private speculators, unwilling to commit funds in stabilizing speculation in support of a positive outcome of these uncertainties, can drive the exchange rate down and thereby help to bring on the convulsion. Under such circumstances, commitment of official funds in an "optimistic" direction, can be a rational investment in social insurance. In this set of cases, the advantage in stabilizing speculation that is held by the official exchange managers is precisely they are *not* risking their own money, because if they were, then they could not

96

afford to do this social insurance of the kind that the private speculators quail from.

Cooper reminded us of why we needed public agencies to be Bagehot-type central banks. There is a clear analogy there. So it is not just a matter of equally available information. It is a matter of providing the "public good" service of a wider form of social insurance.

A similar consideration, and this may be more controversial, seems to me to justify capital controls in some important cases, at least as a second-best policy in a world of imperfect capital markets. This leaves aside the practical matter that different forms of taxation in different countries may make capital controls perfectly rational in order to obtain improved allocation of capital. Therefore, the prohibition of capital controls as suggested by Giersch cannot be accepted as an overriding element in exchange-rate guidelines. I think the emphasis on this in the original articles of the IMF—which I am glad to see have not been changed here—is still correct in making the current-account–capital-account distinction, even if, as we know, that is now more difficult to apply.

Giersch's proposal for preannounced rates of monetary growth has obvious attractions, but seems to me to have the limitations of a fair-weather solution. The fact that the countries that have adopted this policy are those with their money supply most firmly under control is likely to reflect at least some elements of two-way causation. Announcement of monetary targets is to some extent a result as well as a cause of firm monetary control. I think the point made by Emminger this morning, perhaps from a different direction, might be another facet of this; namely, that behind the firm monetary control and credible monetary targets lie other variables, such as firm budgetary policy. Thus a similar announcement policy by countries in which the prerequisites for modest monetary growth were not present, at least without real economic costs, could not be expected to elicit the same market credibility as had been achieved by the countries whose monetary and budgetary positions are in good shape already. The case for an active intervention strategy at both national and international levels hence seems to me conclusive on these grounds.

I now turn to the crucial and much more difficult question of the form of international influence and guidance. Cooper's paper leaves me un-convinced that meaningful guidance can be achieved without biting the bullet of a calculation of norms or target zones on a multilateral basis. Cooper himself touches on the potential ambiguity of the concept of un-fair competitive advantage in the absence of targets on balance-of-payments structure. He emphasizes the need to avoid undue constraints on short-term cyclical management. But this could be met, at least to some extent, by establishing the norms on a medium-term basis. This would leave a degree of freedom in domestic management of the business cycle, which will affect balance-of-payments structure in the way that Cooper describes, while still retaining an international discipline of coor-dination and consistency across the cycle.

Cooper's skepticism about the practicability of the exercise of calculat-ing reference norms seems to me unconvincing. We are wise, I would certainly agree, to have abandoned the confidence that was implicit in a fixed rate regime that we could calculate implicitly or explicitly an inter-national set of fixed parities. But it seems to me a double jump in skep-ticism to go all the way from that to the position that we have nothing useful to say on a set of exchange-rate norms subject to continuous ad-justment and free of the binding commitments of a fixed parity. The sec-ondary point that markets and government may at least at the outset *treat* reference norms as parities is a weak argument that should, in my view, find no place in consideration of the appropriate new regime. We have enough unhappy examples of needed financial reforms being rejected or delayed by preconceived views of how the public and the practical men are bound to misinterpret them. On these grounds, I remain strongly at-tracted to the Williamson–Bloomfield–Ethier reference-rate proposal; or as a weaker alternative, to calculations of multilateral exchange-rate norms on a primarily indicative basis, providing information for the mar-ket. In either variant, a strong case exists for the calculations to be under-taken by two international organizations—or perhaps I should say *at least* two—for example, the IMF and OECD, on the ground that this may be vital to defuse the undesired semblance of finality that would be given by a single set of numbers. In the reference-rate approach, the associated limitations on intervention policy would then be confined to the area in which the competing set of numbers overlapped. Thus, if the market rate of country A is at 100 and the IMF put the reference norm at 95 and the OECD at 90, A would be permitted to reinforce a market depreciation through intervention down to 95. Before people get too horrified at the notion of these numbers being bandied about through the public domain, one might just recall the amount of speculation that can take place when imaginary numbers are hypothesized as pertaining to official institutions. Good information, put out on a systematic basis, can be much less disturbing than what people will make up if such information is not made available.

It is, of course, clear that the norm approach would leave the IMF more exposed to controversy and to risks of apparent failure, as compared with a more cautious guidance strategy based essentially on moderating short-term changes. But I believe that this exposure has to be accepted if the IMF is to accept its fundamental role as "the guardian of the interests of other countries," to use Cooper's language. I suggest that a second fundamental role for the IMF is to provide international support and guidance for what I have called "social insurance" against self-aggravating financial instability.

This danger is back with us in a floating-rate regime that on the whole has worked well. This regime is looking after the easy countries very well, so to speak; but if at the periphery the problem countries get into a self-aggravating spiral of a kind that admittedly may in part be their own responsibility, but in some other part result from lack of sufficient international commitment to what is judged to be a viable position, then I think our retrospective view of the floating-rate regime may be much less favorable than some of us may now realize.

A more fundamental alternative for the IMF than either of these exchange-leadership approaches would be to minimize its direct exchange-rate involvement and concentrate its attention heavily on the domestic financial policy of its member countries. This more fundamental alternative would indeed imply, again using Cooper's language, that the IMF would "oversee all aspects of macroeconomic policy in all its member countries."

This has obvious institutional attractions, but I fully agree with Cooper that this is not the IMF's distinctive role. It is true and somewhat disturbing, at least to me, that the new Article IV can be read in this sense of in-

99

volving more intensive influence by the IMF on domestic financial and economic policies than the earlier articles. This interpretation has received some support from the Managing Director. The Giersch policy of nothing more than "surveillance over notification" would also, on balance, lead us down this road, I believe. The end of this road would be an IMF that quailed from the risk of opposing market forces or even of guiding them in any serious way, but instead put its primary emphasis on disciplining countries to accept the market forces that existed.

There is a rather general point that I want to make here in conclusion. I believe that this approach of minimizing attempts to either shield countries from the market, or to guide it, would neglect the domestic political forces that underly the impulsion to exchange flexibility. Those forces are fundamentally the reluctance of countries to do what they feel to be wrong and dangerous domestically in the interest of some notional international goal. We know those forces came primarily from the side of surplus countries protecting themselves against inflation, but that should not lead us to neglect the fact that similar political forces are strong also in weaker countries in deficit positions. The end result of the approach, I believe, would be to push the problem countries into more drastic departures from convertibility and from free trade.

It is relevant to recall here that in the original Keynes–White tussle, Keynes's insistence on a greater element of exchange flexibility than the Americans had in mind, was directly related to his fear of excessive international incursions on domestic financial, social, and political policies. More exchange flexibility there went along with less international interference, to use a loaded word. Admittedly, perceived relationships between exchange rate policy and domestic economic objectives have changed somewhat in the intervening thirty years, and particularly in the last five. We now expect less autonomy from an independent exchange rate. But I do not believe that the relationships have changed so drastically as to make sense of a regime that yields to impulsions for exchange flexibility but tries to tack onto it more, rather than less, monetary discipline imposed by international pressures. I believe the end result of that would be not more discipline, but rather more countries copping out of the system.

100

DISCUSSION

THE DISCUSSION focused on three general questions relating to IMF surveillance of exchange rates. In the first place, is it technically feasible to calculate the medium-term path of a country's exchange rate given the stance of its macroeconomic policies? Second, is IMF surveillance of exchange rates practicable and desirable; and if so, how is it to be carried out? Third, what should be done about erratic short-term movements in the exchange rates of particular countries?

Regarding the possibility of forecasting exchange rates, several participants, including Salant, Hirsch, and Williamson, felt that countries should attempt to predict "target zones" for their rates. Williamson agreed with the argument in Giersch's paper that the authorities should state clearly their intentions regarding their monetary policy targets, but he wondered why Giersch drew the line at money-supply targets and why he stopped short of advocating that each government should try to project the time path of the exchange rate that was implied by its policy stance. Referring specifically to the "reference-rate proposal,"[1] he contended that it would be advantageous to organize—at an international level—an attempt to draw out the implications for exchange rates of whatever other targets were being pursued, and to publish this information both for purposes of discussion and to improve the information available to the private sector. At the least, this might provide a focus for stabilizing speculation and help to prevent wild fluctuations in market exchange rates. Williamson also sought to counter two of Cooper's main objections to reference rates. The first was the argument that governments could mistakenly con-

[1] See John Williamson, "The Future Exchange Rate Regime," Banca Nazionale del Lavoro *Quarterly Review* (June 1975), pp. 3–20.

sider their target zone as a kind of parity. Such a development was most unlikely, he believed, because the private markets would soon overrule them if they did. The reference-rate proposal would not obligate central banks to stabilize their exchange rates; it would merely prohibit them from attempting to push market rates away from their target zones. Furthermore, the zone itself should be sufficiently flexible to allow for revision in the light of new developments. The second and more fundamental of Cooper's objections was that it is not possible for governments or international organizations to agree on the exchange-rate targets that are appropriate under present circumstances. But Williamson argued that if the official sector proved to be incapable of making these calculations, the private sector would not be able to form a stable view of what exchange rates ought to be, or to engage in stabilizing speculation. Under these conditions, exchange rates would continue to be highly volatile in the future. Alternatively, it might be that officials are hesitant to make projections because there is currently a basic inconsistency in balance-of-payments objectives in the world economy—a problem that has occurred because of the OPEC surplus and its counterpart in the oil-importing countries. One of the attractions of the reference-rate proposal, in Williamson's view, is that it would force the international community to face up explicitly to the question of distributing the oil deficit. Cooper, however, felt that the process by which private sector expectations are formed is quite different from that by which official forecasts are made, since the market is a clearinghouse for quite divergent views about such matters. The private sector does not, in its individual components, have a single view but rather a spectrum of views for which the market produces a net result.

Several participants questioned the feasibility of calculating exchange-rate targets. In particular, they emphasized the practical difficulties of attempting to forecast the exchange rate on the basis of preannounced money-supply targets and anticipated real growth rates. Emminger observed that the relationship among these variables is extremely complicated, and in order to forecast exchange rates it would be necessary to take a medium-term view on such factors as sustainable capital move-

102

ments, the distribution of oil deficits, and the like. Previous experience with such projections does not inspire much confidence in them.

A second difficulty with target zones raised by Emminger, Fellner, and Grubel is the problem of differences in national inflation rates. All participants accepted the propositions that in the long run there is at least some zone of unemployment that represents equilibrium in the labor market; and that since this natural rate of unemployment is largely independent of the inflation rate, there is no longer-term trade-off between them. They disagreed, however, on the question of whether discretionary policy could be used to affect the level of employment in the short run. Giersch felt that in most industrialized countries the degree of private sector money illusion is now so small that demand-management policies have a negligible effect. Thus changes in the level of employment can be obtained only by structural labor-market policies to influence relative wages, and so on. However, it was argued by Haberler and Williamson that although the degree of money illusion has declined as a result of recent experience, thus reducing response lags, activist demand-management policies may still be used to move the level of employment in the appropriate direction whenever it deviates from the long-term equilibrium level. Several participants, including Fellner, Grubel, and Emminger emphasized that, notwithstanding these theoretical conclusions, there are still some governments that continue to act as though they believe that there is a long-term trade-off between inflation and unemployment. This is an important cause of continuing inflation differentials. Emminger and Grubel felt that as long as these differentials exist, markets themselves will not produce a smooth upward crawl in the exchange rates of low inflation countries. Even if this were the case, however, Emminger noted that a number of governments of quite important countries are not prepared to rely on money-supply targets, and that countries announcing these targets frequently fail to achieve them because of such factors as unanticipated budgetary developments. Furthermore, it should be recognized that the link between monetary policy and the exchange rate is highly complex. Political crises have a large impact on exchange markets irrespective of announced movements in monetary aggregates. If distur-

103

bances occur in the economy from the fiscal side, it may be necessary to change interest rates a great deal in order to maintain the preannounced rate of monetary expansion, and these interest rate adjustments may lead to disturbing capital movements that in turn could affect the exchange rates. In summing up this part of the discussion, Cooper acknowledged that his paper reflects extreme skepticism concerning the feasibility of projecting exchange rates in the way that proposals such as the reference-rate scheme require. However, he endorsed the idea that the IMF should develop a model for calculating a mutually consistent set of reference rates, both for purposes of discussion and in order to see if such projections might eventually become a focus on which the discussion of appropriate exchange rates could center. He personally felt that the analytical difficulties would be sufficiently formidable for this approach to fail.

The practical problems of forecasting exchange-rate movements led the participants into the second major issue; namely, the question of how the IMF should fulfill its obligation to exercise firm *surveillance* over the exchange-rate policies of its members. Emminger introduced two questions regarding this topic. First, he wanted to know what is meant by the phrase "manipulating exchange rates" in the new text of Article IV in the IMF Agreement. Second, he wondered whether indeed the IMF can and should take a view on the appropriateness of a particular exchange rate. If the IMF were to take such a view, should it be publicized? And what consequences would follow if it were? On the first of these questions, several participants, including Whitman, Emminger and Grubel, observed that since the economic system is highly interdependent, there is no unique equilibrium level for the exchange rate. The exchange rate depends on both official policies and structural relationships. It follows that "manipulation" comprises not only official intervention in the exchange markets but also other policies that affect the exchange rate, such as official (or officially induced) borrowing, trade and payments controls, and certain types of monetary and fiscal policies. The question arises as to which policies are permissible and which constitute unfair manipulation of exchange rates. Haberler suggested that a distinction might be drawn between "managed" floating and "dirty" floating. The latter category

104

might include all those countries with split exchange markets, multiple exchange rates, import quotas, deposit schemes, and the like. Such arrangements, he noted, violate one of the fundamental objectives of the IMF, namely, that there should be no restrictions on current transactions. This should be distinguished from a float that is managed simply by interventions in the market. However, he acknowledged the difficulties of separating these two categories in practice. In this connection, he felt that the IMF's traditional distinction between current and capital transactions is no longer very realistic. The IMF charter assumes that current transactions should in principle be free while capital transactions can, and in certain cases ought, to be restricted. But capital has now become very mobile. Even in cases where there are capital controls, legal current-account transactions can take the place of capital movements. The prevention of legal substitutes for capital transactions would require detailed enforcement of current-account trade. Thus capital movements can be controlled in the long run only if current transactions are regulated as well. The participants felt that it is unclear how far the IMF can go in "firm surveillance" of the many factors that can potentially influence exchange rates. It will be necessary to find some formula that provides a practicable dividing line, and Grubel observed that the IMF should move cautiously and in an *ad hoc* manner in this area.

On the question as to whether the IMF can and should take a view on the *appropriateness of a particular exchange rate,* there was a considerable difference of views. Several participants, including Emminger, Bernstein, and Giersch, were very skeptical as to whether the IMF would be in a position to take a view on the appropriateness of a target zone, as this would involve IMF surveillance over the entire spectrum of a country's macroeconomic policies. While conceding the difficulties posed by this problem, Witteveen pointed out that in practice the IMF staff frequently gives advice to countries on what exchange rate is appropriate for them and what policies they should pursue in order to achieve it. This advice is frequently accepted and is given without disturbing the exchange market before the government has had a chance to take action. Such advice is often easier to give to small countries, but even in the case of larger countries this approach might have possibilities.

105

Referring to the earlier discussion of inflation differentials, several participants observed that the IMF could hardly exhort those countries that placed a high value on domestic price stability to inflate faster in the interests of more international stability in the exchange markets. While acknowledging the existence of beggar-thy-neighbor policies, Whitman and Solomon felt that the distinction between domestic and international stability is sometimes too sharply drawn. In the present highly integrated world, countries must necessarily take into account the actions that other countries are likely to pursue when designing their own macroeconomic policies. They must also consider likely international feedbacks in order to avoid either stimulative or deflationary overkill. The discussants felt that in addition to differences in national economic goals the iterative process of responding to these feedbacks has led to some of the recent problems and "policy errors." They suggested that the IMF might be of assistance in this latter area. If the authorities of a country feel at any given moment that their macroeconomic policy is as expansive as possible without causing accelerating inflation, it would be politically unrealistic to ask them to follow some global welfare norm rather than their own national interests. On the other hand, the macroeconomic consultations that would be involved in IMF surveillance might help certain governments to formulate policies that they would themselves like to implement, but which are sometimes politically difficult. From this perspective, the IMF should be seen not as a dictating body, but rather as a forum in which countries can come to a mutual agreement on many of these matters.

Other participants, however, found this view overly optimistic. Cooper felt that the community of economic interest among nations was unfortunately much narrower than the Solomon–Whitman position assumed because there are considerable externalities resulting from domestic economic policies. He contended that when major countries, such as the United States and Germany in 1973–74, deflate their economies for reasons reflecting their judgment about the trade-offs among domestic policy objectives, a part—and, over time, a growing part—of the costs of such policy changes are borne by people in foreign countries who have no say in these decisions. As examples, he cited the foreign suppliers

106

whose incomes fall because U.S. imports decline, or the *Gastarbeiter* in Germany who have to go home and are not replaced. Similarly, in the late 1960s the United States financed a large increase in real expenditure on the Vietnam war by drawing resources from the rest of the world through the imposition of an inflation tax on foreign countries without their consent. These are instances of domestic policies that have spill-over effects on other countries, and the externalities that they cause are greater the more interdependent the world economy is.

On the question of *erratic short-term movements in exchange rates* and their implications for IMF surveillance, there was a certain convergence of views. The discussion centered on countries that do not actively use policy measures to affect their exchange rate, but where market behavior gives rise to considerable short-term fluctuations in the value of the currency in the spot market. There was some difference of opinion about the causes of these movements. Bernstein argued that if the supply and demand for foreign exchange came exclusively from exports, imports and "normal" capital flows the exchange rate would soon reflect underlying forces. Thus if the exchange rate oscillates outside a reasonable range around its trend value (and especially when it rises 15 or 20 percent and then falls back to the old level over a period of six or eight months), these movements are not due to underlying factors but to "speculation" in the form of short-term capital flows, leads and lags, and so on. On the other hand, Grubel maintained that even when two countries have similar inflation rates, random shocks—such as bad harvests, differences in the phasing of business cycles, policy errors, and so on—would not be fully offset by private speculators, so that the market rate would tend to fluctuate around its trend value. Both participants agreed with Kenen, however, that in this case it would not be appropriate to manipulate the money supply in order to achieve exchange rate stability. Thus in countries with inflation rates similar to those of their trading partners, exchange-rate stabilization should be achieved through use of international reserves, whereas free floating and changes in the rate of monetary expansion might be used in those cases where the differentials in inflation rates are substantial. In this connection, the participants noted that in practice it is often difficult to determine whether the appearance of a

107

payments imbalance is due to speculation, random shocks, or a continued attempt by the domestic authorities to achieve a trade-off between unemployment and inflation. This problem would make the IMF role more difficult, because in such a world it is not feasible to develop guidelines that rely exclusively on objective indicators such as (levels or movements in) reserves, exchange rates, and so forth.

A related issue was that of profits arising from official intervention in exchange markets. Most participants agreed that stabilizing intervention should at least yield running profits for the authorities. However, Bernstein disagreed with the contention in Giersch's paper that the central bank should *maximize* its profits from intervention. Observing that the authorities would only maximize profits if they refrained from intervention except at the peaks and troughs of exchange-rate oscillations, he argued that the test of successful stabilization was not whether it maximized central bank profits, but the broader question of whether it enhanced national (and international) welfare.

SESSION 3

How Important Is
Control Over
International Reserves?

GOTTFRIED HABERLER

AMERICAN ENTERPRISE INSTITUTE, WASHINGTON, D. C.

THE PROBLEM of the adequacy of international liquidity—or, better, of international monetary reserves—has been discussed almost as long as there has been serious discussion of the international monetary system. According to Jacob Viner, "from the late 1820s on to the end of the century a continuous succession of writers called attention to the inadequacy of gold reserves [in Great Britain], but without any visible results," and Peel himself was said to have been "aware that the metallic base of the currency was extraordinarily narrow, but did not think that either the Bank or the people would willingly bear the expense of broadening it." [1] Both before and after the Bank Act of 1844, numerous writers made proposals for a reform of the international monetary system, most of which aimed at increasing international liquidity. [2]

The Bimetallist Controversy and Commodity Reserve Currencies

The long period of falling prices from the 1870s to the 1890s, the "downswing of the Kondratieff cycle," gave rise to lively discussions in all major countries on international monetary reform; namely, the bimet-

---

[1] Jacob Viner, *Studies in the Theory of International Trade* (New York: Harper, 1957), pp. 265 and 267. See the sections entitled 'Adequate Reserves," "Foreign Securities as a Secondary Reserve," "Silver as a Reserve," and "Cooperation between Central Banks," pp. 264–76.
[2] On the English literature see Viner, *International Trade*, "Currency Reform Proposals," pp. 280–89.

111

allist controversy. The basic issue was the alleged inadequacy of international reserves resulting from the decline in gold production that occurred roughly during 1854–83. To my knowledge there is no satisfactory history of published works on this subject comparable to Viner's history of the English literature during the period of the bullionist controversies (in both its inflationary and deflationary phases) and during the later period of 1825–65. This is a pity, because much of the discussion was on a high level and many leading economists participated. Interestingly enough, and probably surprisingly for many contemporary economists, a galaxy of famous names was ranged on the side of a double standard of gold and silver, either bimetallism or symmetallism, against the monometallism of gold—Alfred Marshall, L. Walras, F. Y. Edgeworth, N. G. Pierson, and I. Fisher, among others.

Especially interesting is Marshall's proposal of symmetallism. The difference between bimetallism and symmetallism is, it will be recalled, that under the former, the money prices of both gold and silver are fixed by central bank pegging,[3] while under the latter the money price of a constant physical bundle, or a bar containing, say, one ounce of gold and fifteen ounces of silver, is fixed and the relative price of gold and silver in terms of money (and in terms of general purchasing power) is free to vary in the market under the influence of changes in demand and supply (cost of production).[4] The system of symmetallism is interesting because it is a

[3] In other words, under bimetallism the rate of exchange between gold and silver is fixed. If convertibility between the two monies is preserved and the chosen rate deviates from market equilibrium, Gresham's law comes into operation.

[4] A. Marshall, "Remedies for Fluctuations of General Prices," 1887, reprinted in A. C. Pigou, ed., *Memorials of Alfred Marshall* (London: Macmillan, 1925), and Marshal's evidence before the Gold and Silver Commission of 1888, reprinted in *Official Papers by Alfred Marshall* (London: Macmillan, 1926). See especially Question 9837, pp. 101–2. F. Y. Edgeworth, "Questions Connected with Bimetallism," *The Economic Journal* (1895), reprinted in F. Y. Edgeworth, *Papers Relating to Political Economy*, vol. 1 (London: Macmillan, 1925). The term "symmetallism" seems to have been coined by Edgeworth (*Political Economy*, p. 431). It should be mentioned, however, that for Marshall (and probably also for Edgeworth), symmetallism was only a second-best solution, better than monometallism (of gold or of silver), but inferior to what Marshall called a "tabular standard," a sort of general optional indexation of debts including government securities (consols).

It is interesting to observe that, according to Edgeworth, one of the advantages of symmetallism over bimetallism is that the former can be introduced independently by different countries and does *not* require international agreement on a common bundle of gold and silver. He points out that if two countries stabilized their currencies in terms of different

forerunner of the commodity reserve-currency proposals. Marshall himself mentioned that if other commodities "suitable" for the purpose could be found, "they could be added to gold and silver to form the basis of the currency."[5] The commodity reserve-currency system has found impressive sponsors, but equally prominent critics. First proposed by W. S. Jevons in 1873, the idea was revived in the 1930s and 1940s by Benjamin Graham and Frank D. Graham and was strongly endorsed by F. A. Hayek. It has been criticized by J. M. Keynes, Milton Friedman, and Herbert Grubel, and has been supported by A. G. Hart, J. Tinbergen, and N. Kaldor.[6]

In the 1890s the bimetallist movement died down, earlier in Europe than in the United States, because in Europe the special interests (the

---

bundles of gold and silver, the exchange rate between the two currencies would have to be allowed to fluctuate. Edgeworth does not recommend this system. He shows, however, that despite a fluctuating exchange rate the system may well ensure greater internal stability for the two currencies in terms of general purchasing power than would occur under a common monometallic standard of gold or silver, let alone in the case where one country was on the silver standard and the other on the gold standard. It should be recalled that the coexistence of the gold standard and silver standard, a situation implying that fluctuating exchange rates had lasted for a long time. China and Mexico remained on the silver standard well into the twentieth century.

[5] Pigou, *Memorials of Alfred Marshall*, p. 206.

[6] W. S. Jevons, *Money and the Mechanism of Exchange* (London: H. S. King, 1875); B. Graham, *Storage and Stability* (New York: McGraw-Hill, 1937) and *World Commodities and World Currency* (New York: McGraw-Hill, 1944); F. D. Graham, *Social Goals and Economic Institutions* (Princeton, N.J.: Princeton University Press, 1942); F. A. Hayek, "A Commodity Reserve Currency," *The Economic Journal* (June–September 1943), 53:177–84; J. M. Keynes, "The Objective of International Price Stability," *The Economic Journal*, (June–September 1943), 53:185–87; Milton Friedman, "Commodity-Reserve Currency," *Journal of Political Economy* (June 1951), 59:203–32, reprinted in Milton Friedman, *Essays in Positive Economics* (Chicago: University of Chicago Press, 1953); Herbert Grubel, "The Case Against an International Commodity Reserve Currency," *Oxford Economic Papers* (1965), n.s., vol. 17, and the reply by A. G. Hart, "The Case For and Against International Reserve Currency," *ibid.* (1968), vol. 18; A. G. Hart, J. Tinbergen, and N. Kaldor, "The Case for an International Commodity Reserve Currency," paper submitted to UNCTAD, E/Conf. 46D Geneva, 1946 and reprinted in N. Kaldor, *Essays on Economic Policy*, (London: Duckworth, 1964), 2:131–74. See also A. G. Hart, "The Case as of 1976 for International Commodity-Reserve Currency," *Weltwirtschaftliches Archiv* (1976), 112:1–32. In the recent proposals the basic objectives of the commodity reserve-currency proposal have changed. The objective is no longer purely monetary, that is, to provide the world with a more stable international monetary system. Equally or perhaps more important in the eyes of the recent proponents is the objective to transfer resources from the rich industrial countries to the poor raw-material-exporting countries.

113

silver producers) were too weak to maintain the pressure needed to give silver a greater role in the monetary system. Gold production picked up rapidly because of new discoveries (in the Rand district of the Transvaal in South Africa and in the Klondike–Yukon valley in Canada) and technological improvements in mining and refining. As a consequence of the increase in gold production (i.e., a more adequate supply of international liquidity) and other factors—such as the increasing use of deposit money (checks) and the early adoption of the gold exchange standard by some countries (Russia and the Austro-Hungarian monarchy)—the declining trend of prices gave way to an upward trend. Thus there could be no further question about the adequacy of international monetary reserves until after World War I.

After the gold standard had been firmly established, a leading German bimetallist wrote, "The gentlemen of the gold standard, when they reflect on what happened must feel like 'der Reiter auf dem Bodensee'," the legendary horseman who inadvertently rode over the frozen lake and suffered a deadly shock when he suddenly realized that he just had narrowly escaped a horrible death. "Every reasonable gold standard man must admit," he continued, "that a further catastrophic price decline has been avoided only because gold production quite unexpectedly jumped from 400 million marks in 1883 to 1,600 million marks in 1906."[7] The nineteenth-century bimetallists probably had a better case than some recent prophets of disaster when they attributed the failure of their prophecy to come true, not to a defect in their argument, but to a run of undeserved good luck.

The Interwar Period

In the 1920s the problem of inadequate international reserves again became acute. The world price level in terms of dollars had about doubled since before the war, while the price of gold remained unchanged at twenty dollars an ounce. This implied a sharp drop in the value of the

[7] O. Arendt, *Geld, Bank, Börse: Reden und Aufsätze* (Berlin, 1907), p. 15.

stock of monetary gold, the principal component of international reserves, compared with the volume of international transactions. Moreover, the lower value of gold caused a decline in the annual production of gold. To cope with the growing inadequacy of international reserves, the more general adoption of the gold exchange standard was recommended by financial experts attending the Genoa Conference in the spring of 1922.

The perils of the gold-exchange standard—which after World War II became, first *de facto* and then, with the suspension of the gold convertibility of the dollar in 1971, explicitly, a dollar standard—have dominated the discussion of reserve adequacy until recently.

Many writers, especially Jacques Rueff and Robert Triffin in recent years, saw in the gold-exchange standard and its unavoidable collapse a major, if not the predominant, cause of the exceptional severity of the Great Depression of the 1930s; and both Rueff and Triffin have warned repeatedly that the unavoidable collapse of the dollar standard would have the same catastrophic consequences in the 1960s or 1970s as the collapse of the gold-exchange standard had in the 1930s. They were fond of quoting Santayana, "Who does not learn from the lessons of history is condemned to repeat them."

As far as the 1930s are concerned, the partial liquidation of the gold-exchange standard may have contributed a little to the severity of the world depression. But the major reasons surely were others. The gold-exchange standard was not responsible for the breakdown of the American banking system and the catastrophic deflation in the United States. One need not be an out-and-out monetarist to recognize that this was the major explanation for the severity of the U.S. depression and that, under fixed exchange rates, the U.S. depression was bound to spread to the rest of the world.[8]

There were, to be sure, other weak spots and foci of deflation in the world, for example, in central Europe and Great Britain. The central Eu-

---

[8] By out-and-out monetarists—if any exist—I mean economists who explain even minor fluctuations in business by minor fluctuations in the quantity of money and refuse to consider any other causes and cures of recessions, depressions, and the business cycle than money and monetary policy.

ropean crisis had nothing to do with the gold-exchange standard. The British weakness and difficulties, although rooted in the overvaluation of sterling since the revaluation of 1925, were possibly aggravated by the gold-exchange standard. But the American depression, which was almost entirely homemade, was the most powerful blow to the stability of the world economy, though chronologically not the first.

It is true, however, that after the depression became worldwide, there developed a severe shortage of international liquidity in the sense that international "liquidity preference" (for gold) became very strong. This was largely the consequence of the slow-motion devaluation of all currencies in terms of gold—sterling and its retinue of currencies in 1931, the dollar in 1933–34, and the "gold bloc" currencies in 1936. This was an early case of a very slowly adjustable peg, of stable but slowly adjustable exchange rates. In the end, international liquidity increased sharply through the painful process of prices declining in terms of national currencies (deflation) and national currencies being discontinuously devalued in terms of gold. An early large injection of international liquidity, such as by doubling the price of gold, would have shortened the painful process.

The Postwar Period

In the post-World War II period the problem of international liquidity and the adequacy or inadequacy of international reserves came into its own. It has loomed very large—disproportionately large, many (including the present writer) would say—in the discussions of the reform of the international monetary system.

Following Keynes's proposal for an International Clearing Union and Robert Triffin's early seminal writings, dozens of schemes for the orderly international creation, supplementation, control, and management of global monetary reserves have been advanced, ranging from proposals for making the IMF a real world central bank or a lender of last resort for national central banks, to proposals for doubling the price of gold, for com-

116

modity reserve-currency schemes, and for multiple-currency standards.[9] In the 1950s proposals to increase international liquidity had largely been "a British-based speciality," in the words of John Williamson.[10] The "British specialty" was "transformed into a widely dispersed growth industry following Triffin's "diagnosis of a prospective liquidity shortage."[11] When the long-predicted deflation and international economic warfare *à la* 1930s failed to materialize and it became clear that inflation, not deflation, was the menace, the diagnosis of an existing or impending shortage of international liquidity gradually shifted to one of excessive international liquidity.

The theoretical literature on the subject of international liquidity has become enormous. There have been several surveys of this literature. The latest and most extensive one by John Williamson lists about 250 items.[12] One of the highlights of this discussion was a three-day international seminar of twenty-nine experts on international reserves held by the IMF in 1970. The papers and proceedings of the seminar were pub-

[9] An excellent selection of these plans can be found in *World Monetary Reform, Plans and Issues*, H. Grubel, ed., Stanford University Press, (Stanford: 1963) and an incisive analysis of many plans in F. Machlup, *Plans for Reform of the International Monetary System*, revised edition (Princeton, N.J.: Department of Economics, 1964).

[10] John Williamson, "Survey in Applied Economics: International Liquidity," *The Economic Journal* (September 1973), 83:718 and 735. Most of these proposals misinterpreted the chronic British balance-of-payments difficulties as a worldwide shortage of liquidity. Ten years ago I wrote: "Countries with chronic balance-of-payments deficits like to blame their troubles on a lack of international liquidity. This is much more appealing than to attribute them to lack of discipline or policy mistakes. The outstanding example is Great Britain. The great majority of British experts right and left, irrespective of party affiliation, are convinced that Britain's chronic balance-of-payments difficulties are a consequence or symptom of a lack of international liquidity and more and more American experts inside and outside the government have become inclined to take the same view. . . . While a real scarcity of international liquidity would almost certainly manifest itself in balance-of-payments deficits of some countries, not every balance-of-payments crisis, even of a reserve currency country, can be regarded as a symptom of an international scarcity of liquidity." Gottfried Haberler, "The International Payments System: Postwar Trends and Prospects" in *International Payments Problems*, a symposium sponsored by the American Enterprise Institute, Washington, D.C., 1966, pp. 9–10. R. G. Hawtrey was one of the few British dissenters. See Sir Ralph Hawtrey, "Too Little Liquidity—or Too Much?" *The Banker*, (November 1962), 67:707–12.

[11] Williamson, "International Liquidity."

[12] *Ibid.*, pp. 655–746. Apart from a few French items, Williamson's list covers only the literature in English, and his English list is by no means complete.

117

lished in a massive volume, together with the lengthy earlier analytical and factual-statistical papers prepared by the IMF staff in connection with the implementation of the SDR scheme.[13]

The Problem of International Reserves under Floating

While this discussion was in full swing the international monetary scene changed completely. Inflation, which had been a serious problem during most of the postwar period, accelerated to the two-digit level, even in the United States and Switzerland. As a consequence, the Bretton Woods system of stable but adjustable exchange rates broke down, giving way to generalized managed floating—which is about to be legalized through the Second Amendment of the IMF Articles of Agreement.[14]

The demise of the fixed-rate system has invalidated, or sharply reduced the relevance of, much of recent theorizing on international liquidity. For as far as I can see, almost all of the discussions of the subject (including the IMF seminar of 1970 where floating received only fleeting mention) were based on the assumption of stable, or stable but adjustable, exchange rates. The same was true four years later, after floating had become worldwide, of the deliberations of the Committee on Reform of the International Monetary System (Committee of Twenty).[15] It is true,

[13] *International Reserves. Needs and Availability*, Papers and Proceedings of Seminar at the International Monetary Fund, June 1–3, 1970 (Washington, D.C.: IMF, 1970), pp. xiv and 552.

[14] In the present paper I take it for granted that high inflation and sharply divergent inflation rates have forced the widespread adoption of floating, and not the other way round, although the opposite view that floating was responsible for the inflation still finds some support in the literature.

[15] See *International Monetary Reform: Documents of the Committee of Twenty* (Washington, D.C.: IMF, 1974).

Tom de Vries, in his inside account of the reform negotiations, says: ". . Neither the Committee [of Twenty] nor the Deputies discussed the future exchange rate regime in any depth. This is quite remarkable in view of the fact that the world moved from a fixed-exchange rate system to a regime of floating rates during the very deliberations of the Committee. . . . This made the work of the Committee look increasingly unreal. . . . The Committee was saved from these contradictions by the quadrupling of the price of oil in . . . 1973. So enormous was the uncertainty created by the disturbance . . . and so evi-

of course, that there was a growing demand for floating, and greater exchange flexibility was often listed as one method among others for dealing with the liquidity problem.[16] But most proponents of floating took it for granted that there would be no liquidity problem under floating or that the problem would be reduced to insignificance—an assumption that many opponents of flexibility seemed to have accepted. There has been very little systematic analysis of the problem of international liquidity under floating.[17]

Admittedly, years ago Sir Roy Harrod argued that under flexible exchange rates larger official interventions in the exchange market and, therefore, larger international reserves, would be required than under fixed rates, because under fixed rates, stabilizing private capital flows that reduce the need for official financing are much more dependable than under floating.[18] But Sir Roy was very careful to add that "this, of course, assumes that there is complete confidence in the maintenance of the fixed rates." Thus, in effect, he compared flexible rates with the gold standard and not with the Bretton Woods adjustable-peg system.

Most other writers have not been so careful to distinguish sharply between credibly fixed and stable but adjustable exchange rates. Under the gold standard, when there was "complete confidence in the maintenance of the fixed rates," small interest differentials would induce large short-

---

dent became the fact that flexible rates were here to stay, that the Committee decided to give up its attempt at comprehensive reform." Tom de Vries, "Jamaica, or the Non-Reform of the International Monetary System," *Foreign Affairs* (April 1976), 54:585–88. Marcus Fleming once remarked in candid and rueful self-criticism, "at every stage in the discussion [of the reform of the international monetary system] reform proposals have lagged behind events and have been quickly outmoded by new events." See J. Marcus Fleming, *Reflections on the International Monetary Reform*, Princeton Essays in International Finance No. 107, Department of Economics, Princeton University, Princeton, N.J., 1974, p. 17.

[16] See, for example, F. Machlup, *Plans for Reform of the International Monetary System*.
[17] Fleming's article, "*Floating Exchange Rates, Asymmetrical Interventions, and the Management of International Liquidity*," *IMF Staff Papers* (July 1975), 22:263–83, seems to be the only attempt to squarely face the problem of international liquidity under floating. The highly involved presentation, the "meandering course" of the argument (the author's own description of his paper, on p. 281), and the author's reluctance to draw firm policy conclusions reflect the great difficulties of applying to a world of floating exchange rates the concepts and prescriptions that were developed for the par value system.
[18] Roy Harrod, *Reforming the World's Money* (London: Macmillan; New York: St. Martins Press, 1965), pp. 45–47.

term capital flows. This is precisely what had enabled Britain to get along with a small gold reserve in the nineteenth century. Under the Bretton Woods system, in contrast, "complete confidence" in the existing rates was no longer possible. It has become increasingly clear and by now should be common knowledge that the method of changing rates by occasional large jumps, the adjustable peg, made it easy and almost riskless for speculators to anticipate changes in the exchange rate. Speculators could speculate against the central banks whose hands were tied rather than against each other, which is a much more hazardous proposition and which is what they have to do under floating. The consequence was a succession of currency crises with increasingly massive and disruptive capital flows. As John Williamson (and others before him) had predicted, "the adjustable peg is unlikely to be viable indefinitely. Ever increasing destabilizing speculation will result if pegs are apt to jump." [19]

Official interventions in the exchange market on an enormous, ever-increasing scale were required to hold the line. This has forced one country after another to give up pegging and to adopt floating. The only alternative would have been tight exchange control. [20] The clear implication of all of this is that the adjustable peg requires much larger international reserves than either the gold standard (credibly fixed exchange rates) or floating rates.

It does not follow, of course, that the problem of international liquidity vanishes altogether under floating. If there are official interventions in the exchange market, as there probably always will be, there is some need (or demand) for reserves. But since under floating the authorities are not restricted in their interventions by a rigid barrier, unless they restrict themselves, which would be tantamount to giving up the float, the need for reserves cannot be greater under floating than it is under the adjustable peg.

This has been denied by John Williamson, largely on the ground that

[19] J. Williamson, *The Crawling Peg*, Princeton Essays in International Finance No. 50, Department of Economics, Princeton University, Princeton, N.J., 1965, p. 8.

[20] Experience has shown that in the long run, capital controls require current account controls, not only to prevent evasions such as illegal over- or underinvoicing of imports (or exports) for the purposes of camouflaging capital movements, but also because trade flows, for example, accumulation or decumulation of inventories of imported commodities, can serve as substitutes for international capital flows. The prevention of such perfectly legal evasions of the capital controls requires tight controls of current transactions.

120

during the first years of the float a number of countries used reserves in interventions to a greater extent than before the float.[21] But this is unconvincing. It does not tell us what the volume of interventions *would have been* in that same period under the same circumstances, if the world had been on the adjustable peg. The first years of widespread floating, 1973–76, was a period of high turbulence, rapid inflation, and severe recession, with sharply divergent rates of inflation and recession. This was also the period of the oil shock, which had different effects on different countries and caused different policy reactions. Can anyone doubt that under the adjustable peg there would have been enormous speculative flows of funds that could have been contained only by equally enormous interventions or by very tight controls? Given the fact (if it is a fact) that in such a disturbed period there were greater interventions, despite floating, than there were in an earlier, calmer period under the adjustable peg—should one draw the conclusion (which Williamson did not draw, although others did) that it was a mistake to give up the adjustable peg and adopt floating? I do not think so. It would be like advising sick people against going to the hospital on the ground that the death rate of hospitalized people is higher than that of the rest of the population.

While it may be an exaggeration to say that international liquidity or the volume of international monetary reserves poses no problems under floating, there can be no doubt that the problem is not pressing any more. The nature of the problem has changed in the last few years, and floating has not constituted the sole reason for the change.

To explore this subject further it will be well to follow J. Marcus Flem-

---

[21] John Williamson, "Exchange Rate Flexibility and Reserve Use," IMF Document 1974, incorporated in "Exchange-Rate Flexibility and Reserve Use," *Scandinavian Journal of Economics* (1976), 78:327–39. Williamson also presents an ingenious theoretical model in mathematical terms that is supposed to throw light on the question whether there would be any difference in the amount of reserve use under managed floating than under a par value system. The model suffers, however, from several serious shortcomings as Stanley W. Black ("Comments on J. Williamson's 'Exchange Rate Flexibility and Reserve Use,' " pp. 340–45) has pointed out. The results of Williamson's model, as he himself summarizes them, are not very enlightening. The model hardly adds anything to the verbal argument. It seems that he, too, compares floating not with the adjustable peg systems, but with more or less credibly fixed rates, that is in effect with the gold standard. See also the comments by Otmar Emminger on Williamson's thesis in O. Emminger, *On the Way to a New International Order* (Washington, D.C.: American Enterprise Institute, 1976), pp. 16–17.

ing and "go back to first principles," as he did in his first paper on the subject and on later occasions.[22] Fleming claimed that "practically all the important economic effects of reserve change come to pass by way of their effects on national policies; namely monetary and budget policies, policies with respect to restrictions on international trade and capital movements and policies with respect to exchange rates." Similarly, "despite the popularity of the name 'international liquidity' as a synonym for reserves, the decisive characteristic of reserve assets is not so much that they are liquid as that they are under the control of the monetary authority."[23]

Because of the essential role of policy, Fleming rejects what has been dubbed the "international quantity theory," which postulates a close parallelism between the association in each country between changes in the national money supply and changes in the national price level (or money GNP) and, on the other hand, between changes in the amount of international reserves and changes in the world price level (or volume of international transactions).[24] Jacques Polak and Egon Sohmen, too, have stressed the basic differences between national money and international

[22] J. Marcus Fleming, "International Liquidity: Ends and Means," *IMF Staff Papers* (December 1961), vol. 8, reprinted as chapter 4 in J. Marcus Fleming, *Essays in International Economics* (Cambridge, Mass: Harvard University Press, 1971). See also the chapters 5 through 7 and Fleming's powerful paper, "Reserve Creation and Real Reserves," in *International Reserves: Needs and Availability* (Washington, D.C.: International Monetary Fund, 1970), pp. 521–52. In a lengthy, closely reasoned essay, "Floating Exchange Rates, Asymmetrical Intervention, and the Management of International Liquidity," *IMF Staff Papers* (July 1975), 22:263–83, Fleming tried to assess the changes in the liquidity problem wrought by widespread floating.

[23] Fleming, *Essays*, p. 97, and "Reserve Creation and Real Reserves," p. 524.

[24] On the international quantity theory, see Williamson "Survey," p. 711. It should be observed that few modern quantity theorists (or monetarists, as they are usually called) have embraced the international quantity theory. Williamson mentions only Robert Mundell. Arthur Laffer also comes to mind, and Harry Johnson and Jürg Niehans came close to embracing it in their comments on Cooper's paper at the IMF seminar *International Reserves* (pp. 149 and 152). The international quantity theory seems to be coextensive with what Marina v. N. Whitman calls "global monetarism." See her paper, "Global Monetarism and the Monetary Approach to the Balance of Payments," in *Brookings Papers on Economic Activity* (Washington, D.C.: Brookings Institution, 1975), 3:531–55 and my review of J. A. Frenkel and H. G. Johnson, eds., *The Monetary Approach to the Balance of Payments*, in *Journal of Economic Literature* (December 1976), 14:1324–27.

monetary reserves.[25] Sohmen states his criticism of the international quantity theory this way: "Its basic fault seems to me to lie in the tendency to attribute to governments and central banks the same type of behavior with respect to monetary assets that we can expect with some confidence from private profit or utility maximizers"—that is to say, from private enterprises and households.

Fleming, Polak and Sohmen fully recognize that there are "formal similarities" between private money holdings and official reserves. But they are surely right that the essential involvement of government policies and the underlying political processes introduce decisive dissimilarities, which are bound to loosen the correlation between changes in international reserves and world inflation. In Fleming's words:

The behavior of monetary authorities with respect to international reserves is governed by considerations far more complex than those which determine the behavior of individuals with respect to money balances. Up to a point, the authorities will react to an increase in their reserve ease as individuals would react to an increase in their monetary ease, namely by taking action intended to reduce the assets in question, reserves and money, respectively. But the authorities will be hampered in so doing by national objectives with respect to internal financial stability, exchange rate stability, etc., that have no parallel in the case of individuals.[26]

We may add that the behavior of *private individuals* with respect to their money holdings can be assumed substantially to remain the same over time (a fact that gives the velocity of monetary circulation a certain stability except in extreme situations such as hyperinflation or comprehensive rationing in wartime), whereas *public* policies bearing on the holding of international reserves are subject to frequent and large changes over time. These changes, both cyclical and long run, often differ from country to

---

[25] See Polak's important paper, "Money: National and International," in *Essays in Honor of Thorkil Kristensen* (Paris: OECD, 1970), and reprinted in *International Reserves*, the IMF seminar volume of 1970. Sohmen's paper, "International Liquidity under Flexible Exchange Rates," is a draft for *Exchange Rate Flexibility*, proceedings of a conference held by the American Enterprise Institute and the U.S. Treasury in April 1976 (forthcoming).

[26] *International Reserves*, p. 525.

country and are sometimes unpredictable or even internally inconsistent.[27] A particular type of change in official attitudes with respect to the desirable level of international reserves, one that has often been mentioned in the literature, is that "views held by monetary authorities on what is to be regarded as an adequate reserve seem to be subject to change without any obvious change in the underlying situation accounting for it. Once countries have enjoyed an ample reserve position for some time, they seem to get used to a comfortable cushion and to raise their sights on what is sufficient."[28] Essentially the same idea later became known as "Mrs. Machlup's wardrobe theory" of the authorities' demand for reserve.[29]

The most searching criticism of the international quantity theory has been expounded by Richard J. Sweeney and Thomas D. Willett.[30] The authors deal not only with the theory but also with the statistical measures and procedures that have been used in several recent publications to establish a close correlation between world inflation and global reserve growth. Sweeney and Willett conclude that these theories and their statistical implementation suffer from excessive aggregation. Especially with extensive floating the very concept and measures of global reserves have become highly ambiguous, if not meaningless.[31] The policy connection between international reserves and domestic money supply differs greatly

[27] The international quantity theorists or global monetarists seem to be harking back to the days of the gold standard. In those days the similarity between official and private behavior with respect to cash and reserve holdings was indeed much greater than it is now, because the rules of the gold standard tended to make central banks behave like individuals: to contract the money supply, thereby inducing reductions in overall expenditures when reserves declined, and to expand the money supply when reserves increased. The growing tendency to violate the rules of the gold standard—to standardize or make constant *domestic* policy objectives, that is, employment, growth, and price stability in some combination (which often differs from country to country), ahead of the objective of keeping the *external* value of the currency (the exchange rate)—has progressively destroyed the similarity and has rendered the gold standard more and more unworkable.

[28] Gottfried Haberler, *Money in the International Economy* (Cambridge, Mass.: Harvard University Press, 1965), p. 42.

[29] For references to that theory, see Williamson, "Survey," p. 694.

[30] Richard J. Sweeney and Thomas D. Willett, "Eurodollars, Petrodollars, and World Liquidity and Inflation," in *Journal of Monetary Economics* (Amsterdam: North Holland, 1976). The reference list of this paper updates the bibliography in Williamson, "Survey."

[31] The reasons have been spelled out in greater detail in Peter Kenen's contribution to this conference.

from country to country and is subject to change in time. Hence, any correlation between changes in global reserves and in the world price level is apt to be spurious even if domestically the quantity theory works well. It follows that there is no presumption that stabilization of global reserves in some sense would tend to stabilize the world price level in some relevant sense. There simply are too many slips between the cup and the lip.

Recent Developments and Problems

There have been important recent cases of policy divergence between countries and of policy and institutional changes in several countries that have beclouded the very concept of international reserves and its role in the world economy. Two such developments deserve mention.

It has been charged that widespread floating since 1973 did not prevent a further inflationary expansion of international monetary reserves. It is true that global reserves as conventionally measured by the IMF grew sharply in 1973, 1974, and 1975. But the great bulk of that increase went to OPEC countries. (In 1975 and 1976 there were also substantial reserve increases resulting from intra-European "snake" interventions—a case of stable but adjustable exchange rates.) It is now generally agreed that the largest part of the increase in OPEC reserves should go "above the line," that is to say, should be counted as "autonomous" investments and not as "accommodating" reserve changes.[32] Moreover, OPEC balances are not inflationary in the same sense as dollar balances accumulated by Japan and European countries because, unlike the latter, OPEC governments do not routinely issue national money to buy dollars (or Eurodollars) from their private exporters. Oil revenues accrue to the governments and the petrodollars are then invested abroad, partly in liquid form.

The other recent development that has blurred the dividing line between changes in monetary reserves and changes in autonomous foreign

[32] On the treatment of OPEC reserves, see especially William R. Cline, *International Monetary Reform and the Developing Countries* (Washington, D.C.: Brookings Institution, 1976), ch. 4.

investment or disinvestment is the foreign borrowing by public and semi-public enterprises or by nominally private enterprises at the government's urging.[33] This has occurred on a huge scale in Britain and Italy. It is generally taken for granted that these operations have been undertaken, wholly or at least to a very large extent, for balance-of-payments reasons so that they are on a par with utilizing monetary reserves to finance a deficit of "autonomous" transactions. There have always existed borderline cases that made the distinction between "autonomous" transactions and "accommodating" reserve movements somewhat fuzzy. But it stands to reason that the rapidly increasing involvement of government policy in the adjustment process and the enormous growth of the public sector in many countries have made the distinction between "accommodating" reserve changes and "autonomous" investments increasingly arbitrary, if not meaningless. One consequence of this development is that it casts doubt on any attempt to define, however cautiously, an optimum level of reserves. It similarly casts in doubt the feasibility and relevance of the many proposals that detailed rules be laid down for the composition of reserves (stipulating, for example, that minimum proportions of total reserves should be kept in SDRs) and for interventions in the exchange market in order to achieve an optimum growth of global reserves or, more modestly, to prevent excessively large departures from the optimum.

Fears have been expressed that the present system as defined in the Second Amendment of the IMF charter—the "nonsystem," as it is often called by those whose blueprints have not been followed—does not eliminate the danger of global inflation (or deflation) resulting from excessive (or deficient) supply of international liquidity. The reason given, for example by John Williamson, is the "total lack of control over the international liquidity."[34] Williamson admits that this is not likely to result

[33] The growing reliance on external borrowing for financing balance-of-payments deficits and propping up the exchange rate is stressed in the *IMF Annual Report, 1976* (Washington, D.C.: IMF, 1976), pp. 39–40.

[34] John Williamson, "The Benefits and Costs of an International Monetary Nonsystem," in *Reflections on Jamaica*, Essays in International Finance No. 115, Department of Economics, Princeton University, April 1976, p. 57. We can surely disregard the danger of deflation. For no country is likely to permit deflation for balance-of-payments reasons. Furthermore, the imposition of import controls for balance-of-payments reasons (rather than on

"from variations in the foreign-exchange component of reserves," because floating, unlike the par value system, enables countries to ward off inflationary (or deflationary) influences from abroad. But Williamson thinks that

no such reassurance exists so far as the gold component of reserves is concerned. The Jamaica Agreement gives central banks the freedom to trade gold among themselves at mutually agreeable prices. If it transpires that a willing buyer at a near-market price can always be found when a central bank wishes to sell (which is a possibility, though perhaps not a probability), the Jamaica Agreement may reverse the *de facto* demonetization of gold that occurred in August 1971. If gold is thus effectively remonetized, any new speculative bubble in the gold market would increase the value of gold reserves, and countries in general could find their reserves carried far above their optimal level. The fact that exchange rates were floating would then do nothing to prevent a competitive scramble to dispose of excess reserves, with inflationary consequences.[35]

I think we should not have sleepless nights over that danger, either. To be sure, no international agreement can prevent the world's leading economic countries from committing collectively at some time in the future the folly of remonetizing gold. But the amended IMF charter does not compel anybody to accept gold. And if the United States refuses to accept gold, other countries, even if they were in complete agreement, could not effectively remonetize gold. They could, of course, collectively go on an inflationary spending spree by buying gold from each other at an

---

protectionist grounds) has not become a very serious problem under floating, at least not yet.

Marcus Fleming stated in his last paper: "In spite of these disturbances [mainly the oil price rise, which Fleming characterized as "one of the biggest exogenuous balance-of-payments shocks of all time"] there has thus far been remarkably little resort to restrictionism by industrial or even by primary producing countries. This has been due to a combination of circumstances. Some of the credit must go to the much-abused Eurocurrency market, together with the willingness of countries to borrow where necessary from the private market. Some of it must go to the system of managed exchange rate floating which, at some cost to exchange stability in the short term, has succeeded in containing disequilibrating capital flows, and has also permitted exchange rates to adjust in the longer run to differential rates of inflation." Marcus J. Fleming, "Mercantilism and Free Trade Today," IMF Document, April 5, 1976, mimeographed (forthcoming), p. 15.

[35] Williamson, "Benefits and Costs," p. 57. Similar fears that the gold provisions of the amended IMF charter may have global inflationary effects have been expressed by others.

inflated price, but they could do that, if they wanted, without the help of gold.

This last thought suggests a possible inflationary danger. It is conceivable that some day in the future the holders of the huge liquid official (or private) dollar balances abroad (largely a legacy from the prefloating period but now voluntarily held) may start to spend them. That could take the form of foreign countries engaging in inflationary policies and financing the resulting balance-of-payments deficits by drawing down their dollar balances. Not many people take this danger very seriously, for as the Bank for International Settlements states in its 1976 report:[36]

the argument, based on the global reserve statistics, that there is now a potentially inflationary overhang of liquidity in the system, the effects of which will be increasingly felt as the world economic recovery proceeds, comes rather close to saying that Germany, Switzerland, Saudi Arabia and Kuwait are about to spend the bulk of their rather large foreign assets on increased net imports of goods and services.

Since this is not a likely development, it is hardly worthwhile to discuss how the United States could protect itself against this threat.

Another scenario would be rapid inflation in the United States, which could induce other countries to try to get rid of their depreciating dollars—an attempt that would in turn intensify the U.S. inflation. This too is unlikely to happen. At any rate, it would not be the fault of the existing international monetary system of floating exchange rates and could not be prevented by controlling the volume of global reserves—unless the power of controlling global reserves were interpreted in an unconventionally broad sense to include the power of controlling the money supply in at least the major countries. Giving the IMF that power would come close to setting it up as a world government.

However, in a highly attenuated form, the possibility that the United States could be put under inflationary pressure by the operation of the present system is taken seriously by some analysts. What I have in mind is the theory that the almost universal use of the dollar as the intervention

[36] Annual Report of the Bank for International Settlements, Basel, 1976, p. 109.

128

currency can lead to a depreciation of the dollar in the exchange market, even if the U.S. balance of payments is in perfect equilibrium.

Suppose, for example, that the French franc is declining and the German DM rising (or that the franc is at the "belly" and the DM at the "back" of the "snake"). If the French then sell dollars to stop or slow the slide (to keep the franc in the "snake"), the dollar will be pushed down, although there may have been no change in the U.S. balance of payments. I do not believe, however, that this is a serious threat requiring elaborate precautions such as a complicated multicurrency intervention system.

In the first place, if the dollar is the universal intervention currency, the chances are that the sales of dollars by deficit countries will at least partially be matched by purchases on the part of surplus countries. Second, if France has a deficit, the United States may be one of the surplus countries, so that the dollar will rise, and dollar sales by France will only delay the rise. Third, even if the U.S. balance is initially in equilibrium, the changes in trade flows set in motion by France's attempt to balance its accounts may change the U.S. balance. The upshot is that in our immensely complicated multilateral world trade and payment system nobody can really forsee all of the ramifications of any particular change. It is impossible to anticipate and match them by *ad hoc* tailored interventions. This task can safely be left to the market. If the dollar were the currency of a small country—say, of Switzerland—there would perhaps be cause for worry. But in the multi-hundred-billion world dollar market, including the Eurodollar market, net intervention sales even of several hundred million dollars can be absorbed without causing more than a small ripple.

Concluding Remarks:
The Role of the IMF

My conclusion is that generalized floating and other developments have rendered obsolete any attempt to define an optimum level of interna-

129

tional reserves; similarly, control of international reserves is no longer an important business for the IMF. It is the adjustment and not the liquidity problem that is of paramount importance, now more than ever before. The main task of the IMF should be "surveillance" over exchange-rate policies, prevention of "dirty floating," and of what has become known as "aggressive interventions," that is to say, "manipulating exchange rates . . . in order to prevent effective balance of payments adjustment or to gain an unfair competitive advantage over other members," as the Amended Articles of Agreement put it.[37] By "dirty floating," as distinguished from merely managed or controlled floating,[38] I mean split exchange markets, multiple exchange rates, import deposit schemes, and similar devices that grossly violate one of the basic objectives of the IMF, namely, that current transactions should not be restricted.

However, to say that control of global international reserves is no longer an urgent problem does not mean that for individual countries the size of their reserves and their external borrowing potential are unimportant, nor that the use countries make of their reserves and borrowing power cannot become a matter of international concern. It is possible that in the last few years there has been much international overborrowing and excessive lending by banks to shore up shaky balance-of-payments positions. All this may, indeed, cause serious troubles in the future. But if so, it has nothing to do with a lack of international control over the volume of global reserves, and it could not have been prevented by such controls unless control over global reserves is unconventionally interpreted to include control over money supply in at least the major countries. Giving the IMF the power to control money supply in major

[37] International Monetary Fund, Article IV, Section 1 (III).

[38] "Merely managed or controlled floating" implies that the only measure to influence the exchange rate directly is buying and selling in the foreign exchange market. Influencing the exchange rate *indirectly* by general monetary and fiscal policy is a different matter. For example, I would not speak of a "managed float" if a decline in the exchange rate induced a country to tighten monetary policy. It is sometimes said that the monetary authorities can influence the exchange rate by interventions in the money market, by buying and selling bonds, just as well as by interventions in the foreign-exchange rate. This may be true with high capital mobility if exchange rates are credibly fixed as they were under the gold standard. But when that credibility is gone, monetary policy becomes a very imperfect substitute for interventions in the exchange market.

130

countries would, I repeat, be almost equivalent to setting it up as a world government.

Furthermore, discounting the importance of global liquidity and its control does not mean that inflation is no problem. On the contrary, I agree with the IMF annual report for 1976 that inflation is the most pressing monetary problem.[39] But today the danger of inflation does not emanate from the working of the international monetary system. During the last years of the par value regime, the international monetary system greatly contributed to the worldwide spread of inflation, but under the present system of floating, inflation has its roots entirely in *national* monetary, fiscal, and exchange-rate policies. The primary responsibility for fighting inflation obviously falls on the leading industrial countries, especially the United States. This is so because the majority of smaller countries peg their currencies either to the currency of one of the leading industrial countries, most of them to the dollar, or to a basket of important currencies or SDRs.

One last point. To say that fighting world inflation is the task of the major industrial countries does not imply that the IMF can do nothing about inflation except preach. The IMF policies have some, though under realistic assumptions only a marginal, direct effect on world inflation. But it is easier to identify policies that would be inflationary than measures that would help to curb inflation. Steps that would add to inflationary pressures are a general increase in the IMF quotas and additional distribution of SDRs, especially if linked to foreign aid. Similarly, adding to inflation would be a further proliferation and expansion of special lending facilities—such as the Oil Facility, the Buffer Stock Facility, the Extended Fund Facility, and the Compensatory Financing of Export Fluctuations.

However, this does not mean that under no circumstances should any such measures be taken. On the contrary, emergencies must be ex-

---

[39] To avoid a possible misunderstanding, I should like to stress that this statement does not reflect a value judgment to the effect that rising prices are a greater evil than high unemployment. On the contrary, my personal value judgment would be the reverse. What it does reflect, and what the authors of the IMF annual report probably had in mind, is that the objective of sustainable growth and full employment cannot be achieved unless inflation is curbed.

131

pected to occur from time to time that would justify even large-scale credit operations by the IMF to forestall some major or minor disturbances of the world economy, including protectionist reactions. What it does mean is that the inflationary implications of such lending should not be overlooked, just as a fire brigade when throwing water on an attic fire should not be oblivious of the damage that flooding can do to the rest of the house. The two dangers—the threatening disturbance and the inflationary side effect of the measures taken—should be weighed against each other, overreactions should be avoided, and the rescue operation should be properly dosed and pinpointed so as to minimize the danger of inflation. To illustrate the last point: Whereas an across-the-board distribution of additional SDRs would clearly be an inflationary move, the use of additional liquidity for a loan to our inflationary country as part of a comprehensive stabilization agreement that enables the country in question to get out of the inflationary rut, can be defended as an anti-inflationary move.

To pursue this highly important problem any further would burst the frame of the present study. However, one more observation may be permitted, specifically, that conditional lending by the IMF—"provision of conditional liquidity," to use official language—can be used as an inducement for countries to put their financial house in order and to pursue anti-inflationary policies. Liberal unconditional lending is likely to be counterproductive because it may well tempt countries to delay needed structural reform and antiinflationary measures and to postpone changes in exchange rates or floating that may be required.[40]

[40] Some of these problems are further discussed in G. Haberler, "The International Monetary System after Jamaica and Manila" in *Contemporary Science Problems*, William Fellner, ed. (Washington, D.C.: American Enterprise Systems, 1977).

HERBERT G. GRUBEL

SIMON FRASER UNIVERSITY, BURNABY, B.C.

A POWERFULLY argued and widely accepted literature in economics concludes that the optimal international monetary system is one in which national governments refrain entirely from intervention in foreign exchange markets and let exchange rates fluctuate freely. In such a world the productivity of and demand for international reserves are zero and the question for which I was asked to provide an answer, namely, how important is control over international reserves, is meaningless. Therefore, I believe that as a first step in answering this question it is necessary to establish rigorously and on the price-theoretic level employed by the proponents of freely floating exchange rates why exchange market intervention and the necessary holding of reserves are socially productive.

Therefore in this paper I present first the price-theoretic case for government exchange-rate stabilization policies in general and then show that it implies the existence of a national and an aggregate world demand functions for reserves. At a given cost of holding reserves, the demand curves of each country and the world aggregate indicate that there is an optimum stock demand for reserves. If this optimum stock is not supplied, then countries are forced into making adjustments that involve avoidable social costs, the nature of which is specified in the derivation of the demand curves proper. My answer to the question about the importance of control over international reserves is, therefore, couched in terms of the costs incurred by the deviation of actual reserve supplies different from optimal demand. Finally, I use the concept of an optimum quantity of money—derived by M. Friedman to specify a Pareto optimal quantity of reserve supply and demand.

In the concluding section of the paper I draw the policy implications

133

flowing from the theoretical analysis. In two brief appendixes I present some ideas on two additional problems of crucial importance to the design of the new international monetary system: first, the development of objective indicators of "proper" policies by national governments; and second, the consequences of the availability of substitutes to IMF controlled means for the financing of payments imbalances. These appendixes supplement the analysis presented in the main part of this paper, but because they are somewhat more abstract and not essential to the main arguments, they fit more readily into appendixes than the body of the paper.

The Environment:
A World of Perfect Markets and Uncertainty

As students of the literature on freely floating exchange rates are well aware, the existence of market imperfections does not justify pegging exchange rates because the optimal or first-best solution to the problems raised by the existence of market imperfections is to eliminate them directly. Price pegging is only a second-best solution that creates additional, socially costly distortions. However, the same price-theoretic models that reject the existence of market imperfections as a justification for government intervention accept that certain types of externalities do constitute a case for such government activities.

In the light of these facts, it is useful to construct a model of exchange-rate determination and government intervention that assumes that all markets are perfect and that governments behave "properly" in a sense to be defined. Therefore, let us make the following three assumptions. First, trade elasticities are high, even in the shortest run, so that the Marshall–Lerner condition holds and exchange-rate changes induce "normal" changes in current accounts. Second, speculators stabilize exchange rates, investing in their activities and the gathering of information up to the point where marginal private costs and benefits are equal. Third, government activities related to the provision of public goods, income redis-

134

tribution, and stabilization of economic activity are explained publicly, and their implications for foreign trade and capital flows are evaluated properly by speculators.

In a regime of freely floating exchange rates, the preceding assumptions imply that the market exchange rates are "efficient" at all times in the sense that they embody all of the implications of economic developments and government policies that it paid the private sector to analyze from available information. However, it is clear from both theoretical and empirical studies of capital markets from the point of view of the efficient market hypothesis, that the exchange rate under these conditions is not perfectly stable, but that it exhibits a distribution with a variance greater than zero.

Such exchange-rate fluctuations are inevitable and necessary because while speculators form rational expectations about the exchange-rate implications of past and current events and policies, they preceive the future only dimly and new information about events continuously affects expectations about the proper current level of exchange rates. Speculators tend to form expectations about all uncertain future events, such as the quality of harvests, government policies, and even earthquakes, but as these events actually take place, predictions are often erroneous, and views about the proper level of the exchange rate have to be revised.

Given that even in a world of perfect markets, exchange rates must exhibit some variance, there exists the opportunity for governments to reduce this variance through stabilization policies. Such governmental activities are justified only if the reduction in the variance leads to welfare gains in the form of externalities. In the next section we discuss the nature of these externalities. Here we need to deal with the important potential objection to such governmental stabilization policies that it can succeed only if bureaucrats know better than the private sector what the proper level of the exchange rate should be in the light of available information about the economic effects of present and future events and policies. This is an important point since it is not at all clear that the bureaucrats running exchange-stabilization policies are better interpretors of information than are private speculators. Moreover, even if they are, the

135

most efficient use of the official analysis of likely exchange-rate trends is to present it to the private sector, which can combine it with its own analysis to form more accurate expectations and act on them.

These objections to the exchange-rate-stabilization policies of governments are invalid if the policies are formulated according to the maxim that exchange-market intervention should "lean against the wind," leading to the purchase of foreign exchange when free-market forces threaten to lower foreign-exchange price and to its sale when they threaten to force it up. The strength and duration of this "leaning against the wind" should be determined by the relationship between actual and target levels of reserve holdings. The greater the difference between actual and target levels, the less intensive should be intervention to increase the gap and the more intensive, to close the gap.

Under this code of behavior exchange rates would not be fixed, as under the gold standard; they would not move in large discrete jumps, as under the parity exchange-rate system. Rather, they would move gradually and exhibit a smaller variance than that which the free and perfect market would have produced. [1]

It may be useful to consider how such government behavior would narrow exchange rate fluctuations with the help of a simple example. Thus, consider that a drought produced a bad harvest. Expert metereological opinion expressed the view that with a high degree of probability, droughts would take place also in the next few years, because of some fundamental shift in global wind patterns, which in the past tended to produce cycles in the levels of precipitation in key agricultural areas of the country. Speculators acting on this best information would tend to depreciate the exchange rate. The government, with reserves initially at their long-run average target level, would resist this depreciation by selling foreign exchange.

---

[1] In appendix A the preceding analysis is formalized with the help of a model depicting the disturbances as producing a random walk of changes in exchange rates (or reserve holdings). In the present paper, we also abstract from the use of balance-of-payments adjustment policies other than exchange-rate fluctuations, which may be triggered by deviations of actual from target reserve holdings. In principle, adjustment should be obtained most efficiently by pushing the use of all instruments to the point where at the margin the social costs of their uses are equal. For further analysis of this point, see H. G. Grubel, *The International Monetary System*, 3d ed. (Harmondsworth, England: Penguin, 1977), ch. 3.

Now there are two polar possibilities, namely, that the metereologists and speculators are proven to be wrong or correct. If they are wrong, harvests return to normal, and the need for the higher price of foreign exchange will have been circumvented. Under these conditions, the government prevented a temporary fluctuation in the exchange rate and its variance will be smaller than it would have been without intervention. If metereologists and speculators are correct, then the government loses reserves and gradually lets the exchange rate move to the level consistent with a series of droughts. Under these conditions, the exchange-rate variance can never be larger than it would have been in the absence of intervention, and probably it is smaller.

In the real world, of course, there are many different kinds of random events influencing the exchange rate continuously. As a result, earthquakes, strikes, and changes in the behavior of consumers or policies of governments can override or reinforce the effects of droughts. Whatever the net effects of these events may be, "leaning against the wind" reduces variance and cannot increase it. That this must be so can be seen most readily by consideration of a set of circumstances where a country has been hit by a large number of events that led to a depletion of reserves and then experiences further influences that cause a depreciation of the exchange rate. Under these conditions, during the subperiod of low reserve holdings there is no intervention, and exchange rates are the same as in the absence of any intervention policies. Following such a run of adverse influences in the balance of payments, favorable events would lead to upward pressures on the exchange rate, which are prevented by the purchase of foreign exchange in order to restore the country's stock of reserves until, at the opposite extreme, excess reserve holdings cause a cessation of intervention and an upward movement of the exchange rate. In between the times when intervention is zero, the policies will have narrowed the magnitude of the exchange-rate fluctuations.

The conclusion from our preceding analysis is that in a world of perfect markets, a government possessing international reserves and stabilizing exchange rates, by following policies of "leaning against the wind" and with an intensity determined by its reserve holdings, can reduce the variance of exchange rates without necessarily having superior information about current or future events and policies affecting the exchange rate than does the private sector. It does so in essence by taking advantage of the fact that most disturbances affecting the exchange rate are unpredictable, but are self-reversing or affected by other random events with influences in the opposite direction over some period of time. The next step in the argument is to show that the reduction in the variance of exchange rates resulting from such policies produces social benefits and, therefore, endows international reserve holdings with a positive social productivity.

The Welfare Gains from Stabilization

The welfare gains accruing to the public from the exchange-rate stabilization activities of the government take the form of externalities that were identified in the literature on optimum currency areas during the 1960s and consist of three sources.[2] They will now be described in the context of exchange-rate stabilization within a given country.

First, there are real income gains due to reduced price-level instabilities. This effect is brought about by the smaller fluctuations in the prices of traded goods that enter into the consumer price index and fluctuate together with the exchange rate. The increased price stability raises the usefulness of money, moving the economy further from the inefficient system of barter toward the most efficient money-exchange economy with its optimal level of trade and specialization. Similarly, the risk from exchange-rate fluctuations introducing a discrepancy between domestic and foreign trade is reduced, and the gains from greater international specialization accrue to the public as a whole. Finally, there are direct income gains to the public due to the reduced cost of portfolio management resulting from the greater stability and predictability of foreign money and asset values.

[2] For a detailed and perceptive view of this literature, see E. Tower and T. Willet, *The Theory of Optimum Currency Areas and Exchange-Rate Flexibility*, Department of Economics, Princeton University, Princeton, N.J., 1976. I have applied the arguments for optimum currency areas to optimum exchange-rate stability previously; see H. G. Grubel, "The Case for Optimum Exchange Rate Stability," *Weltwirtschaftliches Archiv* (1973b), Band 109: 1–13, p. 351–81.

Second, the gains from greater exchange-rate stability can be expected to be reduced by the constraints that the exchange policy imposes on the freedom of the government to pursue domestic stabilization policies. Thus, shortages of reserves may inhibit vigorous monetary expansion in the case of a recession; large reserve gains during a boom may interfere with restrictive monetary policy. Also, it has been argued that reductions of real income resulting from exchange-rate depreciation induce price ` increases that are necessary to achieve lower absorption when it is at a disequilibrating, high level. In other words, the reduced use of exchange-rate changes decreases the usefulness of money illusion as an instrument of adjustment to cyclical or structural excess demand conditions. As a result of these constraints, macroeconomic disequilbrium tends to last longer and reduce welfare more, the greater is the constraint on exchange-rate flexibility due to government stabilization of the rate.

Third, countries lose their freedom to choose an optimum point on the Phillips curve of inflation–unemployment trade-off without concern about inflation rates in the rest of the world. Such a move away from the social optimum induced by the program of exchange-rate stabilization leads to a loss of welfare.

How important are these three elements of costs and benefits from exchange-rate stabilization? In recent years, theoretical and empirical evidence has accumulated that sheds serious doubts on the existence of an inflation–unemployment trade-off. Rapid rates of inflation have led to the condition where even in reletiely closed economies, such as the U.S. economy, money illusion has become of negligible importance. These considerations suggest that two types of cost associated theoretically with exchange-rate stabilization in practice are probably small or nonexistent.

The importance of the constraint imposed by exchange-rate stabilization on the use of countercyclical monetary policy depends very importantly on the quantity of reserves available to finance payments imbalances, the size of business cycles, the degree of international synchronization of these cycles, and a host of other conditions. There is no simple way in which one can reach a judgment on the magnitude of these costs, though it may not be unreasonable to expect that in the future, business-cycle problems will not be as severe as they have been in

139

the past because of the built-in stabilization effect of large government sectors in the economy and because the abandonment of Phillips curve trade-off targets is likely to lead to programs of stable and noninflationary money-supply increases.[3]

The benefits from exchange-rate stabilization are even more difficult to evaluate since they accrue through marginal changes in the overall allocative efficiencies of economies. Yet, as recent experience with large exchange-rate fluctuations has shown, costs may be high. There have been high costs of managing international portfolios, and many multinational firms had difficulties in capital markets due to large fluctuations in earnings and asset values accompanying exchange-rate changes. There is little doubt that the usefulness of domestic money as a store of value and medium of exchange suffers when a country's exchange rate fluctuates widely, as has the British pound.

However, there is no hope of measuring precisely the benefits and costs in the form of externalities accruing from increased exchange-rate stability. For this reason, it is necessary in the remainder of this chapter to assume that exchange-rate stabilization on balance raises welfare. The remaining arguments concerning the demand for reserves and the benefits from having an optimal supply rest on this assumption. Readers who believe the assumption to be unrealistic will, therefore, also reject the validity of conclusions reached in the following analysis.

The Demand for Reserves

The assumption that official exchange-rate stabilization increases welfare through the reduction in externalities from exchange-rate instability implies that international reserves have a positive social productivity and that they will be demanded by governments. Such demand for reserves by an individual country can be represented as the demand curve DD'

[3] The announcement of moderate or prospectively declining rates of growth in the money supply by the governments of the United States, Canada, Britain, and Germany, among others, and the recommendation for the adoption of such targets by the Bank for International Settlements may be taken as evidence of the abandonment of monetary policy as an instrument for the permanent lowering of unemployment rates.

shown in Figure 6.1, where we measure the quantity of reserves and rates of return along the horizontal (abscissa) and vertical (ordinate) axes, respectively. For reserves, the rate of return is the expected marginal social productivity per unit of reserves held. The demand curve slopes downward because of the ubiquitous principle of diminishing returns so that marginal benefits are a decreasing function of the quantity of reserves held. The demand curve tends to shift upward and to the right as a result of economic growth and increased trade and capital flows.

Figure 6.1

Equilibrium Demand For Reserves

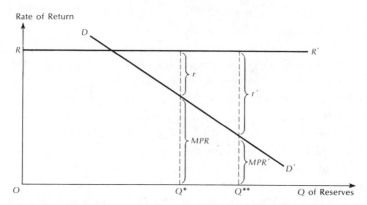

An individual country has given to it exogeneously the interest yield on reserves (r) and the marginal productivity of real resources in domestic use, equal to the long-term real interest rate, OR. In equilibrium the country under consideration holds OQ^* reserves, which results in the maximization of returns on all wealth because the marginal productivity of reserves used for stabilization (MPR) plus the interest yield on them is just equal to the marginal productivity of real resources. If reserve holdings are greater than OQ^*, the combined marginal social productivity and interest yield on reserves is less than the marginal returns on real resources, and a shift from reserves into real resources would increase the total return on wealth. Analogous reasoning for reserve holdings below the optimum can be employed to show the optimality of OQ^*.

141

The model can be used to demonstrate the rationality of using reserves in the financing of imbalances. Thus, in a case of random disturbance in the form of a bad harvest, the productivity of real resources is increased and the schedule RR' is shifted upward. The temporary equilibrium stock of reserves must be below OQ^*, and the difference between the normal and temporary optimal stock demand is used to finance the payments imbalance caused by the bad harvest at the fixed exchange rate. In effect, the government has used its stock of liquid assets to sustain real income of the community during the period of the bad harvest and to stabilize inter-temporal consumption patterns. This behavior corresponds to that of private wealth-holders who meet unforeseen contingencies by drawing on savings-account balances rather than cut back drastically their current standard of living.

In a complete cycle of bad and bumper harvests and other adverse and favorable random shocks, the rate of return on real resources is shifted up and down, producing the accumulation and decumulation of reserves observed in the real world. However, our simple geometric model does not lend itself to the analysis of conditions when actual reserve stocks are so far from the desired normal level that balance-of-payments adjustment policies are necessary to influence the probability pattern and size of expected imbalances. According to our analysis of the preceding section, there exist critical regions of reserve holdings that trigger such a policy response. Presumably the regions are determined by preferences toward risk, the estimated costs of weak adjustment policies applied more frequently against the costs of applying strong policies more rarely, all of which are determined by the flexibility, resiliency, and size of the domestic economy and foreign sector.

The preceding analysis implies that for every country faced with a given pattern of expected balance-of-payments disturbances, rate of return on real resources, yield on reserves, and cost of balance-of-payments policies, including exchange-rate changes, there is a unique level of optimal reserve holdings attained on average in the long run and a resultant unique, determinate pattern of exchange-rate changes. For subsequent purposes of analysis it is important to note that the equilibrium level of reserve holdings is greater and that the efficient pattern of exchange-rate changes has a smaller and less costly variance, the greater is the interest yield on reserves. This point can readily be appreciated by inspection of Figure 6.1, where the equilibrium reserve holdings are shown as OQ^{**} when the rate of return on reserves is assumed to be r', which is greater than r.

The Benefits of Optimal Reserve Supplies

The horizontal addition of individual countries' demand curves produce a world demand curve for international reserves, which in principle looks just like the demand curve of an individual country shown in Figure 6.1. It shows that there exists a unique quantity of reserves that the world wishes to hold in equilibrium at a given interest rate on reserves and with a given stock of real resources and output. The optimally efficient dealing with disturbances by all countries of the world takes place only if the supply of reserves is equal to this equilibrium quantity demanded.

If the aggregate supply falls short of the optimum quantity demanded, some individual countries are induced to engage in restrictive payments policies, including currency devaluations, to influence the expected pattern of imbalances toward the achievement of more or greater surpluses. But these deflationary policies of individual countries are offsetting each other and are not matched by corresponding inflationary policies by other countries holding excess quantities of reserves, as is the case when aggregate supplies are optimal. As a result, the world experiences an average of greater or more exchange-rate depreciations than is efficient or normal under conditions of optimal aggregate reserve supplies. Furthermore, the deflationary effect of the balance-of-payments policies of countries short of their optimal supply tend to put downward pressure on prices, incomes (due to reduced efficiency), and trade levels, which cause the demand curves for reserves to shift downward and to the left until equilibrium is attained and desired aggregate reserve holdings equal supplies. Thus, while there is a natural tendency of the international system to move toward equilibrium of demand and supply, such adjustments lead to losses in real output. In parallel with the well-known analysis of domestic

143

price adjustments necessary for the attainment of equilibrium real money balances, the deflation tends to be prolonged and especially costly if prices are inflexible in the downward direction and other institutional characteristics cause real adjustments to be slow.

In analogy with the cost of having aggregate reserve supplies short of demand, there are social costs from having supplies exceed demand. Countries with excess supplies tend to engage in expansionary balance-of-payments policies, including currency appreciation, to change the probability toward a smaller frequency and size of payments surpluses. But because such policies are undertaken simultaneously by more countries than are policies in the opposite direction, the world economy suffers from an inflationary bias. The resultant price increases lower the real value of reserves until equilibrium is restored. But the process of moving to this equilibrium produces inflation, which was undesired by the individual countries and has certain socially costly effects on efficiency and equity well known in the Western world from recent experiences.

In summary, under the assumption that exchange-rate stabilization results in positive external welfare benefits, national governments were shown to possess a demand function for international reserves and, at a given interest rate on those reserves, a welfare-maximizing equilibrium stock demand. The summing of individual countries' demand functions results in an aggregate optimum world stock demand. If the IMF supplies such an equilibrium quantity, then the world economy functions at peak efficiency. If the supplies are short or in excess of the equilibrium, then the world suffers through deflationary or inflationary adjustment periods, with the well-known costs accompanying them. From this analysis it follows that it is important for the world community of nations to cooperate and institutionalize a system that assures the creation of optimal aggregate supplies of international reserves.

The Problem of Pareto Optimality

The preceding analysis was carried out under the assumption of an exogeneously given interest rate on international reserves, which determined the behavior of individual countries and the optimal aggregate demand for reserves. While in the real world the yield of reserves is exogeneously given to the individual country, for the community of nations seeking a cooperative solution to reserve creation and control, this yield is being determined by explicit design.

As is well known, the interest rate on SDRs was set initially at 1.5 percent at the Rio de Janeiro meetings of the IMF in 1967. At the same time, the capital value of the SDRs was defined in terms of gold so that their total yield was expected to be greater than 1.5 percent, but not so much greater as to make SDRs much more attractive than the U.S. dollar, which was then the dominant reserve asset. Since then, agreement has been reached for the demonetization of gold, a decreased official role for dollar reserves, and increased importance for SDRs. In 1974 the interest rate on SDRs was raised and generally made to be a fraction below the weighted average of short-term interest rates in major industrial countries.[4]

The development of the concept of the optimum quantity of money by M. Friedman, published in 1969, led several economists to apply the concept also to the specification of an interest rate on reserves.[5] The arguments may be summarized briefly as follows. Pareto optimality has as a necessary condition that the price of any good or service be equal to the marginal social cost of producing it. The price of the liquidity services derived from the use of SDRs is the opportunity cost of holding them rather than real assets with a marginal social productivity equal to R. With an interest rate of r on SDRs, the opportunity cost K, therefore, is $K = R - r$.

It has been argued that the marginal scial cost of producing SDRs is near zero. Under these conditions Pareto optimality requires that $R = r$,

[4] The determination of the value and yield on SDRs is discussed in J. J. Polak, "Valuation and Rate of Interest of the SDR," *Pamphlet Series* No. 18 (Washington, D.C.: IMF, 1974), pp. 1–26.

[5] See P. B. Clark, "Interest Payments and the Rate of Return on International Fiat Currency," Duke University discussion paper (Durham, N.C.: Duke University, 1970); H. G. Johnson, "Efficiency in Domestic and International Money Supply," *University of Surrey International Economics Series*, no. 3, March 1970; H. G. Grubel, "Interest Payments and the Efficiency of the International Monetary System," *Economic Notes* (1973a), 2:63–82, which also contain references to the literature on the optimum quantity of money.

that the interest rate on SDRs is equal to the marginal productivity of real resources. I have argued that the entire cost of running the IMF should be considered as a long run, necessary cost of operating the international monetary system because the data-collection services, consultation facilities among member countries, research activities, and general administrative services involve costs that are likely and legitimately growing at much the same rate as the creation of SDRs. In other words, while the short-run marginal cost of creating more SDRs may be zero, in the larger run, the greater quantity of SDRs will require increased IMF activities of the sort just mentioned if the system is to function properly.[6] In recent years, the real resource costs of the IMF amounted to about 1 percent of the outstanding stock of liquidity created. Thus, assuming that there may be some economies of scale in the future, Pareto optimality requires that the interest rate on SDRs be set somewhere within 0.5–1 percent below the marginal productivity of real resources

It is difficult to translate the theoretical arguments about a Pareto optimal interest rate on SDRs into a policy recommendation for a precise rate, both because of the absence of any real evidence on the marginal social productivity of capital in the world as a whole (or average) and differences in this rate among countries. However, it is possible to estimate what would have been the real rate of return on SDRs, given the current formulas for calculating their capital value and interest rate, and compare it with the real yield on competing forms of international reserve assets, to obtain a general idea of the appropriateness of current formula determining the yield on SDRs.

For this purpose, Table 6.1 has been prepared.[7] It shows for the years 1952–74 and the average of these years, the nominal and real rates of return from holding gold, U.S. short-term dollar obligations, SDRs, sterling, and DM. Columns (2) and (3) show the capital gain of gold in terms

[6] This argument is in strict analogy with that suggesting that the short-range marginal cost of using patentable knowledge is zero and that patent legislation hence causes inefficiencies. In a dynamic world, such a proection is necessary to obtain the efficient mix of capital formation in the form of knowledge and real capital. In dynamic equilibrium, patent protection provides no rent to the producers of knowledge on average.

[7] This table is taken from P. Callier, S. Easton, and H. Grubel, "Nominal and Real Yields on International Reserve Assets 1952–74," *Kyklos*, IV, 1977.

of U.S. dollars for the market and official prices of gold, respectively. For the U.S. dollar, the nominal interest yield on U.S. Treasury bills shown in column (4) represents the only form of return since the dollar serves as the *numeraire* in terms of which the capital value changes of all other assets are calculated. In columns (1)–(7) the interest yield, capital gains, and total nominal yield of SDRs are shown, using the formula of calculation in effect in 1974. Analogous data are presented for sterling and the DM in columns (8)–(13), based on capital value changes in terms of dollars and the British and German money market interest rates.

As can be seen from Table 6.1, the average annual yield on SDRs was 2.67 percent, lower than that on U.S. dollars (3.77 percent), sterling (4.45 percent), DM (6.77 percent), and gold evaluated at free-market price (9.24 percent). The yield on SDRs exceeds only that on gold evaluated at the official price (0.89 percent). These figures suggest that even in nominal terms the current method for valuing SDRs does not promise its holders a rate of return competitive with that attainable from holding some other national currencies, especially the dollar and DM. Since the yield on short-term money market instruments typically is below that on real assets, the SDR yield evidently is well below its theoretical optimum.

The preceding conclusions are strengthened if we consider not nominal but real rates of return on the reserve assets shown in Table 6.1. To deflate nominal yields it is possible to use either of two indices of inflation. In column 14 we show price changes in a world consumer price index constructed from national consumer price indices weighted by 1970 gross domestic products of all countries, as calculated by the IMF.[8] While this index measures what most people consider to be the cost of holding money, in our application it tends to involve some double counting. Thus, consider that the world consists of only the United States and Britain, both of which are of equal size, with an exchange rate of 1, interest rate of 10 percent, and a price index of 100 initially. Now assume that at the end of period 1, U.S. prices remained stable while British prices had doubled and the value of sterling had fallen to half of its initial price in terms of dollars. The rate of return calculations would show that

[8] This index was taken from H. R. Heller, "International Reserves and World Wide Inflation," *IMF Staff Papers* (March 1976), 23:61–87.

147

Table 6.1
Nominal Rates of Return 1952–74

(1)	(2)	(3)	(4)	(5)	(6)	(7)	(8)	(9)	(10)	(11)	(12)	(13)	(14)	(15)
	Gold		U.S. Dollar	SDRs			Sterling			DM			Inflation	
Year	Market Cap. Gains	Official Cap. Gains	Interest Rate	Interest	Cap. Gains	Total	Interest	Cap. Gains	Total	Interest	Cap. Gains	Total	CPI[a] World	U.S. Export Prices
1952	0.0	0.0	1.77	2.00	−0.20	1.80	2.15	1.02	3.17	5.00	0.24	5.24	4.1	−0.4
1953	0.0	0.0	1.96	1.88	0.07	1.95	2.29	0.03	2.32	3.63	0.0	3.63	1.4	−1.1
1954	0.0	0.0	0.97	1.50	−0.13	1.37	1.78	−0.93	0.85	3.03	0.0	3.03	2.2	−1.3
1955	0.0	0.0	1.75	1.75	2.64	4.39	3.97	0.64	4.61	3.26	−0.48	2.78	1.5	1.1
1956	0.0	0.0	2.66	2.25	−2.48	−0.23	4.93	−0.65	4.29	4.88	0.47	5.35	3.0	3.6
1957	0.0	0.0	3.26	2.50	−2.70	−0.20	4.80	0.82	5.62	4.28	0.0	4.28	3.7	3.3
1958	0.0	0.0	1.71	2.00	−1.13	−.87	4.78	−0.22	4.57	3.15	0.48	3.62	5.5	−0.9
1959	0.0	0.0	3.41	2.13	−0.62	1.51	3.37	−0.10	3.26	2.67	0.0	2.67	2.7	0.0
1960	0.0	0.0	2.95	2.38	−0.18	2.20	4.75	0.14	4.89	4.54	0.24	4.78	3.4	0.8
1961	0.0	0.0	2.38	2.00	0.26	2.26	5.13	0.14	5.26	2.96	4.04	7.00	2.7	1.9
1962	0.0	0.0	2.66	2.00	−0.18	1.82	4.18	−0.18	4.00	2.70	0.00	2.69	3.4	−0.7
1963	0.0	0.0	3.16	2.00	−0.09	1.91	3.66	−0.21	3.45	2.97	0.50	3.47	4.3	−0.2
1964	0.0	0.0	3.55	2.38	2.20	4.58	4.61	−0.25	4.36	3.29	0.0	3.29	4.7	1.0
1965	0.0	0.0	3.95	2.50	−2.18	0.32	5.91	0.46	6.37	4.11	−0.75	3.36	5.0	3.3
1966	0.0	0.0	4.89	3.06	−0.16	2.91	6.10	−0.47	5.64	5.34	0.75	6.09	6.0	3.0
1967	0.0	0.0	4.33	2.50	−1.66	0.84	5.82	−15.88	−10.05	3.35	−0.50	2.85	4.8	2.0

1968	20.07	0.0	5.35	3.25	-0.10	3.15	7.04	-0.96	6.07	2.58	-0.01	2.57	4.8	1.5
1969	-16.98	0.0	6.71	3.94	-0.07	3.86	7.63	0.71	8.33	4.51	7.75	12.26	5.1	3.3
1970	8.30	0.0	5.44	4.44	0.55	4.99	7.02	-0.29	6.73	8.74	1.08	9.83	6.2	5.7
1971	15.34	0.0	4.34	2.88	4.63	7.51	5.57	6.32	11.89	6.10	10.78	16.88	5.9	3.3
1972	44.91	8.57	4.09	2.56	0.35	2.91	5.54	-8.65	-3.11	4.30	2.11	6.41	5.9	2.8
1973	73.75	11.84	7.03	4.56	4.92	9.49	9.34	-1.60	7.73	10.19	14.53	24.71	9.6	16.9
1974	67.04	0.00	7.50	4.88	2.73	7.60	11.14	1.03	12.17	8.20	10.62	18.82	15.1	27.0
Average	9.24	0.89	3.77	2.67	0.28	2.95	5.28	-0.83	4.45	4.51	2.25	6.77	4.83	3.3
Real CPI	4.41	-3.94	-1.05			-1.88			-0.37			1.94		
Real U.S.														
Export Price	5.94	-2.41	.47			-0.35			1.15			3.47		

SOURCES AND NOTES:

1. *Gold Prices*

   a. Free Market. *Picks Currency Yearbook*, various issues and *Times*, business section. Prices are for end of month for each quarter and refer to the price on the London market for nonresidents.

   b. Official price: *IFS Statistics*, various issues.

2. Exchange rates: *IFS Statistics*, various issues. Prices are at the end of period.

3. Interest rates: *IFS Statistics, OECD Main Indicators*, various issues. Interest rates are the discount rate in France, the call money role in Germany and Japan, and treasury bill rates in the United States and United Kingdom. The interest rate on SDRs has been computed from these national rates according to a formula presented in the text.

   4. Consumer price index: H. R. Heller, "International Reserves and World-Wide Inflation," *IMF Staff Papers* (March 1976), 23: 87. The world rate is the average of national price changes weighted by 1970 GDPs and has been calculated by the IMF.

   5. U.S. export price index: *IFS*, U.S. Country Table, line 74.

   6. The variances are based on quarterly observations expressed as annual rates.

   7. Annual rates are simple averages of quarterly observations. Interest is assumed not to have been reinvested.

[a]CPI-consumer price index.

sterling yielded −90 percent,[9] whereas the world price index shows a gain of 50 percent. Deflation of the nominal yield on sterling would imply that its purchasing power during the period under consideration would have decreased by 140 percent. Clearly, this is an exaggeration and results from the fact that the British inflation is taken account of through both the change in the asset's capital value and its effect on the world price index.

In spite of this short-coming of the World consumer price index of column (14) in table 6.1, the nominal yields are adjusted for this figure partly to provide a lower bound on the estimate of real yields and partly to take account of the fact that in the real world, exchange rates do not adjust in the short run to changes in purcasing power, as was assumed in the theoretical argument made in the preceding paragraph. As can be seen from the next to last row in table 6.1, deflation of the nominal yield on SDRs of 2.95 percent by the average annual changes in world consumer prices of 4.83 percent results in a negative average yield of −1.88 percent. At this inflation rate, over the full period only gold at market prices and the DM had positive yields and the U.S. dollar yield dominated that of the SDRs.

The second measure of inflation is the index of U.S. export prices, which is shown in column (15) of table 6.1. Since in the two-country model presented above the inflation in Britain and the loss of the purchasing power of sterling are equiproportional and fully reflected in the capital value of sterling in terms of dollars, additional changes in the purchasing power of the sterling are a function of the cost of U.S. exports only. This measure represents, therefore, a lower bound on the estimate of loss of purchasing power of national assets used in international trade. As can be seen from table 6.1, the average annual rate of increase in U.S. export prices had been 3.3 percent, resulting even with this measure in a negative real yield on SDRs of −0.35 percent while that on all other assets was positive, with the exception of that on officially valued gold holdings.

---

[9] That is, 100 percent less through devaluation, offset by an interest yield of 10 percent, assumed not to have adjusted for the inflation devaluation. Clearly, the situation described is one of disequilibrium.

The calculations on nominal and real yields on SDRs and other assets protentially useful as international reserves have shown that during 1952–74 SDRs, had they been in existence, would have yielded negative real rates of returns to holders. Since the rates of return on real resources during this period clearly were not negative, we can conclude without doubt that the rates of return on SDRs based on present methods of calculation were far below their theoretically Pareto optimal level. Unless these methods are changed, rates can be expected to be negative in the future, induce an inefficiently low holding of SDRs on average, and encourage debtor nations to use and favor the new creation of SDRs to finance deficits and surplus nations to resist their use and new creation.

Practical Implications of the Analysis

The theoretical model of the demand for reserves presented in the preceding sections of this paper suggest that reserves have a positive social productivity and that the world would benefit from having the IMF supply aggregate reserves in the form of SDRs in Pareto optimal quantity and with a Pareto optimal yield. While this analysis is mainly theoretical, combined with the data on implicit past SDR yields, it results in two important policy implications.

First, the yield on SDRs must be raised. If the basket method of valuations of their capital value is retained, then adjustment of the method for calculating the interest rate is required. I would suggest dropping the current method of calculation based on a weighted and adjusted average of six major countries short-term money market rates. These market rates have often failed to reflect expected and actual inflation rates since they are influenced so heavily by current monetary policy. In its place I would substitute a nominal rate of 1.5 percent which is adjusted quarterly, ex post, for world inflation as measured by a world consumer price index or some other global index of cost. The choice of the appropriate index requires some careful further analysis, which cannot be undertaken here.

It should be noted that this resultant higher real return on SDRs does not imply that debtor nations would not use them and all nations would

151

try to hoard them, as has been argued by some economists. This can best be seen by considering what could happen if private checking accounts were made to yield the same interest rate as savings accounts. Under these conditions, the public clearly would hold greater checking account balances, but they would not reduce and because of greater income may even increase marginally, their consumption and investment expenditures giving rise to the need to write checks. Market processes would produce substitute means of payment and credit extension, but unless barriers to competition exist, the cost, availability, and use of such substitutes would be efficient. In the international monetary system, deficit countries may be tempted to finance imbalances by borrowing in private markets if the cost there were lower than the cost of using SDRs. But the cost of such borrowing, adjusted for risk and the expense of negotiations, would tend to reflect market views on the credit-worthiness of the borrowers, thus giving efficient price signals to both borrowers and lenders. The outright ownership and liquidity of SDRs would assure their use even if nominal interest rates on funds borrowed in private markets were below those on SDRs.

The second practical implication of the theoretical analysis is related to the determination of an efficient aggregate supply of reserves. There have been many attempts by economists to estimate the demand for reserves from historic data.[10] These efforts have been based on the idea that demand is related in some systematic way to the level and variability of countries' past balance of payments. While efforts in this direction should be continued, they are unlikely to overcome the fundamental difficulties that past payments imbalances are a function of the adequacy of reserve stocks and that changing institutional arrangements tend to render past experiences irrelevant. Thus, in a world of deficient aggregate reserve supplies countries on average tend to finance fewer and smaller payments

[10] For a review of the literature, see H. G. Grubel, "The Demand for International Reserves: A Critical Review of the Literature," *Journal of Economic Literature* (December 1971), 9:1148–66 and John H. Williamson, "Surveys in Applied Economics: International Liquidity," *The Economic Journal* (September 1973), 83:685–746. J. H. Makin, "Exchange Rate Flexibility and the Demand for International Reserves," *Weltwirtschaftliches Archiv* 110 (Heft 2) (1974), 229–43 and E. C. Suss, "A Note on Reserve Use Under Alternative Exchange Rate Regimes," *IMF Staff Papers* (July 1976), 23:387–94 represent recent additions to the literature.

imbalances and let their exchange rates fluctuate and impose controls on international transactions more than would be the case if aggregate supplies were at their theoretically efficient levels. Conceptually, in the extreme, with a complete absence of reserves, balance-of-payments instability would be zero and traditional studies of the demand for reserves would conclude that zero reserves are adequate. As for the importance of changed institutions, one may note that the general system of managed floats as compared with the system of fixed parity rates, significant changes in the rate of interest paid on reserves, the creation of central bank lending consortia to bail out countries in difficulty, and the ready availability of Eurodollar credits for borrowing by deficit countries, tend to affect the demand for reserves in ways that cannot be predicted because the range of historic observations does not include such changes.

These considerations about the difficulties encountered in measuring reserve demand directly, together with the theoretical analysis of the sources of the social productivity of reserves, lead me to the conclusion that the determination of aggregate reserve growth should be approached very pragmatically and based on principles employed in the determination of domestic money supply growth rates. Thus, the IMF should be made to increase SDR supplies at a steady and constant rate for a number of years, say five. The rate may be made initially equal to the rate of growth in the nominal value of international trade in the preceding ten years, or it may be set one or two percentage points below that rate in recognition of the likely temporary nature of the world inflation rates in the early 1970s.

During this period the performance of the international economy should be monitored continuously for evidence of the adequacy of reserves, much like governments continuously monitor the performance of national economies to evaluate the adequacy of monetary and fiscal policies. However, while national governments monitor unemployment and capacity utilization rates, the inflation rate, growth, and balance of payments, the IMF should monitor performance characteristics of the international economy suggested by the theoretical analysis of this paper, namely, the stability of exchange rates, the level of direct controls, and inflationary or deflationary tendencies produced by balance-of-payments

153

constraints. The construction of performance indices for the international economy could be a challenging task for economists,[11] but I believe that the IMF has the capability in its research staff and data resources to produce such indices. The availability of such indices would permit a rational discussion of the adequacy of reserves and the determination of proper growth rates at periodic intervals. In the longer run, such a process of determining aggregate reserve supplies would enable countries to deal in the theoretically efficient manner with the unavoidable disturbances afflicting the international economy.

In closing, I should note that the arguments in this paper are based on the premise that governments behave rationally and attempt to maximize national welfare, always remembering that this welfare is dependent on their international economic relations and that they have, therefore, a stake in the proper functioning of the international economy. As a result, rational governments should consider it to be in their own self-interest to manage their exchange rates with a view toward the welfare of other countries and hence not to engage in beggar-thy-neighbor policies or in policies that lead to the export of inflation caused by domestic excess demand creation.

The probability that this assumption about the rationality of national governments' behavior is correct can be increased by the activities of the IMF. It can set out general principles of good behavior and monitor actual policies in the light of these principles. The IMF should also be endowed with methods for enforcing adherence to these principles. Thus, there should be progressively more stringent methods such as informal consultation with maverick governments, followed by formal but still confidential meetings, much as is done in the present setting; in cases

[11] As argued in O. Emminger, "On the Way to a New International Economic Order," *American Enterprise Institute Foreign Affairs Studies*, no. 39, August 1976, stability of exchange rates ultimately must be a function of the stability of domestic economies, primarily of the major countries. Indexes of performance of the international monetary system clearly must be adjusted for the stability of major countries' economies, though care must be taken in accounting for reverse causality. Significant progress has already been made in the construction of international economic performance indexes by the IMF, as was reported in the 1976 Annual Report, p. 39. However, further work would be useful , and a regular publication of the index should encourage its use by outside analysts. For example, it would be interesting to test the relationship between the index and other conventional measures of reserve adequacy, such as ratios of reserves to trade.

154

where such consultations are ineffective, official public censure should be applied and followed, if necessary, by restrictions on the use of IMF facilities and, as a last resort, the imposition of a revised scarce currency clause, applicable to countries in both excessive surplus and deficits. Such a role for the IMF, carried on flexibly and guided by a few basic principles rather than lengthy legal codes, is in the interest of all countries and should be acceptable to all.

Appendix A
A Random Walk Model of the Balance of Payments

In the first section of the paper I have argued that rational and efficient speculation using the best information about the effects of current and future events and policies on the exchange rate does not lead to a stable exchange rate. The reason for this is that continuously new information becomes available and previously only expected events or policies take place. This information tends to influence the perceived equilibrium exchange rate and thus speculators continuously enter the market to bring it to this level. The very essence of this process of adjustment is that it is based on the availability of new information that by its nature could not be known in advance. If it had been known or even knowable by investment in research or if it were systematic, speculators would have acted on it and no price adjustment would have been necessary. Because of the unpredictability of the events giving rise to this information, it is analytically most useful to consider that they are random.

This view of likely balance-of-payments developments has an important bearing on the past futile attempts of economists to make operational the distinction between fundamental and nonfundamental payments disequilibria. It also implies that attempts to codify rules for exchange-rate adjustment cannot succeed, however detailed and refined these codes may be. The reason for this inability to specify operationally fundamental disequilibria and equilibrium exchange rates is that while agreement can be reached on the balance-of-payments effects of current events and policies with relative ease, the nature, timing, and impact of many future

155

events cannot be known with certainty and there is much legitimate room for disagreement. It is one thing to know from the law of large numbers that over the next 100 years the world is almost certainly likely to be hit by a certain number of devastating earthquakes, droughts, and epidemics. But it is quite another matter to predict when and where they will occur and what their impact will be. As a result, countries with large deficits or surpluses could be returned to equilibrium by any of a range of possible developments.

Important elements of further uncertainty arise from the unpredictability of the effects of certain governmental policies. There are innumerable instances in history when changes in monetary and fiscal policies and exchange rates have had effects that in the light of the conventional wisdom of economic theory were "perverse" or operated only with unpredictable lags. For our purposes of analysis, it is irrelevant what causes such unpredictability of the effects of economic policies—errors of theory, omission of variables in econometric models, development of new institutions, or changes in expectations held by the public. Whatever the cause, the fact is that the effects of policies are highly uncertain and random.

Finally, the institution of policies themselves are unpredictable. It is not possible to know the outcome of elections and what the policies of governments will be. Such uncertainty is important because the policies of some countries have effects on others. At the end of 1976 considerable uncertainty existed about the policies of the newly elected U.S. President Carter. If he would have increased aggregate U.S. demand substantially, the payments deficits of many countries would have been remedied, otherwise the opposite would have been true.

Because of this uncertainty about the future caused by random events, policies and their effects, there is much room for legitimate disagreement about the "appropriateness" of any current exchange rate. Consequently, it has proven to be impossible to define operationally when a country is suffering from a fundamental disequilibrium and therefore needs to change its exchange rate in a manner acceptable to the majority of economists and politicians. For the same reason, attempts to specify condi-

156

tions as to when past behavior of certain economic variables, exchange rates, reserves, basic balances, or any other, should lead to current exchange rate fluctuations, have not been acceptable to a majority of economists and politicians.

A *Random Walk Model of Payments Imbalances.* The preceding considerations about the nature of balance-of-payments disturbances lead me to conclude that it is best to abandon the distinction between fundamental and nonfundamental payments disequilibria and instead to treat all imbalances as if they were part of a "random walk process."[12] The nature of such a process is best understood by assuming that under freely floating exchange rates in each period a country's exchange-rate change is decided by the toss of a true coin and the rule that the head of the coin represents a 1 percent increase and the tail a 1 percent decrease in the price of foreign exchange. On average and in the long-run, our best guess is that under these assumptions the plus and minus events have netted to zero since heads and tails of the coin show up an equal number of times. But for any particular time in the future we can calculate the probability of cumulative changes of different sizes or the number of times heads or tails show up in sequence. In figure 6.2, showing a so-called probability tree, we start with a given initial exchange rate at period zero. At this point the probability is 0.5 that the change is plus or minus 1 percent of the rate at the end of period one. By looking at period 2 we can see that if the change has been −1 percent in period 1, in period 2 it is −2 percent or 0 with probability 0.25 each; if it has been +1 percent in period 1, then it is +2 percent or—with probability 0.25 each in period 2, and so on for all later periods. The main point is that for any given period there is the nonzero probability of very large cumulative exchange rate. The model could equally have been developed under the assumption of a managed exchange rate where disturbances result in changes in reserve holdings. In such a model, conventional balance-of-payments policies, including exchange-rate changes, affect the probability of cumulative re-

[12] Heller first used a random walk model to describe balance-of-payments behavior; see H. R. Heller, "Optimal International Reserves," *The Economic Journal* (June 1966), 76: 296–311.

serve gains or losses, but because the similarity between the random walk model under freely floating and managed exchange-rate systems is fairly obvious, this topic is not pursued further here.

In the main body of this paper I have argued that a country whose exchange rate is characterized by such random influences can reduce the variance of realized rates simply by "leaning against the wind." In so doing, it can prevent many of the disturbances from actually affecting the

Figure 6.2

A Random Walk Process

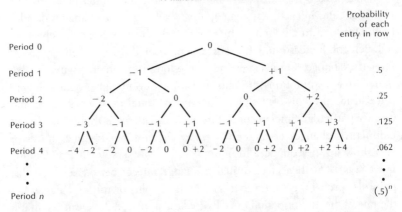

exchange rate while changes in reserve holdings absorb their impact, leaving average reserves unchanged. For example, after four periods in our model, six out of 24 times, the exchange-rate changes could have been eliminated by an extreme form of "leaning against the wind," complete pegging of the exchange rate, without any change in reserves taking place. On the other hand, 50 percent of the time the cumulative reserve loss or gain would have been 2, and only two out of twenty-four times there would have been large cumulative losses or gains of 4, assuming that the pegging implies a one unit reserve change for every 1 percent change in the exchange rate. In the small cases of long runs of balance-of-payments influences in the same direction, the country's reserves might have run low and it might have permitted changes in the exchange rate, so that cumulative reserve losses were smaller than under complete pegging or modified "leaning against the wind," as argued in the main part of this paper.

The preceding exposition is merely suggestive. The model can be made much more rigorous and realistic. For example, the probability distribution of positive and negative influences on the exchange rate and balance of payments could itself be made a function of the exchange rate. The use of other balance-of-payments policies could be incorporated and shown to influence the probability distribution. Certain postulated behavior of the intervention authorities, guided by deviations of actual reserve holdings relative to targets, could be used to simulate the variance of exchange rate implicit in different levels of reserve targets. These ideas cannot be pursued here but have been presented to indicate the potential richness of application of the random-walk model to balance-of-payments analysis in an uncertain world with efficient private speculation.

Random Walks and Price Theory. If one accepts the theoretical propositions and empirical evidence on the random-walk behavior of exchange rates, then it follows that the price of a currency at some point in the future has an equal probability of being very low or very high, regardless of what are the real economic events of the future that, according to basic price-theoretic considerations, determine the value of an exchange rate. This disturbing fact has been pointed out and analysed by P. Samuelson who argues that "Few economists can cheerfully believe in the random, lawless world (described by random walk behavior of prices)." [13]

Samuelson dealt with the conflict between economists' "simultaneous belief in ultimate economic law and in efficient speculative markets" by constructing a mathematical model in which prices are determined by economic forces in the long-run and yet fluctuate randomly in the short-run. He thus concludes that under a reasonable set of assumptions ultimate economic laws of price and random fluctuations are consistent.

However, I believe that there is no such conflict between ultimate economic laws and random walks of prices at even the simplest level of

[13] Paul A. Samuelson, "Proof that Properly Disconnected Present Values of Assets Vibrate Randomly," *Bell Journal of Economics and Management Sciences* (1973), 4:369–74; Paul A. Samuelson, "Is Real-World Price a Tale Told by the Idiot of Chance?" *Review of Economics and Statistics* (February 1976), 58:120–22.

159

analysis because the determinants of true economic prices themselves are random. As a result, a price does have an equal, albeit small, probability of becoming either very large or very small. For example, the dollar price of sterling fifty years from now could either be 10^{-20} or 10^{20} because we cannot rule out the possibility that either country experiences long-runs of economic shocks influencing the exchange rate to move in the same direction, be it by small amounts per time period or by large amounts, as might be the case in a hyper-inflation.

The preceeding argument does imply, of course, that once real economic changes have taken place, they do influence prices according to ultimate economic laws. But as long as these changes are unpredictable and random, price changes will follow a random walk.

Appendix B
The Supply of Reserves

In the main part of this paper it was assumed that the IMF controls the quantity of reserves. This assumption is not realistic under current institutional conditions and may not be even under many of the contemplated reform proposals. The reason for this is that the private sector of the world economy can always be expected to generate new institutions that permit countries to finance payments imbalances through methods other than the use of SDRs of other IMF facilities. In recent years the Eurocurrency market represents such a new institution, which has permitted countries to avoid using SDRs and other "official" reserve assets. Indeed, the use of U.S. dollars in this activity since the end of World War II represents a market response to the demand for means of financing national payments imbalances.

Whether or not the market development of such substitutes for international liquidity interferes seriously with the ability of the IMF to control the quantity of international liquidity has its parallel in the postwar discussion of the influence of financial intermediaries on the effectiveness of national monetary policy. The well-known Radcliffe Committee Report in Britain and the work by John Gurley and Edward Shaw in the United

States claimed that financial intermediaries did interfere strongly with the ability of monetary policy to stabilize the economy and argued for the extension of controls over their activities. These ideas were discussed widely during the 1950s and while no official concensus has yet emerged, the fact is that major western countries have not extended their controls to cover liquidity creation by the full range of financial intermediaries.

This fact would appear to support the argument that financial intermediaries can and probably do influence the elasticity of response of the policy targets, such as interest rates, income, or inflation, with respect to changes in the high-powered money base or money defined narrowly, but they do not prevent monetary policy from having the desired effect. It may be useful to consider that in parallel with these ideas on national monetary control, the development of private means of financing payments imbalances adds to the overall stock of international liquidity, and may even vary it countercyclically. But ultimately the liquidity creation by any institution must have a limit, so that IMF control over official liquidity retains its potential influence on the efficient functioning of the international monetary system. Such a conclusion does not imply, however, that the influence is perfect or that it may not have to take into account the effects of recent financial market innovations, such as the Eurodollar market. However, as experience with domestic policies has shown, on average such developments tend to be gradual and, within some margin of error, predictable. Thus, if the preceding analysis and analogy between financial intermediaries creating national and international liquidity is accurate, then the arguments in the text that assumed the existence of a controllable supply of liquidity, need to be modified only slightly and in fairly obvious ways.

COMMENTS

ROBERT TRIFFIN

YALE UNIVERSITY, NEW HAVEN, CONN.

I HATE speaking—and taking time away from others—when I don't have something really new to say. I don't today and shall try to be very brief—to keep well within the eight to ten minutes allotted to me.

We have listened to two extremely interesting and provocative papers, and I wish I could shorten my introductory remarks by saying that I fully agree with both of them. This would be difficult, however, as they give diametrically opposite answers to the question under discussion, namely, the relative importance of control over international reserves.

Grubel argues that "is is important for the world community of nations to cooperate and institutionalize a system which assures the creation of optimal aggregate supplies of international reserves," while Haberler concludes that "generalized floating and other developments have made obsolete any attempt to define an optimum level of international reserves" and that "control of international reserves is no longer an important task for the Fund [IMF]."

What are those new developments?

One is that an expansion of reserves does not necessarily prompt—though it undoubtedly facilitates—the adoption of additional expansionist policies by governments and central banks. This certainly is not new and does not affect in any way the *direct primary* impact of reserve increases,

162

that is, the equivalent issue of high-powered reserve money,[1] likely to trigger under a fractional system of cash reserves a multiple expansion of deposits and money supply by commercial banks.

A second development is that most reserve increases now accrue to OPEC countries rather than to western Europe and Japan, and are, therefore, less inflationary. It is true that a substantial portion of OPEC reserve accumulation increases government deposits rather than money in the hands of the public, and is not likely to be fully and quickly spent on imports. Yet, this contrast should not be exaggerated. Money supply—as conventionally defined—has doubled or tripled in the last few years in most OPEC countries, their imports have risen spectacularly, and many are already in deficit. Note also that the reserves of Japan and most European countries—particularly Germany—also increased enormously and nearly uninterruptedly throughout all the postwar years. Finally, of course, the present heavy concentration of surpluses by OPEC countries should not be projected into the indefinite future and determine long-term reforms of the international monetary system.

What is true, however, is that we would not wish the OPEC countries to correct their surpluses through cutting their oil exports and keeping their oil in the ground. We prefer to have them accumulate claims even if this increases reserves more than would be normally desired. And as long as decisions on SDR creation cannot be made expeditiously enough, we may be lucky to be able to expand dollar and Eurocurrency reserves instead. Yet, this entails placing on the U.S. and Eurobanks the entire burden of recycling—with all of the political responsibilities and financial risks entailed in such recycling.

Third, it is certainly true that a better control of international reserves may not solve all problems of balance-of-payments adjustment, and that persistent disequilibria have been increasingly financed in the last few years by "much over-borrowing and excessive lending by banks which may cause serious trouble," rather than by transfers of reserves. Other policies may be needed to handle this new development, but a more moderate expansion of reserves, and therefore of *high-powered reserve*

[1] Of course, this does not apply to SDR allocations.

163

money, would certainly have helped limit such overborrowing and excessive lending.

Last, but of course not least, floating rates have undoubtedly made it possible for surplus countries to regain control over their money-printing presses and to stem the inflationary flood of dollar balances that they had to absorb under fixed exchange rates. Yet, the alternative of currency appreciation was by no means barred under the Bretton Woods system, and countries continued to accumulate huge amounts of reserves well after they began floating (Canada in May 1970; Germany and the Netherlands in May 1971) or readjusted their exchange rates upward under the short-lived Smithsonian agreement.

Some limitation on market interventions—and therefore on reserve creation—should be welcome by those who wish to emphasize prompter exchange-rate adjustments as an essential feature of a reformed international monetary system. Limitations on intervention and particularly on the accumulation of foreign-exchange reserves are probably the most practical approach to such control at the moment and need not involve a definition of optimum aggregate reserves.

I very much doubt, therefore, whether any of these "new developments" should lead us to abandon the conclusions previously reached (notably in the last report of the Committee of Twenty) about the shortcomings of an unbridled system of reserve creation, and particularly about the inflationary and maladjusting potential of the widespread use of *national* currencies as *international* reserves. The explosion of world reserves, under that system, preceded by several years the explosion of oil prices, played a crucial—even if only *permissive*—role in the worldwide inflation that has engulfed us, and provided the means through which the reserve-center countries (primarily the United States, of course) could perpetuate enormous deficits and other countries' equivalent surpluses without being forced to readjust their domestic policies or their exchange rates.

The net reserve losses of the United States during 1970–75 totalled about $70 billion (i.e., about four times our global reserve assets at the end of 1969), and 96 percent of them were financed by our accumulation

164

of reserve indebtedness to foreign monetary authorities, rather than by losses of reserve assets.

These reserve losses would have reduced our outstanding issues of reserve money from about $76 billion to only $6 billion, if they had not been compensated by so-called "sterilization" policies of the monetary authorities. These sterilization policies led instead to a 49 percent *increase* of high-powered reserve money, from $76 billion at the end of 1969 to $113 billion at the end of 1975, thus frustrating the classical mechanism of balance-of-payments adjustment and throwing the burden of adjustment on the surplus countries.

These could, of course, "sterilize" also the inflationary impact of their reserve increases through a corresponding contraction of their internal credit. But "sterilization" of surpluses, entailing cuts in expenditures and increases in taxes and interest rates is as unpalatable politically as the sterilization of deficits through increases in expenditures and reduction in taxes and interest rates is politically attractive. The combination of sterilization policies in the deficit countries and nonsterilization policies in the surplus countries was, and will always remain, a powerful engine for world inflation.

Floating rates or exchange-rate adjustments may, of course, provide a solution, but political as well as economic considerations also make it unattractive for surplus countries to appreciate, and for deficit countries to depreciate, in order to correct fully balance-of-payments disequilibria. The continued accumulation of surpluses, no matter how inflationary, and of deficits by reserve-center countries able to settle them with their own IOU's, is the path of least resistance, likely to be abandoned only partially and with considerable delays by both groups of countries.

Some attempt to control the mechanism of reserve creation would help improve the functioning of the flexible rate system with which we shall have to live for a long, if not indefinite, time.

Although 88 percent of the inflationary expansion of world reserves has been derived from the accumulation of reserve currencies, the only concrete suggestion made by Professor Haberler to the IMF to fight inflation is to avoid "an additional distribution of SDRs [and] the proliferation and

165

expansion of unconditional lending facilities." This is rather surprising, since the allocation of SDRs and the other lending operations of the IMF—conditional as well as unconditional—have contributed only 12 percent to the inflationary explosion of reserves since the end of 1969. Nearly two thirds of these operations, moreover, have benefited the developed countries rather than the developing countries.

All in all, only 5 percent of the reserve increases of these years have financed the developing countries and 95 percent, the developed countries. This financing undoubtedly enabled these countries to finance more development assistance than they could have done otherwise, but the total flows of official development assistance reported by the Development Assistance Committee are less than half of the financing received by them from the functioning of the international monetary system, and less than one fourth for the United States.

More effective control of reserve creation and investments seems to me essential to redress this situation, so as to combat inflation and impose more adequate adjustment pressures on all countries alike, including the reserve-center countries that have been the main short-term beneficiaries and long-term victims of such an insane system of reserve creation.

If I have time for a last remark, let me observe that, contrary to Haberler's assertion, the need for reserves may conceivably be greater under floating than it is under the adjustable peg in order to offset bearish or bullish speculation by more participants and more continuously than when rates were changed only infrequently. More people and firms may be tempted or well nigh forced to take speculative positions in exchange rates daily, rather than only on the eve of expected currency appreciation or depreciation.

I have centered my comments on Haberler's paper, and time does not allow me to discuss adequately Grubel's brilliant contribution to our topic. Let me merely say that I am less sanguine than he is, in his penultimate paragraph about the rationality of government behavior. I would rather agree with Abba Eban that "nations and governments behave rationally . . . only after having exhausted all other alternatives." This only strengthens, however, Grubel's concluding paragraph about the need for IMF activities designed to stimulate—or even enforce if pos-

166

sible—more rational government behavior than might be expected otherwise. This seems to me to be plain common sense, but common sense is a rare commodity today among economists as well as among governments.

FRITZ MACHLUP

NEW YORK UNIVERSITY, NEW YORK, N.Y.

THE COMMENTS of my friend, Robert Triffin, have almost succeeded in diverting my critical zeal from the two papers to his own comments, but I will resist this temptation. I have concluded a mutual aggression pact with Mr. Grubel in order to free myself from any constraint in my usually provocative way of speaking. Thus, if you find that I am too aggressive, please bear in mind that he accepts it; he says he is a big boy and can take it.

Now, I repeat what Triffin has said, that the two papers, Haberler's and Grubel's, come to diametrically opposite conclusions regarding the optimum level of reserves. The one says that, under given conditions, it makes no sense; the other says that we must have a grand scheme and an elaborate model to find out what that optimum level really is. I am glad that both authors have at least made the distinction between the optimum *level* and the optimum *growth* of reserves, although I wish they had made a little more of this difference. Grubel, although devoting most of his paper to the optimum level, did in his conclusions come back to the optimum growth, and at that point he began to be pragmatic. I think more pragmatism would have helped a great deal in the entire paper.

I would like to comment on Haberler's remarks about the international quantity theory of money or, in the words of Marina Whitman, on the idea of global monetarism. In addition to Haberler's reason for distinguishing national and international monetary aggregates and the effects of their changes, I wish to call attention to another, rather important reason for the difference. We can speak of a demand for money in a nation, because there is a very large number of money holders. Where there is a large number of decisionmakers, distributional effects may—not always but often—be neglected. If there are millions of money holders, it does not really make so much difference whether Mr. A or Mr. B or company X or company Y hold the money. In the demand for international reserves, however, there are not millions of decisionmakers, there are only a hundred, or a hundred and fifty, decisionmakers, and in such a case it is not possible, or at least not very meaningful, to construct an aggregative demand curve. One can, perhaps, ascertain the quantity demanded at given price levels and price structures and add these quantities laterally to obtain the aggregate quantity demanded. But this does not yield a stable demand curve. What point is there in knowing an aggregate demand curve if one or six months later, the international reserves will be differently distributed and the aggregation of the demand curves of individual countries yield a different curve? The reaction of the central bank of Germany to an increase in its reserves will be very different from that of some other central bank. With the relatively small number of central banks, the distributional effects of changes in total reserves must not be neglected; and certainly no policy may be based on theorizing with the aid of the blunt instrument of an aggregate demand for international reserves.

Haberler said that the gold-valuation problem is not very important. He said that the higher valuation of gold by monetary authorities is not directly inflationary. If he thought that I had made a statement to the contrary, I would have to say that I did not. I regretted the gold revaluation not because I thought it was directly inflationary. It had two reasons: one, the higher valuation of gold may reduce a constraint on the nonadjustment policies of certain countries—I don't say adjustment policies— a constraint on the nonadjustment policies; and two, the higher valuation of gold is inconsistent with the concept of a genuine SDR standard. It is inconsistent with the idea that SDR reserves should or might become a crucial element, if not *the* crucial element in liquidity control. This was

168

my main point. I was not afraid that there would be a burst of inflation merely because countries were revaluing their gold holdings. I may have more to say about Haberler's paper, but it would be trivial. But I should make it clear that I find his paper admirable, indeed masterly. It is time to turn to the other victim of my aggressions.

Grubel's thesis regarding the supposedly single-minded, patriotic rationality on the part of the monetary authorities is not only as Robert Triffin rightly observed, exaggerated but almost funny. Let us ask, before all, *whose* rationality is really implied. Think only of the advisers with their contrary advice, the monetary or economic advisers of President Ford and of Governor Carter, and you cannot fail to realize that they have very different views about what policy would maximize the income of the nation. I submit that even we in this room, a select group of economists, have probably very different views as to what would "rationally" be the best thing to do regarding the level and growth of monetary reserves and the monetary and fiscal policies that would be consistent with the particular level or growth of reserves. Think of the United States and ask yourself who determines its policies. There is Congress, there are the administrative agencies, there are the advisers, and there are the pressure groups. Whose supposedly rational ideas would be carried out and whose views on means and ends would be depicted in a demand curve for monetary reserves? Moreover, I would like to remind you of a very interesting statement by Melvin Krauss not long ago. He wrote that "an economist should no more expect the government to serve the public good as he [the economist] sees it, than he expects the industrial corporation or the trade union to serve the public good." The public good, I repeat, as he, the economist, sees it; one economist, not all economists. We all know that certified economists and self-appointed ones daily contest the government's view of what is the public good, and especially so in various political systems in which the governments have a very short-range view of the public good determined by the terms of reelection. Is it not generally recognized that the long and short views are very different? It is often said that nations live forever but individual people live only for a limited number of years. The conclusion from this observation is pre-

169

sumably that nations have a longer view than individuals. Yes, but the governments of the nations have a very short life—just a few years—and, therefore, take a very short view of what is good for the nation.

Grubel's paper would have been much better if he had considered that we are here a group concerned about practical–political problems. As economists we ought to confine our esoteric theorizing to our own discussions within a seminar at the university. Perhaps I am wrong, but I believe we should try to do without the jargon we use in the seminar when we want to address a wider audience, and we are addressing not only the audience around this table, since the proceedings will be published. We address a wide audience of people who have practical–political interests. I was unhappy about bringing in "Pareto optimality" and such esoteric entities that we use in our classrooms and textbooks, but should not use in discussing practical–political problems.

I do not understand the stress Grubel places on random disturbances. Of course, we cannot deny that there are random disturbances: these are the completely unpredictable things that, in the long run, may or may not cancel out. But we economists are specialists chiefly in putting our fingers on things that do lead or force the markets into various directions. So a recommendation based on the assumption that most of the changes that affect the markets are random disturbances is not very helpful to those who have to run the national or the international monetary system.

Grubel speaks several times of the benefits and costs of stabilization; he means, I suppose, stabilization of the exchange rate. But there he did not make it clear—and this is a point we always ought to make clear— whether he means stabilization by interventions in the market. Does he perhaps mean stabilization by some control measures, or stabilization by general monetary policy? All these things are important and should be discussed, but we should never use the word "stabilization" without stating which approach to stabilization we have in mind and what kind of action we are referring to, especially if we discuss problems with policy implications. Most people probably think that in the context of your discourse you mean to refer to stabilization through interventions in the foreign-exchange market, but I was not sure whether you did not have in

170

mind stabilization through coordinated monetary policies of the countries concerned.

I found it disarmingly modest of Grubel when he made a transition to "his remaining arguments" and anticipated that readers who believe his assumptions to be unrealistic might also reject the validity of his conclusions. I think his modesty was disarming but probably justified.

I have one more point and it will really be my last point. It goes back to Grubel's discussion of "the unique level of optimal reserve holdings." This notion implies that we know the "national objective function." In actual fact we do not know it, and we do not know the optimal policies to attain these national objectives. We know only that different people in the government have different views. How then can we ever know a unique level of optimum reserves? Do we know, to give analogous examples, the optimal minimum wage rate? Do we know the optimum tariff for this product and that? Do we know the optimum price for natural gas? And do not the governments actually, in most instances, act in complete disregard of what some economists consider the optimum? How can we, under these circumstances, assume that the government is striving to achieve, or that international agencies are striving to achieve, an optimum level of international reserves? My questions are, of course, rhetorical. I said this was my last point and I will stick to it.

171

REPLY TO ROBERT TRIFFITH

GOTTFRIED HABERLER

I AM GRATEFUL to Robert Triffin for his thoughtful comments which give me an opportunity to clarify and amplify my paper. He questions my conclusions that "generalized floating and other developments have made obsolete any attempt to define an optimum level of international reserves" and that "control of international reserves is no longer an important task for the Fund." He does not offer a definition of an optimum level of reserves but he asks, "What are these new developments that have made the liquidity problem obsolete?"

He lists the following: "One is that expansion of reserves does not necessarily prompt . . . the adoption of additional expansionary policies by governments and central banks." He here refers to my discussion of the criticism that the so-called "international quantity-theory" has received from Marcus Fleming, Jacques Polak, Egon Sohmen, Thomas Willett, and others. Triffin comments that "this certainly is not new" and does not support my position. But I did not say that this was a new phenomenon and I did not claim, nor did the writers just mentioned, that the rejection of the international quantity theory postulating as it does a fairly *precise* relationship between international reserves and world money income or world price-level changes, implies that under fixed exchanges a *sharp* increase in international reserves (an increase in gold production under the gold standard, or gold production plus foreign exchange held by central banks of nonreserve currency countries, etc.) has nothing to do with world inflation. My conclusion that control of global reserves is no

172

longer an important task for the IMF relates to a world of floating exchange rates. Throughout his comments Triffin does not distinguish sharply enough between a floating and fixed-rate system.

Several people, including Triffin himself on several occasions, have complained that contrary to predictions of advocates of floating, floating has not stopped a further inflationary expansion of global reserves. I have tried to counter this argument by pointing out that the additions to global reserves since 1973 have largely gone to OPEC countries and that OPEC dollar reserves are not as inflationary as reserves accruing to industrial countries. Triffin's criticism of my argument is that money supply in most OPEC countries as well as OPEC imports have risen sharply and "that the reserves of Japan and most European countries . . . particularly Germany's increased enormously . . . throughout all the post war years."

I am fully aware that OPEC countries have turned out to be much better spenders than was expected and that they have preferred inflation to appreciation of their currencies.[1] But what has that to do with the expansion of global reserves? Could the IMF have prevented inflation in the OPEC countries by control of global reserves? Triffin does not say nor does he ask the question whether the IMF *should* have tried. Few would answer that question in the affirmative.

It is true that Japanese and European reserves grew sharply during the postwar period. But the greatest part of the growth occurred during the par value system. According to IMF statistics, world reserves grew by about $60 billion from 1973 to October 1976. Of these more than $40 billion were OPEC accumulations. Japanese reserves were lower in October 1976 than in 1972. German reserves doubled from 1970 to 1973. Since then they rose by about 12 percent, largely as a consequence of interventions in the European common float ("snake").

Triffin agrees with me that in the last few years persistent disequilibria have often been financed by borrowing rather than "by transfers of re-

[1] I discussed these problems in a previous paper; see G. Haberler, "Oil, Inflation, Recession and the International Monetary System," *The Journal of Energy and Development* (1976), 1:177–90. Available also as Reprint No. 45, American Enterprise Institute, Washington, D.C., 1976.

173

serves." But he insists that "a more moderate expansion of reserves and, therefore, of high-powered reserve money would have helped to limit overborrowing and excessive lending." How the IMF could accomplish that under floating, Triffin does not explain. I discuss that problem below.

Triffin further agrees that "floating rates have made it possible for surplus countries to regain control over their money-printing press and to stem the inflationary flood of dollar balances which they had to absorb under fixed exchange rates." But, he says, under the Bretton Woods system, countries could appreciate their currencies. The trouble was that surplus countries were reluctant to do so, for the valid reason that under the par value system exchange rate changes were accompanied by disruptive capital flows, and undershooting or overshooting of the equilibrium rate of exchange was all but unavoidable. That is why floating became necessary.

Triffin is, however, mistaken when he says that "countries (e.g., Canada, Germany, and the Netherlands) continued to accumulate huge amounts of reserves well after they began floating." Canadian and Dutch reserves have fluctuated in a very narrow range since floating started (in 1970 and 1973, respectively) and, as noted, German reserves that grew explosively before 1973 have since then increased much more slowly. The main cause of further German reserve growth were interventions in the "minisnake." Thus the reserve growth was not the consequence of floating but of nonfloating.

Triffin repeats the complaint that the United States could run "enormous deficits" without being forced to adjust. According to his calculations during 1970–75, net U.S. reserve losses totaled about $70 billion and "96 percent of them were financed by piling up indebtedness to foreign monetary authorities." But most of these liabilities were incurred before floating became widespread. Liabilities to foreign central banks and governments rose from $16 billion in 1969 to $67 billion in 1973. Since then the growth of official foreign liabilities has slowed sharply, though it has not stopped. By August 1976 these liabilities had grown to $87 billion. However, such liabilities to western Europe, whose currencies float, have remained practically unchanged since 1973.

174

I made it clear in my paper that by discounting the importance of control of global reserves I did not wish to minimize the dangers of inflation. On the contrary, inflation is in my opinion a major world problem. But world inflation has no longer anything to do with a lack of control over global reserves; it has its roots in *national* monetary, fiscal, and exchange-rate policies primarily in the major countries. The primary responsibility for preventing world inflation thus falls on the leading industrial countries, especially on the United States. This follows from the fact that many, if not most, smaller countries peg their currencies to some key currency, most of them to the dollar, or to a basket of such currencies.

It is true that national monetary policies (inflation or deflation) in countries that peg to the dollar are profoundly influenced, if not fully determined, by the inflation, or absence of it, in the United States. If the United States lapses into inflation, dollar balances pile up in the dependent countries and inflation spreads. It follows that if the IMF could control inflation in the United States and in a few other key countries, it would substantially control world inflation. If control of global reserves is unconventionally interpreted to include control of monetary policy and, therefore, of inflation in the United States and some other major countries then, and only then, could it be said that control of global reserves is necessary to prevent world inflation. Perhaps Triffin had that in mind.

Actually the IMF can do nothing about inflation in the United States and only in exceptional cases, about inflation in other major countries. (The British borrowing may offer such an exceptional opportunity.) If the United States lapsed again into high inflation, the only effective measure to prevent the piling up of dollar balances abroad and to forestall the spread of U.S. inflation would be to stop pegging to the dollar. In other words, if there is inflation in the United States, floating is the only effective policy to prevent an excessive growth of international reserves in the form of dollar balances.

Triffin is surprised that my "only concrete suggestion . . . to the Fund on how to fight inflation" is "to avoid an additional distribution of SDRs [and] the proliferation and expansion of unconditional lending facilities." He finds this odd because "88 percent of the inflationary expansion of world reserves has been derived from the accumulation of reserve curren-

175

cies" and only 12 percent "of the inflationary explosion of reserves since the end of 1969" have been contributed by lending operations of the IMF. He complains that "nearly two thirds of these operations [of the IMF] have benefited the developed countries rather than the [developing countries]."

My answer is as follows. First, the subject of my paper was the importance of control of global reserves in a system of floating exchange rates. Triffin's figures relate largely to the prefloating period and hence are not relevant to my topic. Second, my remarks on the possible *direct* impact of IMF operations on world inflation were merely peripheral to my topic and were not meant to be a rounded discussion of what the IMF has done or could do to further a noninflationary expansion of the world economy. Such a discussion would have to consider what can be done indirectly in annual consultations, through prodding countries by conditional lending, and so forth. But that would go beyond the scope of my paper. Third, the question raised by Triffin whether the IMF has done enough for the developing countries I did not address at all. Triffin's answer to that question is clearly and resoundingly in the negative. My answer would be that the small percentage of total IMF lending going to developing countries throws no light at all on what benefits those nations derive from IMF activities. We should keep in mind that the industrial countries account for the great bulk of world trade; that their monetary, fiscal, and exchange-rate policies determine the stability of the world economy; that avoidance of inflationary (and deflationary) disruptions of world trade depend largely on how the major countries, the key currency countries, conduct their affairs. If by conditional lending to the developed countries, by prodding, annual consultations, and other measures the IMF is able to promote noninflationary expansion of trade, to help to avoid monetary disruptions and protectionist reactions and so to keep the channels of world trade open, then IMF activities are of immense benefit for the developing countries, even if only a small fraction of IMF lending directly goes to the developing countries.

DISCUSSION

THE FOCUS of the general discussion was both on the significance of controlling the quantity of international reserves and the impact of foreign private bank lending on international liquidity. The discussion also dealt with specific comments on the two papers presented in this session.

The discussants took both sides on the question of the *desirability of reserve control*. Williamson argued that the overall quantity was not important in a floating exchange-rate world, in which the dollar was the primary form of reserves and the United States was content to be passive about its exchange rate. While he preferred a looser notion of the optimal level of reserves than that depicted in Grubel's paper, nevertheless he could envisage the possibility of "shortages and surfeits" of reserves. Such occurrences, in his view, would result in a general appreciation or depreciation of the dollar in a floating world. Hence he concluded that as long as the United States was content to play the passive nth country role, one could be relaxed about current arrangements. He added that a corollary of this view was that there is "no reason on grounds of monetary control for refraining from immediate substantial and sustained new issues of SDRs," as such action would induce a depreciation of the dollar and a redistribution of the seignorage benefits of reserve creation. Finally, he indicated that the issue of reserve control is very important if the United States is unwilling to play a passive role.

Other discussants, in greater sympathy with Grubel's conclusions, expressed concern about the magnitude of the overall stock of reserves. Much of this discussion was directed at those countries who peg their exchange rates. For example, Emminger noted that Germany, because of its "snake" commitments, has had to accumulate reserves, which has resulted in an increase of high-powered money with its inflationary impact. Moreover, he saw the control of reserves as limiting the permissive policies followed in some countries. Kenen also called attention to the continued significance of the quantity of reserves to the large number of countries who peg their exchange rates. He argued that because of shocks to the currency to which they are pegged, the current situation may require them to hold more reserves.

The remaining speakers acknowledged that a precise optimal level of reserves may not exist, but argued that the lack thereof does not diminish the desirability of some form of IMF control over the stock of and creation of new reserves. Bernstein, proceeding from a discussion of the Great Depression, argued that we would need some growth of reserves in the future, and that the IMF was the appropriate source of these accretions. De Vries noted that domestic money supplies are controlled even in the absence of an optimum. He further contended that the current situation of demand-determined reserve supplies keeps deficit areas from adjusting. This implies that surplus countries have to inflate or appreciate, with the latter policy perhaps causing problems vis-à-vis third countries. He also suggested that the composition of reserves may be a problem in that shifts in demand may cause otherwise unwarranted exchange-rate changes. He thus favored controlling the composition of reserves as well.

Haberler addressed himself to the question, posed by Mundell, of which, if any, components of reserves should be controlled. He indicated that remonetization of gold or an enormous distribution of SDRs would have an inflationary impact, but that these were unlikely events. While acknowledging that control over reserves has some significance, he argued that in general it was a matter of avoiding mistakes and questioned whether such a negative stance should be deemed "control."

Moreover, Haberler argued that control over reserves is unlikely to be a potent anti-inflationary factor. Specifically, he noted that important countries do not predicate their internal policies, inflationary or otherwise, on their reserve positions, and added that floating imparts an ambiguity to the entire whole concept of reserves.

The second point to receive widespread attention was the issue of

178

foreign bank lending, which had been raised initially in Haberler's paper. Lamfalussy put this question into context by asking how a country's reserve position relates to its ability to borrow abroad from private financial institutions. Moreover, he conjectured that in many instances banks are captives of their previous lending policies. Katz also expressed concern over the surge in bank lending. In particular, he hypothesized that the increasing reliance on private channels for international settlements would introduce an additional element of volatility into exchange-rate changes. In a slightly different vein, Solomon discussed the growth in bank lending from the perspective of the OPEC surpluses. In particular, he argued that a large part of the recent increase in bank lending is simply due to the intermediation between oil surplus and deficit countries. Moreover, he suggested that serious consideration be given to official intermediation facilities if it appeared that the private banking system was becoming overloaded.

In response to these comments, Haberler noted that private lending makes effective liquidity control more difficult. Specifically, he noted that large borrowings by the public sector and nationalized industries provide a vehicle for evading international control over reserves. Grubel, on the other hand, drew the analogy between domestic monetary policy and reserve control, and noted that Gurley and Shaw had argued in the early 1950s that monetary policy was ineffective because the private sector was generating substitutes for money.[1] However, as Grubel pointed out, they were shown to be incorrect, and that as long as the elasticity of substitution between different assets is less than perfect, the monetary authorities can control the amount of liquidity in the system. Grubel concluded that a parallel situation exists with respect to SDRs.

While much of the discussion on specific issues raised in the two papers was in opposition to the very precise notion of the optimum quantity of reserves embodied in Grubel's paper, there was some support for his approach. Cooper, for example, defended the reliance on first principles, although he disagreed with the particular formulation and recom-

[1] J. G. Gurley and E. S. Shaw, "Financial Aspects of Economic Development," *The American Economic Review* (September 1955), 45:515–38.

179

mended the approach followed by Kemp in a paper delivered at the IMF 1970 Conference.[2] And Findlay noted that the question of optimality had been implicit in Cooper's paper of the previous session. Claassen, while supporting in principle the notion of finding an optimum level of reserves, argued that because of the manifold variables affecting the demand for reserves, it may well be less stable than the demand for money.

Grubel countered criticism of his theoretical approach, levied primarily by Machlup, first of all by arguing that it is important to lay down and be guided by long-run principles in establishing policy guidelines. Second, he defended his optimality criterion by noting that such considerations distinguish economists from other social scientists. Third, he noted that his formulation of the demand for reserves could be rejected only if reserve holdings were random or if other important variables had been omitted. He precluded the former by alluding to empirical studies that indicate a systematic relationship between certain variables and reserves. He acknowledged the possibility of the latter point, raised by Claassen, and agreed that more research was warranted in identifying the important determinants of the demand for reserves.

Kenen raised two technical objections. First, he chided Grubel for apparently discarding information by assuming in his theoretical formulation that all disturbances are random. He argued that the failure to distinguish between random and systematic disturbances is to fail to utilize information essential for deciding when to intervene and also how much in the way of reserves one should hold. Second, he questioned the wisdom of Grubel's proposal that the rate of growth of SDRs be set and announced at five-year intervals. Specifically, he noted that this would introduce a great deal of uncertainty into the system as the five-year periods drew to a close. Giersch responded to this point and noted that the gap between two periods could be bridged by a timely announcement of the next period's target.

In response, Grubel reiterated his policy prescription of "leaning

[2] See Murray C. Kemp, "World Reserve Supplementation: Long-Run Needs for Short-Run Purposes," in *International Reserves: Needs and Availability* (Washington, D.C.: IMF, 1970), pp. 3–11.

180

against the wind." He argued that it is difficult to distinguish in practice between random and systematic disturbances, and that operationally it makes sense to intervene until reserves begin to be depleted, and then let the exchange rate drift.

With respect to Haberler's paper, three specific points were disputed. First, Williamson contended that Haberler had misrepresented his position by attributing to him the theoretical presumption that reserve needs would be larger under floating rates. He indicated that he had argued instead that there were conflicting influences on the magnitude of reserve use under floating as opposed to fixed exchange rates. On the one hand, the focus for stabilizing speculation is removed with the abandonment of the peg; on the other hand, central banks are no longer obliged to intervene to maintain it. Thus it is an empirical question as to whether reserve use rises or falls with the transition from fixed to flexible exchange rates.

Second, Bernstein objected to Haberler's statement that the Great Depression was of domestic origin. Rather, he contended that it was caused by the international monetary system itself, through a combination of wartime inflation and the gold standard, which tend to exhaust the money-creating powers of gold-standard countries. The postwar attempt to restore historical parities, resulted in deflationary pressures, which were transmitted to other countries. Haberler reconciled their positions by agreeing that it was the system, namely, fixed exchange rates and the gold standard, that caused the Depression to spread, but argued that it was "homemade" in the sense that it could have been prevented by internal measures.

Third, Cooper took issue with Haberler's conclusion that, in the interests of price stability, less unconditional financing should be forthcoming from the IMF. Rather, Cooper argued that the Compensatory Financing Facility operated as an automatic stabilizer; and, because funds borrowed thereunder by the primary producing countries are repaid in periods of increasing exports, it is not inflationary. Witteveen agreed with this point and added that the Extended Fund Facility, also mentioned in Haberler's paper, is the most conditional form of financing available from the IMF, requiring a fundamental improvement in the borrower's economic struc-

181

ture in the course of several years. Haberler conceded that these facilities are small and contain elements of foreign aid and stabilization. Nevertheless, he maintained that these should be kept separate from the question of liquidity.

SESSION 4

Techniques to Control International Reserves

ROBERT SOLOMON

THE BROOKINGS INSTITUTION, WASHINGTON D.C.

LET ME begin by saying simply that the man we honor at this conference was a fine human being, a fine economist, and a fine international civil servant.

This paper, though it ranges beyond a narrow interpretation of the assigned topic, tries to avoid impinging on the subject of the preceding session. Therefore, it does not address the important questions relating to the nature and extent of the impact of reserve growth on the world economy. What the paper does is to trace briefly the history of thinking about controlling world reserves; to identify and analyze the sources of reserve creation; to examine the nature of OPEC "reserves"; and to analyze techniques for controlling the growth of reserves.

The emphasis is on the potential problem of excess growth of international reserves. If the topic were viewed more broadly, attention would also be focused on avoiding deficiencies in the growth of reserves. It is assumed, however, that the problem of inadequate reserve expansion can easily be dealt with by decisions to create additional SDRs.

A Bit of History

The first international effort to "control" international reserves was designed to avoid a shortage rather than an overabundance. The Genoa Conference in 1922 recommended adoption of the gold-exchange standard on the grounds that there was insufficient gold to meet the needs of countries trying to restore the gold standard after World War I and that a deflationary scramble for gold would ensue. Although this recommendation of the Finance Commission of the Genoa Conference was not formally adopted, it had an influence on countries' policies.[1]

Later, in 1930 and 1931, the Gold Delegation of the League of Nations recommended a reduction in gold cover requirements of central banks. Its report of 1932 proposed elimination of these requirements.[2]

In the mid-1930s there was some discussion of a "plethora of gold" and of the possibility of reducing the official price of gold. This gave rise to the so-called gold scare in 1936–37, when private holders dishoarded gold in large volume.[3]

In Keynes's *Proposals for an International Clearing Union* (April 1943), one of the objectives was set forth as follows:

We need a *quantum* of international currency, which is neither determined in an unpredictable and irrelevant manner as, for example, by the technical progress of the gold industry, nor subject to large variations depending on the gold reserve policies of individual countries; but is governed by the actual current requirements of world commerce, and is also capable of deliberate expansion and contraction to offset deflationary and inflationary tendencies in effective world demand.[4]

The White Plan included no such specific objective, nor did the Articles of Agreement that were signed at Bretton Woods.

In October 1953 the IMF published a technical report entitled *The Adequacy of Monetary Reserves*.[5] Although the report contained two brief references to the possibility that too rapid an increase in the supply of world reserves "tends to promote inflationary policies," it was principally devoted to analyzing the adequacy of reserves. It did not discuss the question of controlling world reserves.

A second report, *International Reserves and Liquidity*,[6] was published by the IMF in September 1958. Once again the emphasis was on whether reserves were adequate; no concern was expressed about over-

---

[1] Ragnar Nurkse, *International Currency Experience*, (Geneva, League of Nations, 1944), pp. 27–28.

[2] League of Nations, Reports of the Gold Delegation of the Financial Committee.

[3] Nurkse, *International Currency Experience*, p. 133.

[4] Reprinted in *The International Monetary Fund 1945–1965*, vol. 3: Documents (Washington, D.C., IMF, 1969), p. 20.

[5] *Ibid.*, pp. 311–48.   [6] *Ibid.*, pp. 349–410.

abundant reserves or the need to control their growth. The report observed that the "conclusion that can be drawn from a comparison with the past is, therefore, that the contribution of reserves to the achievement of full employment, to the increase of world trade, and to the genesis of both inflation and deflation is not a dominant one." The major policy conclusion of the report was that IMF resources (i.e., quotas) would probably need to be enlarged.

Robert Triffin's proposals, published in 1960 in *Gold and the Dollar Crisis* but put forward earlier, would have "internationalized" countries' foreign-exchange holdings in the IMF and would have provided for a controlled expansion of world reserves in the future. As a preliminary step, Triffin recommended that members hold in the form of IMF deposits a certain proportion of their gross monetary reserves. While Triffin's proposals would have "controlled" the volume of international reserves, his main concerns were that, in the absence of innovations such as those he was suggesting, the growth of reserves was haphazard, a scarcity of reserves might occur, and instability might develop as U.S. liabilities increased relative to U.S. reserves. Excess creation of reserves was not one of Triffin's preoccupations in *Gold and the Dollar Crisis.*

The notion of "avoiding excesses or shortages in the means of financing existing or anticipated surpluses and deficits in the balance of payments" was included in the statement of the Ministers and Governors of the Group of Ten that was issued in August 1964, together with an annex prepared by their deputies. This statement also approved the establishment of a Study Group on the Creation of Reserve Assets, given the "possibility that the supply of gold and foreign exchange reserves may prove to be inadequate for the overall reserve needs of the world economy."

By 1964, when this ministerial statement was circulated following a year-long study by the deputies, the controversy over monetary matters between the French and other European officials, on the one hand, and the Americans, on the other, was well under way. French objections to the special role of the dollar were being aired and the French proposal for a new reserve asset, the Collective Reserve Unit, had been put forward. Although there was some talk of "imported inflation" in Europe, the concerns expressed in the 1964 reports had to do mainly with the nature of

187

the gold-exchange standard and, in particular, with the role of the dollar rather than with an excess of international reserves.

Meanwhile, under the leadership of Professor Fritz Machlup, a group of thirty-two private economists met in 1963–64 and published *International Monetary Arrangements: The Problem of Choice.* The group did not reach unanimous conclusions, but there was a consensus on several propositions, including agreement that the "mechanism of reserve creation should be overhauled to adjust the expansion of reserves to needs," and that the "process by which nations acquire reserves should not disrupt international trade and payments or interfere with the pursuit of domestic economic objectives; the rate of reserve creation should be sufficient to sustain the growth of world production without inducing price inflation." In general, the report was more concerned with potential instability in the existing system than with excess creation of reserves.

The report of the Group of Ten's Study Group on the Creation of Reserve Assets was published in August 1965. Its major focus was on the deliberate creation of new reserve assets, should this become necessary because of a "general inadequacy of reserves." Once again, there was no comprehensive consideration of "controlling" aggregate reserves.

The further work done in the Group of Ten and in the IMF on the creation of reserve assets—which ultimately led to the establishment of SDRs—did not concentrate on controlling world reserves but on supplementing gold and foreign exchange in order to prevent a shortage of reserves. When the U.S. balance of payments went into (temporary) surplus on the official settlements basis in 1968–69, and a number of European countries experienced reductions in their reserves, conditions seemed ripe for the creation of SDRs, which began in January 1970.

The history recounted above reveals little concern with the need to limit the growth of world reserves in the aggregate. One reason was that, until 1970, reserves increased at a moderate pace. From 1951 through 1969, international reserves expanded at a compound annual rate of 2.7 percent. For countries other than the United States, the increase was about 5.2 percent.

Dissatisfaction, some of it political, was being expressed about the na-

188

ture of the system and the "exorbitant privilege" of the United States as the main reserve center. But virtually no one was claiming that the growth of world reserves was excessive.

All of this changed in the early 1970s. The U.S. current account surplus dwindled and then disappeared while the surpluses of Germany and Japan increased correspondingly. There was a reversal from borrowing to repayment by American banks of Eurodollar funds in 1970–71. Finally, a speculative flight from the dollar developed in 1971. The results were enormous deficits in the U.S. accounts during 1970–72. Over these three years, the U.S. deficit on official settlements amounted to $50 billion. For this and other reasons, world reserves almost doubled, measured in SDRs, from the end of 1969 to the end of 1972.

Thus the "better international management of global liquidity" became one of the objectives of the Committee of Twenty, which began its work in the autumn of 1972. The Outline of Reform published by the Committee in June 1974 stated that it "is agreed that the basic objectives to be accommodated in the reformed convertibility system should be . . . the better management of global liquidity and the avoidance of uncontrolled growth of reserve currency balances.[7] The precise means for implementing this objective were not agreed upon, but they involved a degree of convertibility (or "asset settlement") by reserve centers, which was expected to influence the balance-of-payments policies of those countries (principally the United States). Thus the better management of international reserves was to derive largely, though not entirely, from better management of the balance-of-payments adjustment process.

Sources of Growth of World Reserves

The largest single source of reserve growth during the past quarter-century has been the increase in U.S. liabilities to monetary authorities. From 1951 through 1969, when world reserves increased by SDR 30

[7] Outline of Reform, June 14, 1974, reprinted in *International Monetary Reform*, Documents of the Committee of Twenty (Washington, D.C.: IMF, 1974), paragraph 8.

billion, official liabilities of the United States grew by SDR 12.1 billion, accounting for 40 percent of the total.[8] (The cumulative official settlements deficit of the United States over this period was SDR $19.4 billion, of which SDR 7.3 billion was financed by reductions in reserve assets of the United States.) Most of the remaining SDR 18 billion in reserve growth was accounted for, to the extent of about SDR 5 billion each, by the net flow of gold into official holdings, by increased reserve positions in the IMF, and by the placement of official reserves in Eurocurrency markets.

In the four years 1970–73, world reserves grew by SDR 73.6 billion. Official claims on the United States rose SDR 39.6 billion, accounting for 54 percent of the total. The other major source of reserve growth was the placement of official reserves in Eurocurrency markets by both developed and developing countries. Such placements created reserves, since the Eurocurrency banks loaned out the proceeds, which under "fixed" exchange rates, ended up in the reserves of some country, while the country making the placement continued to count them as part of its reserves. According to IMF estimates, these placements came to SDR 24 billion in the four-year period. Another SDR 8.8 billion of reserve expansion was accounted for by the issuance of SDRs in 1970–72.

Since 1973, the growth of international reserves has been dominated by the accumulation of claims on the rest of the world by OPEC countries. In 1974–75, world reserves increased SDR 42.2 billion. Of this amount, SDR 37.2 billion or 88 percent accrued to OPEC nations.

The Nature of OPEC "Reserves"

The major oil-exporting countries have characteristics that make it advisable to treat their growing claims on the rest of the world as long-term investments rather than as reserves in the usual sense.

The large and abrupt increase in oil prices in late 1973 gave the OPEC

[8] Until December 1971, SDR 1 equaled $1.

countries a very large current-account surplus and imposed a corresponding deficit on the rest of the world. How rapidly the OPEC surplus will decrease is a matter of some uncertainty, depending as it does on future oil prices, the rate of expansion of imports by OPEC countries, and the demand for OPEC oil. It is a reasonable assumption that the OPEC surplus, which was temporarily reduced during the economic recession of 1975–76, will continue in significant but perhaps declining magnitude for the next few years.

In addition to the real and financial problems created by the action of OPEC, there has been a spate of analytical and statistical confusion. One of the confusing questions is how to view the accumulation of financial claims by OPEC countries when one is considering international reserves.

If an advanced industrial country develops a large current account surplus, it is likely also to experience a sizeable outflow of private capital. In some cases, policy actions are taken to encourage such capital outflows. To that extent, the country's increased claims on the rest of the world do not constitute reserves. In most OPEC countries, the scope for similar capital outflows is quite limited. Thus, the bulk of the counterpart of the current-account surplus accrues to the government or central bank and is regarded as an increase in reserves.

Even if one insists on calling these claims "reserves," one should recognize their special character. They are unlikely to be unleashed on the rest of the world in the form of purchases of goods and services. Most OPEC countries are already straining their capacity to absorb imports and cannot accelerate this process further. A number of them are cutting back ambitious investment programs because of labor and other bottlenecks. Thus there is little they can do to shift their "reserves" into the hands of other countries in the short run.

Moreover, it should be recognized that, corresponding to the "reserve" accumulations by OPEC countries, there is a growing volume of debt being incurred by oil-importing nations. Most of the latter chose to finance their current-account deficits, beginning in 1974, by borrowing rather than by drawing down their reserves. In some cases, such as the

191

United States with its large money and capital markets, the borrower was passive. In most cases, countries took active steps to borrow abroad in order to finance their "oil deficits."

One implication of this fact is that when the OPEC countries finally move to a position where they can use their "reserves," by developing current account deficits, the "reserves" may well be extinguished. This will happen to the extent that the current-account deficits of OPEC countries provide scope for countries now borrowing to earn surpluses. If they do so and use the proceeds of their surpluses to repay debt, the "reserves" will disappear. These are some of the reasons why OPEC "reserves" should be viewed in a different light from ordinary reserves. If they were excluded from the reserve totals compiled by the IMF and identified instead as investments, the evolution of international reserves in recent years would look different.

It would turn out that, in the entire period from the end of World War II to the present, there has been an interval of about three years—1970–72—when reserve creation appeared to be excessive or out of control. This was the period when the par value system was breaking down. It is significant that from March 1973—when par values were abandoned—through June 1976, reserves of non-OPEC countries increased less than 4 percent per year. And much of that increase occurred within the EEC "snake"—a microcosm of the former worldwide par value system—as the members of the "snake" loaned to each other in an effort to preserve their established exchange-rate relationships.

Reserves in a Floating World

Given the facts and analysis presented above, one may wonder how important it is to develop techniques to control international reserves, since it appears that excess creation of reserves was a short-lived phenomenon—a pathological happening associated with the breakdown of the Bretton Woods system. Nevertheless, it is worth asking whether and how world reserve growth might get out of hand in the monetary system as it now functions.

In the present system of managed floating, reserve use among the larger industrial countries has decreased but has not disappeared.[9] Apart from use of reserves in the EEC "snake," other industrial nations have used reserves to temper a depreciation of their currencies (e.g., the United Kingdom and Italy), and others have accumulated reserves to temper an appreciation (Japan, Canada, and Switzerland).

Furthermore, to some degree the action of countries to borrow in order to finance oil-related current account deficits has resulted in reserve increases for countries other than OPEC members. Reserve positions in the IMF have grown by more than SDR 10 billion since the end of 1973, when the oil-financing problem began. Of this increase between December 1973 and June 1976, OPEC countries accounted for SDR 5.3 billion, and industrial countries as a group accounted for SDR 5.5 billion. Borrowing outside of the IMF can also add to reserves, when the lender is a government or central bank. Germany's gold collateral loan to Italy added to Germany's reserves without decreasing the reserves of any other country. For the most part, however, the lenders have been private and the heavy official and semiofficial borrowing since 1973 has served to prevent reductions in the reserves of oil-importing nations while adding to the "reserves" of OPEC countries. Private lenders—mainly banks and other financial institutions—have increased their liabilities to OPEC and their claims on oil-importing countries.

If one asks how it might come about that reserves could expand excessively, the answer begins with intervention in exchange markets. If a country tries to moderate upward pressure on its exchange rate by purchasing foreign exchange, its reserves will go up. Whether world reserves will also increase depends on the actions of other countries. To the extent that other monetary authorities are selling foreign exchange to moderate a depreciation of their currencies, there will simply be a shift of reserves from one country to another. On the other hand, if intervention is not balanced in this way—if countries experiencing downward pressure on their exchange rates do not intervene or intervene less than those ex-

[9] Esther C. Suss, "A Note on Reserve Use under Alternative Exchange Rate Regimes," *IMF Staff Papers* (July 1976), 23:387–94.

periencing upward pressure—world reserves will increase. Whether that increase is excessive is another question.

It is clear that what happens to world reserves will depend to a large degree on countries' actions in the face of strains on their balance-of-payments positions. Thus we are driven back to the heart of the international monetary process, namely, to balance-of-payments adjustment.

Forms of Reserve Creation

Reserves are created as the result of imbalances in international payments that are financed by either (1) the acquisition of new balances of one country's currency by another or (2) the extension of credit from one country to another where the creditor regards its claim as part of its reserves. These two forms of reserve creation may collapse to one form if the extension of credit involves acquisition of the debtor's currency. But given the fact that some currencies are "more equal" than others—that is, some currencies are widely used and regarded as reserve currencies—it is useful to make the distinction.

New reserves in the form of reserve positions in the IMF come into existence through process (2), with the IMF acting as intermediary between borrower and lender. New reserves created as a result of placements of official foreign-exchange holdings in the Eurocurrency markets may also be thought of as a form of process (2). In this case, the central bank of a country takes the initiative to lend to an unknown borrower by placing a deposit with a Eurocurrency bank, which in turn lends out the proceeds; if these are ultimately purchased by another central bank (or even the depositing central bank) intervening in its exchange market, total reserves go up. The direct diversification of reserves by holders of traditional reserve currencies involves a similar process.

Although these two latter processes—placement of reserves in Eurocurrency markets and diversification of foreign-exchange holdings—can be formally analyzed in terms of payments imbalances, that interpretation appears to stretch the concept of payments imbalance. One can imagine a country in balance—neither buying nor selling foreign exchange and having a stable exchange rate—switching some of its existing reserve currency holdings to the Euromarket in order to earn a higher rate of interest. The result may be an increase in world reserves. It is preferable, therefore, to regard these actions as a separate category of reserve creation instead of trying to subsume them under the financing of imbalances.

We finally end up with four ways in which reserves may potentially be created: (1) new SDR allocations, (2) purchases of nonmonetary gold by monetary authorities, (3) financing payments imbalances either actively (through loans) or passively (through acquisitions of reserve currencies), and (4) placements of officially held currency balances in other markets.

In case (4), reserves are created only if a central bank intervenes to purchase the currency that has been switched. Little space needs to be devoted to (1) and (2). Special-drawing-right allocations are certainly under control. The flow of new gold into reserves is unlikely to be of large magnitude; under present arrangements, central banks of Group of Ten Countries can buy no more gold than the IMF sells and, in fact, have bought only a small fraction of what the IMF has auctioned off. (The total reserves of a small number of countries could be importantly affected by changes in the market value of gold. But that value has been highly unstable as would be the potential proceeds from sales in the market by central banks. It is assumed here that the agreement not to peg the market price will be continued indefinitely.) This leaves us with (3) and (4).

Payments Imbalances and Reserves

The need for a better balance-of-payments adjustment process was the principal rallying cry of monetary reformers in the 1960s and early 1970s.

The Committee of Twenty devoted considerable time and effort to the twin questions of adjustment and asset settlement in a par value system. The American proposal for a set of reserve indicators[10] was designed to create a strong presumption that countries in imbalance, particularly on

[10] Reprinted in *Economic Report of the President*, January 1973, pp. 160–74.

the surplus side, would adopt corrective policies to adjust. This proposal was never fully accepted, but the Outline of Reform did state that countries "will aim to keep their official reserves within limits which will be internationally agreed from time to time in the Fund and which will be consistent with the volume of global liquidity. For this purpose, reserve indicators will be established on a basis to be agreed in the Fund" (paragraph 4b). However, now that the industrial countries are floating, either individually or jointly in the EEC "snake," the adjustment problem has a different complexion.

For the purposes of this paper, the pertinent question is whether inadequate adjustment is likely to lead to uncontrolled or excessive growth of world reserves. Apart from "oil deficits" and the associated build-up of OPEC "reserves," this could come about only as the result of excessive official lending or excessive purchases of reserve currencies—by countries that are floating or by those that are pegging either to a group or to a major currency—as an alternative to letting exchange rates move. To a large degree, reserve creation will depend on countries' intervention policies and on the exchange-rate policies of those that have pegged rates.

To take an extreme example, it is conceivable that a number of countries might actively purchase dollars in order to drive down their exchange rates relative to the dollar. Their reserves would increase, and the U.S. balance of payments would react to the appreciation of the dollar. The intervention behavior assumed here would be in violation of the guidelines for floating adopted by the IMF in 1974: and it will presumably be proscribed by the guiding principles the IMF is called upon to adopt under the amended Articles of Agreement.

A less extreme example would have other countries intervening to purchase dollars when the U.S. current account moved in the deficit direction or when U.S. capital outflows increased. Such intervention would prevent the dollar from depreciating and the currencies of the other countries from appreciating. This, of course, is what happened in 1970–71. Since that time, the inhibitions on depreciation of the dollar and appreciation of other currencies have been largely swept away. But perhaps not entirely.

Another and possibly more likely basis for payments imbalance under the existing exchange-rate regime will be differential monetary policies. It

196

can be imagined that the United States goes into a recession while Europe and Japan are experiencing strong or even excess demand. The fall in U.S. interest rates would lead to capital outflows and to a tendency for the dollar to depreciate. What would be the reaction of European and Japanese monetary authorities under these circumstances? They would be likely to view the increased disparity in interest rates as cyclical and presumably temporary. Would they intervene to purchase dollars in order to prevent a cyclical appreciation of their currencies? The IMF will undoubtedly find this question difficult to resolve as it attempts to formulate "specific principles" for the guidance of members with respect to their exchange rate policies. In any event, it is clear that the question relates more to adjustment than to techniques for controlling reserves.

Reserve Placement

The fourth means of reserve creation referred to above—placement of reserves in Eurocurrency markets or directly in a national market—was also dealt with by the Committee of Twenty. The Outline of Reform identified three proposals that had been "suggested but not agreed." They all involve restrictions on the freedom of action of monetary authorities in investing their foreign-exchange reserves and were resisted by the representatives of developing countries.

It is conceivable that some such rules of behavior might be agreed to in the future, though such agreement would probably require a *quid pro quo* that benefits developing countries.

On the other hand, there is now less incentive for developing nations (or others) to place their dollar reserves in the Eurodollar market rather than in the United States. The abolition of U.S. capital controls has resulted in a narrowing in the differential in interest rates between the two markets. In 1975, according to IMF estimates, 90 percent of the increase in official Eurodollar holdings by nonindustrial countries was accounted for by major oil-producing countries. Some of these nations may have experienced noneconomic motives for placing their reserves outside the United States.

The diversification of reserves from one currency to another is still a

197

potential problem. As these words are being written in September 1976, the newspapers report a general expectation that the DM will be revalued in the "snake" after the German election of October 3. This expectation would create an incentive for diversification. Whether it also creates reserves will depend on the intervention policies of the Bundesbank and the other countries in the "snake." In this area as well, it is possible to imagine agreement on rules of behavior among monetary authorities.

Direct Techniques for Controlling Reserves

What has been written thus far in this paper, if it is cogent, is not likely to make the reader an enthusiast for the immediate adoption of techniques to control international reserves. Nevertheless, we now proceed to discuss the nature and implications of such techniques as they might be applied in the existing monetary system.

Consideration of these techniques should be related to the processes by which reserves are created, as outlined above. It follows from the earlier discussion that, if control techniques are needed, they should be directed mainly at the financing of payments imbalances. Consideration of techniques to control reserves in present conditions thus overlaps with the question of IMF surveillance of countries' exchange-rate practices.

There appear to be two general categories of techniques; namely, absolute and proportional limits. Absolute limits would be similar to the U.S. proposals for reserve indicators submitted to the Committee of Twenty. One can imagine a structure of reserve indicator points for each country, based on the amount of reserves it held when the scheme began to operate. As a country's reserves rose it would come under increasing pressure from the IMF to let its exchange rate appreciate or to adopt other measures to reduce its accumulation of reserves. For such a scheme to be acceptable, it would no doubt have to be symmetrical, applying to losses of reserves as well as gains.[11]

[11] It is worth noting that one of the working groups of the Committee of Twenty explored the relationship between rules for floating and a reserve indicator structure; see Report of Technical Group on Adjustment, *International Monetary Reform*, Documents of the C-20, 1974, pp. 141–61.

This approach is a means of enforcing adjustment. It would limit the transfer of reserves among nonreserve centers; it would curb the creation of new reserves to the extent that it limited acquisition of net new reserve currency balances.

The other category—proportional limits—is based on analogy with domestic monetary policy techniques. This was presumably the inspiration for Witteveen's suggestion that international liquidity might be regulated "by countries agreeing to hold a certain minimum proportion of their reserves in the form of SDRs," and that "adjustments in the aggregate volume of SDRs and/or in the reserve ratio would then also bring about international management of the global amount of international reserves." [12]

Before we examine this technique, it is worth pointing out that domestic monetary management, via changes in reserves or in reserve requirements, deals only with a part of the liquidity of the private sector. It regulates the money supply, whether broadly or narrowly defined, but not the other liquid assets that businesses and consumers can use to finance expenditures. International reserves, on the other hand, comprise the gamut of liquid assets in the hands of central banks and available to finance deficits. In this sense, proposals for international reserve requirements are more ambitious than conventional domestic monetary policy.

In analyzing the workings of the proposal for SDR reserve requirements, one immediately faces the fact that countries' present ratios of SDRs to total reserves are far from uniform. Thus some transitional arrangements would be needed, involving a reshuffling of SDRs among countries. Let us skip over this problem and examine how the proposal would work after the transition.

Suppose a country found its foreign exchange reserves increasing, so that its ratio of SDRs to total reserves was threatening to fall below the minimum reserve requirement. It would have two alternative courses of action. It could seek to acquire additional SDRs. If another country were losing reserves, that country might be willing to sell SDRs to the reserve-gaining country, probably in exchange for dollars, the most widely used

[12] "On the Control of International Liquidity," address by H. Johannes Witteveen, Frankfurt, Germany, October 28, 1975.

199

intervention currency. Would the reserve-gaining country have a right to demand SDRs from the issuer of the currency it was acquiring? If the answer were "yes," this would mean that convertibility of the dollar into other reserve assets had been reestablished. Given the widespread holding of dollars and the possibility that countries may acquire them as a result not only of developments in the U.S. balance of payments but of imbalances elsewhere, the United States would be unlikely to agree to such a scheme without the sort of adjustment mechanism it sought during the negotiations in the Committee of Twenty.

The other course of action open to the reserve-gaining country would be to reduce its accumulations of foreign exchange so as to keep its ratio from falling below the minimum requirement. In this case the "burden" of policy action falls on the country gaining reserves and, in the absence of convertibility, it is unable to force some of this "burden" onto other countries. (It is assumed that other countries would exchange SDRs for currencies only on a voluntary basis.) Since the action required may be no more than abstaining from intervention, this option might be acceptable.

The question arises whether the reserve ratio would be only a minimum requirement or also a maximum. Would a country whose reserves fell, so that its SDR ratio rose above the minimum, be expected to restore the required ratio? If the answer is "yes," the country with a ratio above the minimum would have two options. It could offer to sell SDRs to countries whose ratios were relatively low. Or it could reverse its intervention policy—presumably it had been selling foreign exchange to prevent or temper a depreciation of its exchange rate—and start buying foreign exchange. This would cause a sharp depreciation, given the conditions that had induced it to sell foreign exchange in the first place. More realistically, the country would reduce the volume of its intervention as its ratio rose toward the maximum.

It appears, therefore, that adoption of a reserve requirement based on a ratio to SDR holdings would tend to discourage intervention in both directions if the ratio involved both a minimum and a maximum. If it involved only a minimum, adoption of the proposal would discourage intervention on the buying side but not on the selling side. If the purpose of

200

the proposal is to limit the growth of total reserves, a minimum ratio would be sufficient.

A consequence of the scheme, if it involved only a minimum requirement, would be a tendency to freeze holdings of SDRs. Countries would be reluctant to sell SDRs when their ratios were above the minimum, in order to save them for a "rainy day"—that is, in order to have scope for increasing foreign exchange reserves in the future.

In general, then, a reserve requirement with mandatory convertibility is unlikely to be acceptable unless it is accompanied by a scheme to assure symmetrical adjustment actions. A scheme without mandatory convertibility would, it seems, tend to meet the objective of its proponents—to limit the growth of total reserves. The relative importance of this constitutes another question, as indicated earlier.

Finally, let me say that, despite the tone of this paper, I am one who believes, with Bagehot, that money does not manage itself. But I see less urgency in limiting the growth of international reserves than in working out guidelines for exchange-rate management and IMF surveillance.

PETER B. KENEN

PRINCETON UNIVERSITY, PRINCETON, N.J.

IN THIS, the bicentennial year of Adam Smith's *Wealth of Nations*, it would be unkind to quarrel with the principle of specialization. A division of labor enhances efficiency in the production of goods. It may also enhance efficiency in the production of ideas. The sponsors of our conference would seem to think so, for they have given each of us a specialized task. But the case for specialization in the production of goods assumes that producers have perfect knowledge, including knowledge of the future, and similar assumptions would seem to be needed to prove the case for specialization in the production of ideas. I am convinced of it, being at a disadvantage as the last specialist on the program.

When I present this paper at the conference table, I will have perfect knowledge. Professors Cooper and Giersch will have explained why and how the IMF should exercise surveillance over exchange rates. Professors Haberler and Grubel will have explained why we should want to control international reserves. My task, to discuss techniques for controlling reserves, will be well defined. The exchange of ideas around the conference table will take place under conditions of diminishing uncertainty. But the act of production—the preparation of my paper—is encumbered by a great deal of uncertainty. I do not know why I am supposed to tell you how we should control international reserves.

When we must make decisions under uncertainty concerning the behavior of others, we can try to guess what they will do by looking at what they have done in the past. But this is an expensive option, especially when trying to forecast the opinions of four distinguished, prolific economists. Furthermore, it does not promise to be helpful at this juncture,

202

when all of us are trying to assimilate new facts, including the law and philosophy of the Second Amendment to the IMF Articles of Agreement, and to understand new problems, including those of managing economic policies at a time when recovery is far from exuberant, inflation far from dormant, and the distributions of trade balances, capital flows, and stocks of debt very sharply skewed.

When we cannot guess what others will do or say, we fall back to a second way of dealing with uncertainty. We ask what we would do or say were we in their places. I use this introspective method here to sort out my own thinking on some of the questions that have to be answered before I can specialize efficiently, as I was asked to do, in the production of ideas concerning techniques to control international reserves. My paper, then, deals with three sets of questions, not just one, and takes them up more or less sequentially:

1. What are the implications of the Second Amendment, especially the portions dealing with exchange rates, for the manner in which reserves are created, the location of the power to create reserves, and the virtues of various techniques to guard against abuse of that power?
2. What role, if any, should be given to reserves, national or global, in IMF surveillance of exchange-rate practices and, more mechanically, in any set of guidelines promulgated to control central-bank intervention in the foreign-exchange markets?
3. What are the implications of answers to these questions for efforts to control the creation or destruction of individual reserve assets, to control relationships among reserve assets, including the terms on which they are exchangeable and the proportions in which they are held, and to control the totality of reserves?

I am not especially happy with my answers to these questions. They lead me to wonder whether the reform of the monetary system embodied in the Second Amendment is sufficiently coherent internally and sufficiently consistent externally with the aspirations of major governments. I wonder, too, whether the reform portends a satisfactory role for the IMF, the custodian of global influence over national monetary policies.

203

To launch an exploration of the issues raised by my three questions, it is useful to identify the chief features of the present reserve system. Risking excessive simplification, let me suggest that there are today three types of reserve assets: those whose supplies are determined collectively, by governments acting through the IMF and other international institutions; those whose supplies are determined unilaterally, by governments acting individually; and those whose supplies are determined by a mixture of these principles—by way of transactions between international and national institutions or by the actions of national agencies pursuant to rules or limitations on which they have agreed collectively.

The supply of SDRs is, of course, the one that is most clearly and decisively determined collectively. Special drawing rights are created and distributed by the IMF under rules that require the consent of countries accounting for an 85 percent majority of the votes in the IMF. The rules are so strict that we may see no substantial growth in the supply of SDRs for some years to come, a prospect that causes me to wonder how IMF members plan to achieve the objective to which they subscribe in Article VII, Section 7, of the amended articles—to make the SDR the principal reserve asset in the international monetary system. These familiar words have now migrated from the pious, inconsequential context of a ministerial communiqué to the formal, binding context of a treaty having the force of law. To make them meaningful in this century, it will not suffice to use the SDR as a unit of account in IMF transactions and statistics. It is necessary also to plan now for a gradual but sizeable growth in the supply of SDRs—a matter to which I return below.

At the opposite pole, the supply of any reserve currency is determined unilaterally, not collectively. Dollars, pounds, francs, and marks become reserve assets when and only when they are acquired and held by governments and central banks. The supply of a reserve currency is not, I emphasize, determined by the issuer. It is determined by the sum of the decisions of holders. I will return to this point too, because it epitomizes the spirit of the Second Amendment and has far-reaching implications for the feasibility and necessity of controlling international reserves.

Reserve positions in the IMF and national gold holdings belong, for different reasons, to the third, mixed category of reserve assets. Reserve

204

positions in the IMF are determined initially by discrete decisions taken collectively concerning the sizes of IMF quotas and the manner in which IMF members must "pay" for their quotas. But the sizes of reserve positions are not fixed thereafter; they vary with the volume and composition of drawings on the IMF, and these are initiated by individual governments, subject to IMF rules and policies.

Changes in reserve positions are not always or exclusively the results of decisions taken by the countries whose positions are affected. The size of any country's reserve position in the IMF depends on IMF holdings of its currency, and these depend in part on transactions undertaken by other countries. Thus reserve positions are jointly determined by collective decisions, holders' decisions, and decisions by other countries.

I say that gold holdings belong today to this third category because of the agreement reached last year among the members of the Group of Ten. In August 1975 they decided that they would refrain from any action to peg the price of gold and that "the total stock of gold in the hands of the Fund and the monetary authorities of the Group of Ten will not be increased" during the two-year life span of the agreement.[1] By virtue of this self-denying ordinance and the decision taken soon afterward to distribute to the IMF members one-sixth of IMF gold holdings and to auction off a second sixth on the free market, the supply of monetary gold to the members of the Group of Ten is subject temporarily to collective control. Decisions of the IMF concerning its gold holdings place an upper limit on the holdings of the Group of Ten. Their gold holdings can, of course, fall below this limit; members of the Group of Ten can decide individually to sell gold. Furthermore, collective control is incomplete, in that other countries are free to buy gold (or will be when the Second Amendment comes into force). Nevertheless, it is accurate to say that gold holdings are jointly determined by the decisions of the IMF, the Group of Ten, and individual governments.

There is reason to believe, however, that this situation will not last. The ten-country agreement may not be renewed in its present form. And

---

[1] The passage quoted is from the communiqué issued by the Interim Committee of the IMF Board of Governors, reproduced as Appendix III to the 1976 *Annual Report* of the IMF.

there have been suggestions, by Italy and other countries, that the IMF suspend or limit its gold auctions in order to prevent the price of gold from falling. We may thus be approaching a worrisome situation in which gold holdings, like currency holdings, will be determined entirely by the decisions of individual countries, by way of their transactions with gold producers and gold hoarders.

This is perhaps the point to pause for lamenting. I am, like many others, deeply disappointed by the manner in which the Second Amendment deals with gold. The aim, we have been told, is to reduce the role of gold in international monetary affairs. But this is to be done by sedulous neglect, not by restricting governments' rights to buy or sell gold at free-market prices or to value as they wish gold that they already hold. It is one achievement of the Amendment to the IMF articles that it brings international monetary law into conformity with monetary practice in matters pertaining to exchange rates. Laws that are not consonant with practice breed contempt for the rule of law and for those who must enforce it. But the Amendment marches in a different direction when it faces the gold problem. It achieves demonetization *de jure* by removing gold entirely from IMF cognizance and depriving the IMF of any right or power to regulate national gold holdings or policies.

As gold will continue to be a reserve asset for some time to come and gold holdings will be governed in growing degree by the decisions of gold holders, demonetization *de jure* will not accomplish demonetization *de factor*. Law and practice may become totally orthogonal. Governments, moreover, are not now and will not soon become indifferent to the price of gold, and their views about gold holdings and the prospects for gold prices will continue to affect their judgments regarding the need to adjust collectively the supplies of other reserve assests, including SDRs.

Those who have participated in the running debate on reform of the reserve system are apt to balk at my assertion that decisions affecting supplies of currency reserves have today to be regarded as resting with the governments that *hold* those reserves. The supply of any national currency is, after all, determined to a first approximation by the decisions of the government issuing that currency.

206

A currency becomes a reserve asset, however, only when another country chooses to acquire it, and the decision to acquire any currency is today discretionary, not an obligation of participation in the international monetary system. This is what I meant by my suggestion that the present classification of currency reserves epitomizes the dramatic change in philosophy that is reflected in the Second Amendment.

When countries were obligated to declare and defend par values for their currencies, as they were in practice before the advent of floating and in law before the Second Amendment, responsibility for the control of reserve-currency supplies was said to rest with the countries issuing the currencies. It was indeed that very view that led to a decade of transatlantic recriminations concerning the responsibilities of the United States. The supply of dollars to the stock of reserves was the joint result of U.S. policies affecting the size of the U.S. payments deficit, the obligation of other countries to take up the dollars supplied by the deficit so as to defend par values, and the obligation assumed by large countries—not all of them to be sure, nor with equal formality—to refrain from converting the dollars they acquired.

It is not my intention to rehearse that transatlantic argument, and still less to apportion moral responsibility for the huge growth of dollar holdings that took place in the final years of the par value system. There are some who still believe that the U.S. deficit, the underlying source of dollar supplies, was fundamentally demand-determined. Other countries, it is argued, had an appetite for dollars that was reflected in their policies, and those policies ordained the U.S. deficit. I recall the argument only to stress its irrelevance under present circumstances.

What was an obligation of each government to declare and defend a par value is today an option, but only one of many. Under the new Article IV, "each member [of the IMF] undertakes to collaborate with the Fund [IMF] and other members to assure orderly exchange arrangements and to promote a stable system of exchange rates." To this end, it must notify the IMF "of the exchange arrangements it intends to apply in fulfillment of its obligations," and these may include "(i) the maintenance by a member of a value for its currency in terms of the special drawing right or another denominator, other than gold, selected by the member,

207

or (ii) cooperative arrangements by which members maintain the value of their currencies in relation to the value of the currency or currencies of other members, or (iii) other exchange arrangements of a member's choice." No member, moreover, is bound by its choice; it is free to change its exchange arrangements.

This text might be described as codified anarchy, and it conceals a number of difficulties. Not so long ago, for example, economists had to explain why it was nonsense to say that floating exchange rates were good for all countries except the United States; if all currencies were floating against the dollar, and that was a good thing, then the dollar would be floating against all other currencies, and that would have to be a good thing, too. Now, it would appear, we are required to warn that no country can choose an exchange arrangement for its currency without impinging on the freedom of others to choose arrangements for themselves. If all countries other than the United States undertake to manage their exchange rates by intervening in foreign-exchange markets, the dollar will be managed too, whatever the wishes of the United States.[2]

---

[2] The U.S. Government seems to be worried about this problem, and not without justification. The managed float toward which we are drifting contains the seeds of grave international disorder. Large numbers of countries would appear to hold strong views about exchange rates. Many have chosen to peg their currencies; others are intervening actively to prevent or attenuate movements in floating rates. It is not too wrong to say that we have devised a system of gliding parities in which the parities and rates of glide do not have to be announced and are thus hidden from the scrutiny required to guarantee overall consistency. There is, then, the danger that the dollar will become again the nth currency in the system—that practice, if not law, will come to resemble in this respect the par value system we have just supplanted. Should this occur, the United States may seek someday to free itself from the constraints imposed by others, by acting as it did in 1971, with convulsive consequences for international financial, economic, and political relationships. Were I to advise the U.S. Treasury, however, I would counsel a response different from the one it appears to have adopted. I would urge the rapid, complete articulation of explicit rules to regulate intervention, rules proscribing any intervention designed to drive exchange rates away from target rates or zones that the IMF, acting on its own initiative, would promulgate from time to time. I leave open a number of complicated questions—whether the IMF should publish the targets and how it should obtain them, to what extent it should rely on its own research, including its own econometric models, and to what extent it should proceed by consultation with the governments concerned. I do believe, however, that we need to move in this direction. Proposals to impose rules for floating that do not include well-defined procedures for setting and altering target rates or zones miss the basic point at issue. The nth country problem will not go away. It is sure to arise from the verbiage of Article IV, to plague us when we are most vulnerable to its implications.

But this is not my chief point. My main aim is to insist that the change in the language of Article IV has, as I have stated, shifted completely the locus of responsibility for determining the volume of currency reserves. No country has any constitutional obligation, other than one it may assume freely for itself or in concert and reciprocity with like-minded countries, to acquire or hold another country's currency. The creation of currency reserves results from the manner in which each IMF member resolves the question posed by Article IV. Is it to acquire currency reserves by intervening to influence the exchange rate, or is it to allow the exchange rate to vary?

From this interpretation there follows a second. It is the logical implication of what I have been saying, and quite directly of Article IV, that no country should be required to redeem in any "primary" reserve asset the holdings of its currency acquired by another in the course of intervention. There may be a case, based on prior law anu practice, for redeeming or converting in some gradual fashion reserve currencies acquired under the par value system. This is the old problem of consolidation. It is not unneighborly or obstinate, however, for the United States to persist in its opinion that it should not be compelled to redeem dollar balances acquired since the termination of the par value system. That obligation was reciprocal to the one accepted by other countries—the obligation to defend par values—and it has lapsed in principle, not only in practice, with the expiration of its counterpart.

The same conclusion follows just as forcefully from a different view of Article IV. The case for the new text is basically the case for national autonomy in monetary policy. In some significant respects, of course, autonomy is unattainable. With tight international integration of financial markets, no country can assert complete control over its own national markets. In one important respect, however, resort to floating under Article IV does confer autonomy. It allows each government or central bank to decide whether, to what extent, and at what times it will assert control over the supply of money. We all know by now that intervention in the foreign-exchange market does not differ in its impact on bank reserves from intervention in the money market. The right to undertake or abstain from purchases and sales of foreign exchange, the right rehabilitated by

209

Article IV, is the right of each country to determine its domestic money stock.

To impose on the United States or any other country the obligation to pay out reserves on demand, because of the policies pursued by other countries in respect of their exchange rates, would be to replace the famous asymmetries of the par value system with new asymmetries. It would withhold from countries with intervention currencies the degree of domestic autonomy that the Second Amendment purports to confer on all IMF members.

In answer, then, to part of my first question, I conclude that the Second Amendment precludes, as a matter of principle and logical consistency, resort to any form of asset convertibility, mandatory or at the option of the holder, as a way to regulate currency reserves or the evolution of total reserves. It does so because no country has any remaining obligation to defend a par value, and no other country has the corresponding obligation to conduct its affairs with a view to sparing its neighbors the domestic monetary consequences of reserve-currency accumulations. The choice between reserve accumulation and a change in the exchange rate is open to every country.

These are strong words, with large implications for the management of world reserves. They are not, however, altogether nihilistic. I propose to argue in the balance of this paper that the close control of global reserves is not the important objective it was (or should have been) under the par value system, that it is not in any case an efficient way to discipline the domestic policies of a large country such as the United States, and that it is not a promising technique for governing the management of floating exchange rates—the volume or character of intervention under the new monetary system.

The United States and other large countries have an obligation to pursue domestic policies, especially domestic monetary policies, that foster global economic stability. By virtue of its size alone, the United States should seek always to avoid insofar as possible policies that force other countries to choose between painful alternatives. And currency appreciation, the chief option open to a country when its neighbors err in an inflationary manner, is far from being painless, economically or politically.

What we have been learning and preaching recently—the asset-market theory of exchange-rate determination—says, among other things, that fluctuations in exchange rates occur in the first instance as responses to disturbances in financial markets and that changes in national monetary policies are among the most influential disturbances. It is a corollary to this proposition that day-to-day changes in exchange rates bear no clear-cut relationship to changes needed for insulation from swings in foreign prices or, by extension, from the expenditure and price effects of other countries' policies. On the contrary, any change in one country's monetary policy can, by its short-term effects on floating exchange rates, destabilize domestic prices and production in neighboring economies. Moving to the real world, a classic case in point is furnished by recent experience in Europe. Market forces, driven by monetary policies in Europe and the United States, have caused certain European currencies to appreciate. The domestic price effects of the appreciations have not been unwelcome, but the cyclical and secular effects on important traded-goods industries have been quite painful.

Yet these considerations do not argue for limiting reserve supplies, even if it were possible to do so without undermining the philosophy of the Second Amendment. If reserve-currency accumulations had been limited in the years before 1971, it might have been possible to avoid that debacle. Acting under a reserve constraint, the American authorities would have been compelled to end the U.S. payments deficit. I venture to suggest, however, that they would have started to consider changes in exchange rates—an earlier realignment—not to contemplate any major change in domestic monetary and fiscal policies. It was in part because they were concerned to maximize the world's appetite for dollars, thereby to finance U.S. deficits without losses of reserves, that they refused to entertain, let alone discuss, thoughts about a realignment, including a concomitant change in the gold price. Had it been known in, say, 1965 that the U.S. deficit would not disappear in two or three years, as forecast by an influential study, and that U.S. reserves had been falling steadily for five years or so under an asset-settlement rule, the U.S. authorities would have had cause to talk about changing exchange rates, rather than suppressing any secret thoughts they or their aides may have harbored. But

211

asset convertibility would not have caused them to deflate the U.S. economy as rapidly or sharply as might have been required to terminate the deficit before U.S. reserves were exhausted.

It is, I believe, a fair generalization that no large country can agree to subordinate the imperatives of domestic policy to the requirements of convertibility. It will instead jettison its external obligations, if not by obtaining agreement to a change in the exchange rate through the ordinary methods of consultation, then by throwing a tantrum to extort the concurrence it requires. I will go further. It may be possible someday to foster in all countries a decent respect for the needs of neighbors. Today, however, it is sometimes difficult for democratic governments to generate adequate support for measures to achieve domestic stability. The disciplines of democracy do not always work to foster sound policies. Under these circumstances, it is utterly unrealistic to suppose that limitations on reserve supplies can prevent or rectify damaging policies. If governments are not rewarded by their own citizens for taking the steps necessary to maintain domestic economic health, they cannot expect to be rewarded for submitting to the arcane constraint of reserve scarcity.

My suggestion that restrictions on reserve creation might have induced an earlier devaluation of the dollar, forestalling the crisis of 1971, has its counterpart in the proposal made by the United States during the deliberations of the Committee of Twenty. Confronting demands for restrictions on the creation of currency reserves, demands for mandatory asset settlement, the United States suggested that movements in reserves be treated as "presumptive" indicators of the need for changes in par values and in domestic financial policies aimed at the correction of payments imbalances. The insistence of Europeans on more symmetry in access to official financing was met by American insistence on more symmetry in the initiation of adjustment.

As described in the Report of the Committee of Twenty (Annex 1 to the Outline of Reform), the plan for a reserve indicator could have been implemented in the absence of mandatory asset settlement. It was not even necessary to have close control over the global supply of reserves. The only requirement—and this pertained to symmetry—was that the reserves of participating countries be defined in net rather than in gross

212

terms. Had that not been done, the signals transmitted to surplus and deficit countries might not have been equally strong.

The use of reserves—levels, trends, or changes—to regulate the management of floating exchange rates is subject only to this same minimal requirement. It would not be essential to control total reserves. It would be important to define reserve levels, trends, or changes in net terms. Otherwise, a rule that prohibited France from selling francs for dollars, because it had acquired large dollar reserves, would not necessarily prevent the United States from doing the same thing; U.S. liabilities to France would not count against U.S. reserve assets, and the latter might be large. The aim of such a rule, after all, is to bar any intervention that would block a change in the franc–dollar rate, and it must therefore operate to prohibit intervention by either country having an interest in that rate.

Furthermore, the use of reserve levels in rules to manage floating rates would be free of one objection made against their use to regulate par values. A mechanical use of reserve levels to mandate changes in par values, combined with the requirement of intervention to defend those par values, could have caused large oscillations in exchange rates. A country with low reserves would have had to devalue until it began to run a surplus, and this would have caused the country's reserves to rise until the reserve-level rule signaled the need for revaluation. Par values would have moved up and down, dragging exchange rates with them.[3] A reserve-level rule to govern a managed float would not necessarily destabilize exchange rates, because it would not be combined with mandatory intervention. A country with low reserves would be required to abstain from further support of its currency, and the currency might then depreciate. But the country would not be required to ratify the depreciation by selling its currency and building up reserves, the source of cyclical instability under a par value system.

These observations, however, fall short of making a good case for using reserves in rules to govern intervention under floating rates. There are, on the contrary, two arguments against reserve-based rules.

[3] For simulations illustrating this possibility, see my previous paper, Peter B. Kenen, "Floats, Glides, and Indicators: A Comparison of Methods for Changing Exchange Rates," *Journal of International Economics* (May 1975), 5:107–51.

First, reserve movements are, at best, historical testimony. They do not necessarily tell us much about the present, let alone the future of exchange-rate relationships. An accumulation or high level of reserves is *prime facie* evidence that a government or central bank has been acting to depress the price of its national currency (or at least, to limit the increase that would have occurred in the absence of intervention). Yet this information does not always indicate that the currency should be allowed to appreciate now or in the near future, and this is the question to which an intervention rule should be addressed. The history of policies told by reserves may not be altogether irrelevant to judgments concerning the future. Data relating to recent changes in net reserves, if current and comprehensive, may shed some light on the propriety of further intervention.[4] But I would want to use that information only as an input to the process of deciding where to set and how to change target rates or target zones, and then to use those rates or zones as the norms in rules to regulate intervention.

Second, it is difficult to interpret changes in reserves, especially in net reserves, under floating rates. I have in mind a feature of the present situation neglected in my brief description of the reserve system. With floating rates, the prices of reserve assets are not fixed in terms of any single asset or in terms of any index. (There is, in addition, no fixed official price for gold under the Second Amendment, but this merely complicates the situation, and I defer discussion of the gold price to another context.) The level of reserves is, of course, more stable in terms of the SDR than in terms of any national currency. But the dollar bulks larger in total reserves than in the "basket" of currencies defining the SDR, so that changes in dollar exchange rates can cause variations in the value of reserves, even when measured in terms of the SDR.

To illustrate, consider the changes in global reserves recorded in 1975.[5] Total reserves rose by SDR 14.4 billion during that year. Omit-

---

[4] Movements of reserves can also be employed to check on compliance with an intervention rule, but they are not perfect indicators even for this purpose. A country that has violated an intervention rule, thereby acquiring currency reserves, would not have great difficulty hiding the reserves. It might indeed be easier to conceal changes in reserves from the statistical scrutiny of the IMF than to conceal the fact of intervention from the market and financial press.

[5] The data come from Table 14 in the IMF 1976 *Annual Report*.

214

ting the reserves of oil-exporting countries, they rose by SDR 4.0 billion. But three quarters of that total, SDR 3.0 billion, reflected changes in exchange rates, chiefly the appreciation of the U.S. dollar. The increase in the volume of reserves was only SDR 1.0 billion. These statistics warn that data on reserves may tell us very little, even retrospectively, about the rights and wrongs of intervention. They also raise questions about the functioning of intervention rules based on the evolution of reserves. Does an appreciation of a country's currency, increasing its net reserves by reducing the foreign-currency value of its liabilities, affect in any significant way the justification for intervention to prevent a further appreciation? If we were concerned with the country's ability to meet demands for the conversion of its liabilities into "primary" reserve assets —demands that do not and should not arise under the Second Amendment—we might answer affirmatively. If we are concerned (as we should be) with the implications of the appreciation for the pattern of trade and payments, we must answer negatively. The story told by such a change in net reserves can signify little.

It is, in brief, my answer to the second question posed at the start of this paper that the need to regulate intervention is no reason for concern with the control of total reserves.

This may be the best juncture to look at a proposal that has been advanced in many forms and contexts, to harmonize the composition of reserves and limit their volume by imposing holding limits. Each country's holdings of other countries' currencies could be no larger than some fixed multiple of its holdings of "primary" assets.

In its most recent incarnation, an address by the managing director of the IMF delivered a year ago in Frankfurt, the proposal would employ the SDR as the "primary" reserve asset and would thereby confer on the IMF the power to limit the volume of reserves by limiting the volume of SDRs—the one component of the total reserve supply over which the IMF has adequate control. Some of the implications of this proposal were explored by J. Marcus Fleming in an internal memorandum drafted in his last weeks at the IMF, and my own views have been influenced by that memorandum. He should not be held responsible, however, for what I have to say.

215

I have already given one reason to doubt the need for a holding limit. With the legalization of floating exchange rates, it is no longer necessary to exercise close control over the volume of currency reserves. Even if there were need to do so, however, a holding limit might not be a good way to achieve control. Consider the plight of a country that has reached its holding limit. If it is unable to obtain additional SDRs, its holding limit is transformed into an absolute injunction against intervention to prevent appreciation of the country's currency. As such, it is exposed to all of my complaints about reserve-based rules to regulate intervention— and to the additional complaint that an injunction against intervention could be imposed by the composition as well as the level of a country's reserves, an accident of history that can have little bearing on the desirability of intervention.

There are, of course, two ways in which a country can acquire additional SDRs: it can buy them or can borrow them. No country, however, is entitled automatically to buy SDRs from another; France is not empowered to demand that the United States sell them in exchange for U.S. dollars. To confer this right on any country would be to impose on other countries the obsolete obligation of asset convertibility. The Second Amendment does allow countries to deal more freely in SDRs than they could before; voluntary transfers, presumably including loans or sales subject to repurchase, can be agreed between two countries without specific IMF approval. But the removal of restrictions on transfers not mandated by "designation" is no guarantee that a country will find a voluntary seller or lender, and the likelihood of finding a supplier is itself inversely related to the effectiveness of a holding limit.

Thanks to the Second Amendment, it is now possible to foresee the development of an SDR loan market akin to the Federal Funds market in the United States. But that possibility may not be realized until the IMF becomes a lender of last resort, and it is not now authorized to perform that function. The Second Amendment makes no major change in the rigid rules relating to new distributions and cancellations of SDRs. And in the absence of an SDR loan market, holding limits could function unevenly across countries and time, affecting arbitrarily the allowable amounts of intervention in various currency markets.

216

The point I made earlier about reserve statistics—how difficult it is to interpret them under floating rates—raises another general issue. When there were par values and a fixed official price for gold, the global total of reserves was easy to define. It was the sum of its parts. There were, to be sure, difficulties in deciding how to measure net reserves. Was it right, for example, to regard Eurodollars held by governments and central banks as reserve liabilities of the United States? But these and other problems, both conceptual and statistical, were simple by comparison with those we face today. The SDR prices of reserve currencies can change from day to day. The gold price is SDR 35 per ounce in IMF reserve statistics, is different in certain national statistics, and is on its way into legal limbo. It is difficult to ascertain whether the total of reserves, gross or net, is larger or smaller than the sum of its parts, valued at any set of prices one might choose to use.

Furthermore, the *liquidity* of certain reserve assets—their transferability at stable prices—has been much impaired. Do the French authorities, who value their gold holdings at market-related prices but cannot be sure of selling gold at those prices, regard themselves to be three or four times richer than they would be if they valued their gold holdings at SDR 35 but knew that they could sell freely at that price?

A few years ago there was a rash of academic papers showing that the national demand for reserves could be derived from models in which the need to use reserves is described by stochastic disturbances affecting external payments and in which the cost of foregoing their use is described by the reductions of real income associated with devaluations or deflations required to stabilize external payments. Under present circumstances, one would have to add another stochastic dimension. The expected value of a country's reserves is itself uncertain. The problem of determining, even in theory, the optimal quantity of reserves has become, *inter alia*, an exercise in portfolio theory.[6]

[6] To use this term is to raise another problem. Because the prices of individual reserve assets can vary in terms of any *numeraire*, holders have incentives to diversify. To diversify reserves, however, a country must swap one reserve asset for another in the foreign-exchange markets, and in so doing, it can contribute to the variability of exchange rates, with the incidental effect of reducing further the liquidity of all reserve assets by increasing uncertainty about the prices at which one asset can be converted into others.

One thing is reasonably clear. The growth of international reserves, measured at prices used by the IMF, has slowed down dramatically. In 1970–72, the years of large U.S. deficits, gross reserves rose by SDR 67.8 billion (by 86 percent of reserves outstanding at the end of 1969). In 1973–75 they grew by another SDR 48.2 billion (by 33 percent of reserves outstanding at the end of 1972), but most of the increase accrued to oil-exporting countries. The reserves of all other countries rose by only SDR 8.9 billion (6.5 percent). It can be argued that these numbers are misleading because the appropriate gold price is higher than SDR 35 per ounce, the one used by the IMF, but this argument cuts two ways. Were gold valued at market-related prices after 1968 (the year in which the two-tiered gold market was abandoned), total reserves would be much larger; using SDR 100 per ounce, for example, global reserves would have been SDR 274 billion at June 30, 1976, rather than SDR 208 billion. The same procedure, however, would underscore the fact that reserves are rising slowly at present. The market price of gold has been falling, reducing the market-related value of gold reserves.

There is, of course, another answer to my numbers. The increase of reserves in 1970–72 was much too large; slower growth is needed to offset it. But the inflation caused by the policies that gave rise to the earlier increase of reserves has by now revenged itself upon the real value of reserves. Using the familiar ratio of reserves to imports, the crudest but simplest available yardstick, the story of slow growth in nominal reserves turns into a tale of rapid decline, to levels below those prevailing before the "explosion" of reserves. Citing once again figures published by the IMF, the ratio of reserves to imports was 30 percent for all countries together in 1969 (and for industrial countries as well). It rose to 33 percent in 1972 (and to 37 percent for industrial countries). But by 1975, it had fallen to 28 percent (and to 22 percent for industrial countries).

In its own judicious assessment of trends in reserves, the IMF in its 1976 *Annual Report* gives reasons for distrusting these familiar calculations. It points out, for instance, that the balance between financing and adjustment has shifted, "so that aggregate payments imbalances are likely to be smaller relative to the volume of international transactions than they would have been if, with the magnitude of balance of payments disturbances given, the world economy were still functioning under the Bretton Woods par value system." Nevertheless, it proceeds to remind us that the majority of countries continue to peg their currencies. The pegs are altered more frequently than in the days when devaluation was regarded as a confession of failure, and some countries have adopted gliding parities or methods of pegging exchange rates (as to the SDR) that allow for gradual changes in exchange rates. At the same time, countries with floating rates intervene extensively in currency markets to smooth out day-to-day fluctuations and to attenuate longer-term trends. There is by now evidence that countries with floating rates make less use of reserves than other countries, but the difference in usage is a matter of degree, not a textbook difference in kind.[7]

When this point is made, another emerges. The reserves of countries with pegged rates are not on average higher than those of countries with floating rates. I summarize some evidence in Table 8.1 (albeit diffidently, because it is so hard to classify the exchange arrangements of various countries). In 1975 the unweighted average ratios of reserves to imports was just under 24 percent for the thirty-six large countries represented in that table. But the ratios for the countries with floating rates were slightly higher than those for the countries with pegged rates. The ratios for the former, excluding the United States, the United Kingdom, and Italy, averaged about 26 percent.[8] Those for the members of the European "snake" averaged only 21 percent, and only 17 percent without Germany.[9] And those for the countries that peg to the dollar, to other currencies, and to the SDR averaged under 25 percent, a shade below the average for the floating-rate countries. There is, in brief, no reason to believe that the countries which have chosen to peg their exchange rates are the ones well endowed with reserves to do so.

[7] See Esther Suss. "A Note on Reserve Use Under Alternative Exchange Rate Regimes," *IMF Staff Papers* (July 1976), 23:387–94.

[8] I remove these three countries because the United States has never used reserves in the same way as other countries, the dollar being the intervention currency, while the United Kingdom and Italy were obliged to float separately from their partners in the EEC *because* they were short of reserves.

[9] If Germany is transferred to the floating-rate group, because for practical purposes the "snake" is a group of countries that peg to the mark while the mark floats freely *vis-à-vis* the dollar, the unweighted average for the floating-rate group rises to 26.5 percent.

219

Table 8.1
Ratios of Reserves to Imports, Large Trading Countries, 1975
(percent)

Country Group	Weighted[a]	Unweighted[b]
All Large Trading Countries[c]	21.9	23.6
Except United States	23.0	23.8
Floating Exchange Rates[d]	19.1	23.7
Except United States	20.3	24.1
Except US, UK, Italy	23.8	25.7
European Snake[e]	27.9	21.4
Except Germany	18.3	17.5
Other Pegged Exchange Rates[f]	23.7	24.6

SOURCES: Data from International Monetary Fund, *International Financial Statistics*, September 1976. Reserves are year-end figures; imports are annual figures (cf.). Country classification from International Monetary Fund, *Annual Report 1976*, Table I.1.

[a] Reserves for country group divided by imports for country group.

[b] Average of ratios of members of group.

[c] All countries reporting exchange arrangements to the IMF and having imports larger than $3 billion in 1975. For individual countries, see notes below.

[d] Australia, Austria, Canada, Finland, France, Greece, India, Italy, Japan, Malaysia, Morocco, New Zealand, Philippines, Portugal, Singapore, Spain, Turkey, United Kingdom, United States, Yugoslavia.

[e] Belgium, Denmark, Germany, Netherlands, Norway, Sweden.

[f] Argentina, Brazil, China (Taiwan), Egypt, Ireland, Israel, Korea, Mexico, South Africa, Thailand.

Much of this paper has been concerned with the problem of limiting reserve creation. It has in this sense echoed preoccupations generated by the "explosion" of currency holdings in 1970–72. The figures I have cited, however, together with the variability of exchange rates and the gold price, lead me to believe that there may now be the serious danger of a shortage in usable reserves and to ask what should be done about it.

It is no answer to say that IMF quotas have just been enlarged. The Sixth General Review of quotas was an exercise in bloc politics, in its intent and in its effect. Its chief results were to increase the quotas of the oil-exporting countries, to preserve in the face of that increase the voting hegemony of other countries, and to compensate for the termination of the Oil Facility (an aim that was not achieved in full, since the once-and-for-all increase in the quotas of the oil-importing developing countries was much smaller than their two-year use of the Oil Facility).

220

Where there is a will to increase reserves there is, of course, a way. It is necessary only to resume the distribution of SDRs. This process should begin quite soon, if only to honor the pledge enshrined in the IMF Articles to move the SDR to the front and center of the international monetary system. It would be wrong, however, to create new reserves in an effort to offset declines in the liquidity of other reserve assets, especially to offset declines in the liquidity of gold holdings.

Perceptions concerning the usability of gold holdings can change abruptly, and attempts to compensate for shifts in perceptions by increasing or decreasing the stock of SDRs would be cumbersome, to say the least, and grossly unfair in their consequences for the distribution of reserves. It would be more sensible to shore up the liquidity of gold reserves, even at the expense of acknowledging what the Second Amendment denies—the continuing role of gold in the monetary system.

I had hoped that the Second Amendment would move to centralize gold holdings in the IMF, and not to disperse the IMF's own holdings. I wish, even now, that it were possible to revive the proposal for a gold-substitution account. It is, I fear, too late for that. There nevertheless remain several ways to underwrite the liquidity of gold holdings or, less ambitiously, to prevent large variations in their usability that could influence the policies of major governments—policies concerning their exchange rates and domestic economies and policies concerning IMF activities, including the creation of SDRs. These would no doubt require a third amendment, but let us not pretend that the second is the last.

The IMF, for example, could shift to the other side of the gold market, becoming a buyer rather than a seller. It could hold periodic auctions to sell new SDRs to the highest bidders, with the bids expressed and payable in gold. The gold acquired in this fashion could be held by the IMF indefinitely or sold at subsequent auctions for the benefit of the trust fund that is the recipient of profits from the current auctions. (I would prefer that the IMF retain the gold, consonant with my view that gold should be demonetized by centralization, not decentralization, but this is not essential to the purpose at hand.)

This first proposal, however, has disadvantages. It might work in the long run to gather gold into the IMF, but would lead to lumpy substitutions of SDRs for gold, could increase the volatility of the gold price, and

221

would do nothing between auctions to maintain the liquidity of national gold holdings. A second plan makes more sense. The IMF might be authorized to lend new SDRs against gold, at an SDR gold price based on (but well below) a moving average of free-market prices. Decisions concerning a country's right to borrow against its gold holdings could be vested in the IMF or based on the sizes of countries' gold holdings at some base date, their quotas in the IMF, or a combination of the two.

It would be neater to remove completely the risk of instability in reserves and, more importantly, in national policies resulting from the complicated composition of reserves. But my proposal may be a partial solution. I offer it here to provoke discussion—to emphasize my concern about the disparity between the roles of gold *de jure* and *de facto*—and to be told what may be wrong with it.

COMMENTS

MARINA v. N. WHITMAN

UNIVERSITY OF PITTSBURGH, PITTSBURGH, PA.

IN COMMENTING, I am faced with a choice that has become obvious by now, namely, whether to discuss the subject in the title of this session or the two papers I was assigned. Because both authors, and in fact three of the four authors who have spoken today, spent the bulk of their time analyzing why the control of reserves is a nonproblem, rather than concentrating on the question of control techniques. There is, in fact, a certain symmetry in this conference. Yesterday afternoon and today, we learned from Professor Kenen that exchange-rate management does not require reserve control. Today it seems to me we've also been told, implicitly if not explicitly, that exchange-rate flexibility provides, to some extent, automatic reserve control. In other words, we're back to the fact that when you don't try to control the price of international money you may be able to control the quantity. Of course, in the world of managed floating, we are in fact controlling some of each. And that control is of a rather different form than we've traditionally been wont to think about when we consider the control of reserves. I'll come back to that in just a moment.

Let me first dwell for a moment on the question of what we mean by control, or control for what? The aspect that has been most emphasized today is control of reserves as a mechanism to force adjustment; that is, the interelationship between exchange-rate rules and reserve rules. The authors have made the point that direct control of reserves is neither a necessary nor a sufficient condition to force adjustment. And it has also been made abundantly clear why this is a less important problem now than it was under the Bretton Woods system.

The second aspect of control has to do with the relationship of world reserves to global inflation or deflation. In that sense, "control" implies the avoidance of either excess or inadequacy of aggregate reserves. This whole concept is, of course, based on what Professor Haberler referred to as the international quantity theory. I think he has already covered quite adequately the looseness of some of the linkages there, but nonetheless it does remain a matter of some concern. However, that concern must be tempered by the recognition that, although under the present system we have neither freely flexible rates, which would circumvent the problem of control by eliminating the need for reserves, or asset convertibility, which would give centralized control of reserves, we do have a much greater degree of what one might call consumer sovereignty than we did before. This is a point made by Kenen, although he doesn't use that phrase. That is, under the present system the initiative for the creation of reserves has very largely passed from the producer of reserves to the consumer. Thus, we have not centralized but decentralized control, in the sense that countries can use exchange-rate policy to equate their actual stocks of nominal reserves with their desired stocks. However, I must add that if one accepts the idea of a feedback from changes in the exchange rate to the domestic price level, then control over the nominal quantity of reserves does not mean control over the real quantity of reserves. I think that is an important distinction.

So, at least in terms of nominal stocks, the present exchange-rate regime is much more likely to generate the optimal level of reserves than was the Bretton Woods system, in the sense that the total is the sum of what each country wants. But it seems to me that there is some asymmetry here. That is, this decentralized control mechanism probably works more effectively in avoiding the creation of excess reserves than in ensuring the adequacy of total reserves. This is because some deficit countries encounter real difficulties in using depreciation to try to build up their reserve stocks. The most obvious case in point is the problems faced by developing countries that find themselves with very large oil deficits, in using depreciation to alleviate these deficits. These limitations become even more acute if we take into account the phenomenon of the "vicious" and "virtuous" circles, and particularly the vicious circle, specifically, the feedback from depreciation to domestic inflation. Finally, as both authors suggest, it appears that excess liquidity-creation was not a major problem in the Bretton Woods era, except for the brief "pathological" period of the early 1970s, which was a period of very rocky transition from one exchange-rate régime to another. As a means of control on the other side, to ensure reserve adequacy, we do have a centralized mechanism—the activation of SDRs. In principle, this takes care of the problem, although it seems to me there are some very real practical difficulties involved there.

The third aspect of control has to do with reserves as a means of smoothing resource transfers. And here excess is much less the problem than adequacy and, of course, the distribution of reserves. These issues pose a host of problems that perhaps should have been raised in the context of this session, but haven't been, and I won't get into them either, other than simply to note this important aspect of the issue. It was alluded to, of course, by Kenen in his discussion of reserve ratios in pegging versus nonpegging countries.

Having asked "what do we mean by control?" the companion question is "what do we mean by reserves?" or, perhaps more precisely, "what do we mean by international liquidity?" One aspect of this question is simply an international version of the old Guley–Shaw problem. There is a continuum at the international level, paralleling the now-familiar one at the national level, from owned reserves to unconditional liquidity to conditional liquidity or borrowing rights. Today, there are more and more numerous and complicated alternatives in this continuum.

The second aspect of this question is a new problem referred to at some length by Kenen. That is the valuation problem created by the fact that, under the flexible rate system, we no longer have a single world money but instead a number of national monies, along with gold and SDRs, many of which bear no fixed value relationship to one another. So it really isn't possible to tally them to obtain something called "world reserves." What this means is that there is now a new stochastic variable in-

225

volved in any attempt to estimate the optimal reserve level, and that is the value of the reserves themselves. What is it that we should control, reserve *volume* creation or total reserve *value?* This measurement problem is complicated even further by another point, made earlier here, having to do with the extent to which the liquidity of various international assets has been impaired by recent developments. This is what Bob Mundell would call the loss of "efficiency of world money" enjoyed under a fixed-rate system. It has produced the desire for diversification of reserve assets that has become a source of reserve creation in recent years. It probably also underlies the fact that the apparent reduction in desired reserves has been on the whole rather less than might have been anticipated from a move to managed flexibility.

Very quickly, let me note a few subsidiary points relating to specific policy issues. First of all, with respect to gold demonetization, I share some of Kenen's concern, although I think I am agnostic where he is atheistic about *de facto* demonetization. For one thing, it seems to me that price variability *is* an aspect of demonetization; if gold is going to be a commodity like any other, then presumably its price should vary with supply and demand. Furthermore, if we do as Kenen suggests, and try to demonetize gold through a gold-substitution account, what happens to that gold once it gets into the IMF, and how does it affect IMF behavior? That is, are we back to some new version of the gold-exchange standard with the IMF at the center rather than the United States, or what? How does gold ultimately get demonetized if we do that?

A second point has to do with what Kenen refers to, and what a number of us have referred to in the past, as the "nth country" problem. He is quite right in assuming that problem to still be with us, and I think it is going to remain with us. There are, of course, several "pure types" of organizing principle on which a monetary system can be based. One can have an automatic system, a hegemonial system, a supranational system that is run by some supranational authority, or even a negotiated system, although pure negotiation is an awkward way to run anything. But any actual system I've ever heard of is some combination of these. Today we have somewhat more automaticity than we did before, but it is by no means complete. We have, I think, somewhat more supranationality than we did before, in the form of collective adherence to the judgments of the IMF. It's a little early to be sure of that, though nearly everyone has indicated that that is what is desired. And we have somewhat less U.S. hegemony than we had before, I believe, although whether we are today on more or less of a dollar standard than during the Bretton Woods era is not quite clear, either.

In any case, it seems to me that in this world of what Kenen calls "codified anarchy" there is ample room for inconsistency in national targets, and so there probably is still a need for some member of the system to be more flexible about its own targets than others are, in order to try to mitigate this inconsistency problem. And it appears that, for a number of reasons, the United States is still the logical candidate to play that "nth country" role, though not by any means in an unlimited fashion. I think it's obvious that we couldn't tolerate an unlimited nth country role, in the sense of total passivity in terms of our own payments and exchange-rate positions. The extent to which we play that role will doubtless have to be arrived at through negotiation; more specifically, it will be implicit in the negotiations regarding the guidelines for intervention. We're back again to the subject matter of yesterday and we can't seem to get away from it.

Before we leave this question, let me note a related technical point; without asset settlement (and I think it is obvious, for several reasons already mentioned, that we're not going to have asset settlement in the near future), it makes a difference, as Bob Solomon points out, to the creation of reserves whether there is floor intervention or ceiling intervention. Therefore, as the work on intervention guidelines progresses, we may need some guidelines with respect to that question as well.

My final points have to do with the idea of reserve management via ratios or proportional holding limits rather than via direct control over the absolute size of reserves. This is an interesting idea and an attractive one in that it would enable the IMF to exercise control through an instrument it already has, that is, through the creation of SDRs. It is also, as was pointed out by one of the authors, rather draconian, unless it is combined with a much more rapid evolution than seems likely of SDRs toward being a real world money and of the IMF toward being a world central bank or bank of last resort.

Furthermore, I must say the history at the national level of this kind of

227

control is not terribly encouraging. At least in the United States, if one looks at what happened to the fractional reserve requirement, when we still had gold backing for the money supply, to see how things were resolved when a conflict arose between those requirements and what the authorities wanted to do in terms of the money supply, it turns out that the requirements gave way every time. And this was true even in the context of a fully developed set of alternatives and a genuine national government, as contrasted with the international situation, in which no genuine world government exists. So I think history suggests a certain skepticism as to how effectively such a control scheme could be expected to operate.

Finally, if one believes that reserve adequacy is as much a matter of potential concern as excess liquidity, the implication is that any such holding requirements should really be symmetrical; they should have ceilings as well as floors. Of course, creating that kind of symmetrical requirement would make for an even tighter system, probably even harder to implement, and one for which, as far as I know, there are really no precedents. But I find, a bit to my own surprise, that as I finished reading these two papers, the symmetrical view is where things seem to come out. Both authors appear to agree, with varying degrees of explicitness, that in regard to reserve control or reserve management, the problem may be more one of ensuring adequacy than of avoiding excess. We seem, after a long detour, to have come back close to where we started with Bob Triffin nearly twenty years ago.

JOHN WILLIAMSON

UNIVERSITY OF WARWICK, COVENTRY, ENGLAND

THE STANDARD VIEW on the subject under discussion today, which evolved in the period up to 1972 in large measure under the intellectual leadership of J. Marcus Fleming, could be summarized in the following two propositions: (a) that asset settlement is a necessary but not sufficient condition for establishing control of the supply of reserves and (b) that control of the supply of reserves is a necessary but not a sufficient condition for stable growth of the world economy. I discussed proposition (b) this morning, and indicated that in my judgment the force of this proposition had been substantially weakened by the move to generalized floating, but that an element of truth nonetheless remained. I propose to confine my comments this afternoon to proposition (a).

The papers of Solomon and Kenen do not, in my view, do anything to undermine proposition (a); indeed, they substantiate it. In the first place, both authors have taken the opportunity in their papers to examine the suggestion advanced by the IMF managing director that control of reserve supply might be established without asset settlement through the mechanism of a fractional SDR reserve requirement. Both conclude that the practical effect of this proposal would be to force countries close to their minimum required reserve ratio to stop accumulating further reserves. (This would be equivalent to introducing a reserve-indicator system with an additional element of arbitrariness arising from accidents of reserve composition.) The object of the proposal is presumably to introduce a deflationary constraint on policy when reserves are threatening to become excessive; yet a prohibition on further reserve accumulation would lead to an upward float of the currency involved, and while this would be deflationary for the country in question, it would simply lead to exportation of inflationary pressures to the rest of the world. In a floating world there is no presumption that limiting reserve accumulation would also serve to limit domestic credit expansion, which is what is required if the proposal is to achieve its intended effect. Hence I find myself in agreement with the preceding three speakers that a fractional SDR reserve requirement does not provide a potential alternative way of achieving the ultimate objectives for which asset settlement has been proposed.

In the second place, it remains true that even if control over the liabilities of reserve centers were achieved via asset settlement, this would not suffice to establish control of the volume of reserves, for two reasons. The first is the gap created by the practice of depositing reserves in the Euro-markets. The second is the status of gold. This problem is brushed

229

aside by Solomon but given considerable weight by Kenen. My own view is that Kenen is right to regard this as a serious potential problem, although I must say I found strange both his concern at the potential illiquidity of gold and his assertion that "gold will *continue to be* a reserve asset for some time to come." Reserve assets are invariably defined as liquid assets immediately available to finance payments deficits; the most basic characteristic of a liquid asset is not that it be realizable at a fixed price (though that is also important), but that it can always be realized immediately. Gold has conspicuously lacked this characteristic since August 1971, since major holders have been unable to realize their holdings quickly without severely depressing the price against themselves, which they were naturally reluctant to do. The only major official use of gold required months of difficult negotiations before Italy finally got a gold-collateral loan. However, this state of affairs may change when the Second Amendment comes into force, since central banks will then be permitted to buy gold at any price. This may mean that gold will once again become a reserve asset: that will depend on whether a willing central bank buyer at the market price can always in practice be found when a country wishes to sell. If it turns out that countries cannot rely on this, then the gold problem can be finally dismissed by the simple expedient of deleting gold from the reserve pages of *International Financial Statistics*. In the converse case, however, one will have to worry very much about the variations in international liquidity produced by movements in the gold price, especially since these are likely to be strongly destabilizing. A period of inflation requiring monetary restraint is just the time when a run into gold is most likely to occur and cause growth in the value of reserves. Unfortunately, neither of the suggestions at the end of Kenen's paper starts to meet this potential problem: his first proposal is not financially viable as long as the SDR carries a rate of interest, while under the circumstances where gold remains a problem, there is no incentive for countries to trade in their gold. More fundamentally, both are addressed to the wrong problem—the maintenance of the liquidity of gold rather than its limitation.

It remains to consider some of the propositions about the possibility of controlling currency reserves that have been advanced. I would first re-

230

mark that I see little point in schemes designed to control reserves as conventionally measured without also bringing the possibility of liability financing under similar control. Indeed, I would suggest, in contrast to both Solomon and Kenen, that the explosion of effective liquidity occurred in the mid- and late 1960s, when the dollar standard was becoming established, and that the period 1970–72 can be better viewed as a period when liquidity was redistributed rather than created. In other words, asset settlement remains the key concept. Kenen argues that asset settlement is precluded by the Second Amendment. I do not venture a judgment on that essentially legal issue, but where he is unquestionably right is in arguing that one cannot have asset settlement without some form of internationally accepted obligation regarding exchange rates, since one cannot expect one country to accept an obligation to convert balances of its currency acquired in intervention to which it has not consented. I have elsewhere argued[1] that a system of agreed reference rates or target zones would provide sufficient leverage for acceptance of asset settlement obligations, so that one would not necessarily have to abandon floating in order to secure asset settlement. However, the Solomon and Kenen papers seem to imply that there may be another, and possibly more promising, route to achieve adequate control of reserves, which essentially works from the demand rather than the supply side. This is the suggestion that net reserves, relative to a norm, and/or changes in net reserves, should be a determinant of adjustment obligations as under a reserve-indicator system. They might, for example, be important determinants of reference rates. This possibility seems to me worth pursuing.

Finally, I associate myself with the thought advanced this morning by Lamfalussy and others that controlling international reserves is probably not the most urgent aspect of controlling international liquidity under present circumstances. International borrowing surely does require regulation—but with a view to stabilizing rather than necessarily curtailing international borrowing, which is fulfilling a very important welfare function.

[1] See John Williamson, "The Future Exchange Rate Regime," *Banca Nazionale del Lavoro Quarterly Review* (June 1975).

DISCUSSION

THE DIFFERENCE of view between the two papers on the question of global reserve adequacy stimulated a lively discussion among the partipants. Salant noted that Kenen's paper had raised the possibility that the danger in the new system might lie in inadequate rather than excessive growth in reserves. On the other hand, Solomon's paper, though recognizing this possibility, had argued that it could be neglected, since too slow a rate of reserve growth could easily be dealt with by decisions to create additional SDRs. Salant observed that under the present arrangements the decision to allocate SDRs requires an 85 percent vote of the members. Assuming that the countries with the largest voting power are more or less satisfied that their reserves are adequate, he wondered whether it would be as easy to get new SDR allocations as Solomon supposed. What arguments, aside from their own self-interest, could countries holding low reserve stocks make in order to get approval for such allocations? Solomon acknowledged the link between global reserve adequacy and the distribution of reserves, but felt that if the aggregate reserve stock grew too slowly, even the countries that were satisfied with their own holdings would begin to feel the effects of reserve stringency elsewhere in the world, as reflected in increased import controls, deflation, or depreciation by countries with inadequate reserves. If these effects became strong enough, even the countries whose reserves were adequate from their own point of view might still approve an SDR allocation out of self-interest rather than altruism. On the other hand, it was argued by Salant and Polak that the countries experiencing a reserve shortage might be too small to have much impact on others, but still be a source of concern to the IMF. When the first SDR allocation was made in 1970 there was a worldwide

232

feeling—possibly due to temporary factors—that an addition to the global reserve stock would directly benefit virtually all member countries. At present, however, it might be possible for, say, one-third of the IMF members to have a considerable shortage of reserves without another third feeling the effects of this shortage. Under these circumstances, certain countries would have to look beyond their own interests to those of the world as a whole in order to see the need for an SDR allocation.

De Vries felt that if there is both agreement on the desirability of control over liquidity and the political will to do so, then techniques can easily be found to implement such control. Specifically, he disagreed with Kenen's paper on one point. Kenen had argued about the "non-necessity" of control, but had also stated that if the reserve stock had been controlled, the United States might have devalued earlier. De Vries felt that this would have made a most important difference in the financial developments of the last few years and was a very important, if not unqualified, argument in favor of controlling the level of liquidity.

Referring to Kenen's observation that intervention in the foreign-exchange market is not very different from intervention in the domestic bond market, De Vries also wondered why the U.S. Treasury continued both to argue that exchange rates should be left to market forces and to operate an active monetary policy that affected the rate, at least indirectly.

Wallich acknowledged that the United States is very comfortable under the existing system, since it is no longer burdened by the convertibility obligations that existed previously. Furthermore, although the benefits to the United States from the dollar's reserve-currency role were never very important, some of these benefits still exist in an attenuated form. The current system also has advantages for other countries since, with flexible exchange rates, they are not compelled to finance the U.S. payments deficit. In view of these mutual benefits, he felt that it is important for the United States to assist in the establishment and maintenance of this system and emphasized that any attempt to implement target zones would revive control of the dollar rate by others. In contrast to Kenen's statement that the United States was "obsessed by" this issue, he felt that the concern was legitimate because the extra degree of freedom is one of

233

the important gains from the new system. He did not reject the suggestion of Kenen, Whitman, and others that the same objective could at least possibly be achieved by good and effective target setting, but felt that it would deprive the United States of its recently acquired elbow room. In any case, Wallich did not think that the U.S. could be accused of wanting deliberately to choose its own rate. Indeed, he noted that there is no way of intervening on a sufficient scale to affect the dollar rate very much because the stock of dollar-denominated assets around the world amounts to something like $5 trillion. Interventions of a few hundred million at a time, which the United States never does, would not have much effect on this stock and would hence be unlikely to have much of an impact on the exchange value of the dollar for any length of time. Obviously, there must be an nth country that is not free to determine its exchange rate, but not every country needs to be actively trying to influence its rate. If enough countries float freely, then the problem for the United States in being the nth country will largely disappear.

Kenen generally agreed with Wallich. In his view, the basic issue is that the nth country problem is still present, whether it is in the asymmetries introduced by asset settlement in a floating world or in the problem of setting reference rates for the nth country. The course of international monetary history for the next several years will be decided in large measure by the attitude of the United States, not only on the question of exchange-market intervention versus money-market intervention, but also on the degree of passivity that it can afford to assume in respect of international monetary problems and the prerogatives that it will feel entitled to claim in return for accepting that asymmetrical role.

Several participants, particularly de Vries and Kenen, expressed disappointment over what the Second Amendment will do to *gold*. Kenen elaborated on this section of his paper by observing that governments refuse to behave as though gold is no longer a reserve asset even though that is what the "rules of the game" now say. He felt, for example, that most observers would regard replacement of the gold in official reserves by SDRs as highly inflationary, even if this were done at $35 per ounce.

Several technical points in the papers also elicited comments. The par-

234

ticipants disagreed somewhat on the implications of recent theoretical work on exchange rates. Findlay drew attention to Kenen's argument that the newly developed "asset-market" theory of exchange-rate determination attributes fluctuations in exchange rates to disturbances in financial markets that are mainly caused by changes in international policy. He felt that this view reflects the style of presentation of the authors rather than its substance. This approach does not preclude such real factors as an earthquake or an oil-price increase from triggering a change in the exchange rate. The factors that stimulate exchange-rate changes do not have to occur in the financial markets in the first instance. Indeed, the most important shock to the international monetary system in the last few years has arisen from the current account side. Kenen, however, disagreed with this view, and maintained that even these real changes initially cause exchange-rate movements via their effect on demands and supplies in international asset markets.

Findlay also raised a question that he felt was lurking in the background throughout the seminar, namely, whether a flexible exchange rate can insulate one country from shocks arising in another. Haberler had said that a flexible exchange rate could insulate a country from monetary shocks but not from real shocks, while Whitman felt that, in some instances, flexible exchange rates can provide insulation even from real shocks. Findlay's personal view was that if the terms of trade, for example, turn adversely to a country, there is nothing the exchange-rate system can do. Although he essentially agreed with Haberler, he preferred to amend his statement by saying that not only real shocks, but also the real consequences of monetary shocks cannot be avoided simply by floating the exchange rate.

Claassen contrasted the statement in Solomon's paper about the possible excessive growth of nominal reserves with the decreasing ratios of reserves to imports noted in Kenen's paper. These two statements, he said, reflected the fact that excessive growth in nominal reserves may be accompanied by a slow growth of reserves measured in real terms.

Finally, Cooper wondered why Kenen favored market exchange rates to guide intervention rules when at the same time he deemed it undesir-

235

able to link intervention to reserve levels or movements in reserves. Cooper felt that linking exchange-rate intervention to the level of the rates themselves is a circular process. At best, market rates simply indicate the direction in which the target zones can be altered. Even then, however, it seemed to him undesirable to divorce such intervention from reserve movements.

CONCLUDING REMARKS

ROBERT A. MUNDELL

COLUMBIA UNIVERSITY, NEW YORK, N.Y.

IT IS NOT EASY to design a smoothly functioning international monetary system by the collective wisdom of a committee. It seems to be a haphazard mixture of laissez-faire, government controls, fixed exchange rates, flexible rates systems, currency groups, and power relations. Yet the function of theory is to find order in chaos, and this has been one of the purposes of this conference. The discussions have brought to light complexities and even confusions. This is in spite of the wisdom and experience of the participants, all of whom are familiar with the problems. Different branches of the subject at this conference have been parceled out along division-of-labor principles. But most economists here have ideas on the system as a whole, and their contributions to each particular topic should ideally be set in the framework of their own individual conception of the entire system. While there may be 29 opinions around the table on each particular question, the convergence of views would be more evident if each participant had been able to state how he thinks the system would evolve over the next ten years. When a paper focuses on a single problem, it is not possible to know the penumbra of ideas in the background of the author's argument. It is for this reason that the U.S. Treasury advanced a proposal for a floating exchange rate system in 1971–73, with the hope that countries would accept or reject it in its entirety, rather than piecemeal.

International monetary reform requires a coherent view of the entire system in its actual historical setting and its political and social framework. Because there is no room for mistakes, wise men have usually recognized human limitations and built reform on the foundations of the past, allowing the system to evolve gradually by itself, at best nudging it only slightly against the swell of the tide. In that sense, reform has, and perhaps must have, a conservative bent. All our legal entrappings of new international monetary orders have been firmly based on the foundations of underlying economic forces and political realities, from the bimetalism of the Middle Ages to the gold standard of the late nineteenth century, the credit mechanisms which developed under gold and the pound sterling and then, after 1915, to a dollar used along with sterling as a worldwide unit of account. What became known as the Bretton Woods Order was an accommodation to the overwhelming significance in the twentieth century of the phenomenal rise of the U.S. as a supereconomy replacing the nineteenth-century role of the British Empire. The emergence of the dollar as the major currency in the monetary sphere, replacing the pound sterling and even gold from the system results from the rise of the United States as a hegemonic power. It was this very rise, reaching an apogee in the 1960s, that created countervailing checks and balances and resistances to further growth in the use of the dollar. The struggle to impose gold convertibility on the United States was increasingly seen as a struggle for power in the political system, fought out in the monetary domain. The collapse of the Bretton Woods Order in 1971 did not, however, fundamentally alter the secular power relationship; it merely stripped the reality of the dross that made it policially acceptable. We felt impoversihed by it because it deprived us of a comfortable hypocrisy. Even the move toward a managed floating rate system has forced us to find ways in which intervention should take place in order to make the new system less different than the old one. The problem is not so much to make exchange rates change to devise new equilibria as it is to make monetary policies consistent with price level and therefore exchange rate objectives. There is still a vast dollar area that commands the central tendency of the world economy and the rates of inflation in that area call the tune of world prices after allowance for exchange rate changes.

238

It is for that reason that U.S. monetary policy is so influential in the world economy, and its regulation, no longer checked by the gold convertibility discipline, is the single most important policy variable in the arsenal of global stabilization weapons. The monetary policies of other countries, of course, affect their respective national price levels, and differential rates of change in inflation rates imply exchange-rate depreciation rates. Under the old system, the fixed rate objectives gave the world a monetary unity, in effect the framework of a single international money based on a gold-convertible dollar, tying the monetary world together into a single global unit. In that system, world liquidity was ultimately controlled by the gold base supplemented by the use of the reserve currencies which were, at least in principle, convertible into gold. Gold convertibility represented the theoretical means by which the control of the monetary policy of the reserve currency center was shared by other countries. With the 1971 collapse that lever was given up and multilateralism broke down into balkanization in Europe and major bilateralism around the dollar, with an outside minor center about the mark.

I find the controversy surrounding "global monetarism" slightly astonishing. The IMF itself gave impetus to this approach in the late 1950s by its use of the reserves/imports ratio as an (albeit imperfect) test of reserve adequacy. The quantity theory of money does not work for an open national economy on fixed exchange rates; it is only valid within the currency area concept, and if the currency area is most of the world economy, then we should all be "global monetarists." The exchange rate determines the price level; and the balance of payments, along with credit creation, determines money creation, which has to be compatible with the public's demand for new money. Credit creation (new bank loans) are thus controlled by the need to protect the stock of reserves. Monetary policy is therefore passive for a single country under fixed rates and the domestic money supply is "endogenous." The *only* plane at which the quantity theory holds is the global (or currency bloc) level, where the quantity of gold plus other reserves in the system provides the high-powered base of the total world supply of money. With fixed exchange rates, the world price level could be defined in a common monetary denominator and a meaning could be given to "the" value of money, deter-

239

mined by demand and supply like all other values. Under the gold standard, gold was distributed around the world according to Ricardo's Theorem on the Distribution of the Precious Metals. The modern counterpart of this is the theory of the international distribution of dollars or, more exactly, gold plus dollars plus other foreign exchange plus IMF money. Some version of this theory, perhaps with a more sophisticated view of the determinants of velocity, has always been a basis for international monetary theory at the global level, and the fact that the quantity theory was never applicable to the individual country under the gold standard or the Bretton Woods system should not lead us to dismiss its critical importance in determining equilibrium of the system as a whole.

It is easiest to see the full influence of monetary events from a long distance, since they unfold in time intervals spanning decades or even centuries. The sixteenth century case of the effect of silver imports in one of the sessions stressed the point that international price deflation in the 1930s was the aftermath of overexpansion of the system due to inflationary finance both during World War I and in the 1920s (through the gold exchange standard). This longer-run view is often scoffed at by those who are devoted only to short-run policy problems, but most economists probably accept the idea that global monetary factors played a role in these long price cycles in the world economy, and this acceptance is made easier by the fact that these events took place in the "distant" past. It is curious, however, to find strong resistance to the idea that in our current problems we are caught up in a long-run movement. But now let us look at recent history. It is clear that the twentieth century has been a period of vast expansion in money and gold. The period of the last eight decades is by far the greatest period of gold production in world history. The stock of gold has doubled every two decades since 1890! This phenomenal growth in international liquidity provided by gold slowed down in the 1950s, but was replaced by dollar expansion, which displaced gold production as the main source of liquidity growth in the 1960s. As a result, a vast imbalance developed between central bank-held dollars and gold evaluated at official prices, leading to the great price break in the 1970s when the price of gold more than quadrupled.

Control of reserves is important insofar as we want to control the rate of dollar inflation as well as inflation of other currencies in the world. If we do not accept this common-sense denominator of global monetarism, we would have to throw out all monetary theory and all purpose to monetary coordination plans. How, then, should international liquidity be managed? Reserves consist essentially of gold, dollars, and Fund-money. The traditional method of controlling dollars is through convertibility into "primary assets." This can be achieved by fixing the exchange ratio between dollars and some other primary reserve asset, such as gold or SDR's. But the United States has always felt uncomfortable with this approach; it is not willing to exchange dollars for gold. Nor is the United States likely to accept SDR convertibility if it leads to a constraint upon U.S. monetary policy. But the whole point of convertibility, of course, is to impose such a constraint. The underlying struggle is based on the *autonomy* of U.S. policy. If the United States insists on complete autonomy unfettered by international rules, it opts out of any international system in which its central bank does not have dictatorial powers. There is little point in talking about stabilizing the ratio of SDR's to total reserves in the system (if dollars are counted as part of total reserves) if the supply of dollars is autonomously determined by the United States, because SDR's would then have to adapt passively to preserve the SDR–Reserve Ratio. If the inflation rate is to be multilaterally determined, every country must accept some element of the convertibility discipline.

What about gold? There are two ways of controlling gold: one can either control the quantity or the price. There is, I am glad to say, a general reluctance to build up quantities of gold beyond the billion ounces now held by central banks. But if the price fluctuates, it is the value of gold that is relevant from the standpoint of international liquidity. Currently, there is an agreement among countries not to fix the price of gold in national currencies; fixing gold in all currencies would reinstate the gold standard. But the gold problem will not go away. A problem will arise if a world boom occurs. Then the price of gold may rise enough to inflate gold reserves, and the increased effective liquidity will exaggerate the boom. Similarly a downward movement, a stalling of the recovery, would create a fall in reserves and exaggerate the recession. Flexible gold prices thus operate to destabilize the world system. This contrasts sharply

241

with the former system in which, when commodity prices move pro-cyclically, real liquidity balances are generated during recessions and constrained during inflations. There already exists an effective quantity stabilization of gold. The only way to stabilize gold is to stabilize its price. Until that is done international reserves will be unstable, and it would be the epitome of hypocrisy to pretend that effective stabilization arrangements had been achieved.

There remains for consideration control of the liquidity created by the IMF in the form of SDR allocations. In the past, however, these allocations have been made on a "stop-go" basis, with the initial creation of a significant amount of SDR's, followed by several years without allocations. This way of augmenting reserves is not conducive to stability, and presents a highly complicated problem. Fluctuations in dollars and gold values swamp SDR allocations. But in the long run a steady policy of increasing SDR liquidity by a few billions each year would establish that asset as a permanent and usable component of the global reserve portfolio. I hope the Fund will investigate ways in which that policy could be implemented and that the present confusion over the nature of the SDR as a reserve asset could be eliminated.

Somehow the current world situation is not nearly as bad as my long catalogue of complaints would seem to suggest. One reason is that 1976 has been a good year, as election years usually are. There is a political cycle, but I am not sure it is altogether bad. If every country achieved full employment and stable prices every four years, we would at least have some insurance against violent swings. It might, however, be better to desynchronize elections in the major countries to avoid global conjuctures. Here the minimum role for international liquidity management is to make sure that international factors do not destabilize the world economy.

The goals of the new system should be full employment, price stability, moderate growth, freedom of international commerce and lending, and wiser global conservation policies, as mineral scarcities and prices increase secularly. Furthermore, in each country there should be a rational balance between available resources and total spending, subject to cushioning by reserve use for smoothing, and some reliance on short-term lending in the system. In groping toward a revised system, a basic pillar of the new framework will be continued stability of the economies of both the basic dollar area and the Snake-DM area. In this respect harmonization between the snake and the dollar area countries becomes extremely important. This harmonization requires relative interest rate differentials equal to expected exchange rate variations. During the past year and a half, stabilization of the mark/dollar rate has contributed to the fact that Germany and the United States have managed to maintain a reasonably good price performance. I would like to see that stability preserved. But if it proves impossible, a policy that agreed on goals for a stable rate of appreciation of one currency for the other would be enough to stabilize the *level* of the interest rate differential.

The goals of the new system will certainly be furthered if the Fund could become more actively involved in big country consultations and could take a larger part in the management of the international system at this level. At the same time, however, the Fund must continue to study the impact of the currency area decisions in the large countries on the small countries, since fluctuations in the exchange rates of major nations can play havoc with the economic policies of the developing world. Thus the Fund must also perform its role as the monetary spokesman for the collective interests of the small countries at the big power meetings.

The participants at this conference have been extremely "monetarist" in talking about flexible money supplies and fixed exchange rates, versus fixed money supplies and flexible exchange rates. But as Sir Roy Harrod emphasized in his intervention, it is important not to lose sight of that other goal of international policy—wage stability. The fundamental significance of wages is underlined by the fact that some people have gone so far as to argue that the world is on an "American wage" standard—that American wages are the crucial variable in the system and play a huge part in inflation control. The dollar price of U.S. labor and the dollar price of oil rank as the two principal determinants of long-run inflation in a world where money supplies are adaptable.

Finally, two words of caution. In the first place, we have to be careful nowadays in making clear what we mean by the term "balance of payments surplus." When a country exports raw materials, it is giving up its

243

reserves *below* ground, so to speak, for reserves *above* the ground. It would be foolhardy for mineral exporting countries to sell off their below-ground reserves merely to accumulate low interest-yielding assets; cheap mineral reserves are not going to last forever. Resource-exporting countries need to have foreign investments and to acquire current oil supplies at good prices. The importing countries have to offer in exchange stable international assets with a reasonable yield. When gold and dollars cease to be attractive new world assets—perhaps stable purchasing-power international bonds should come into being. This would provide a means for channeling redundant OPEC reserves into fruitful development finance. If this cannot be achieved by existing institutions, we shall have to create new ones.

A final and related point concerns the mutual recrimination between countries which are in different international payments situations. Surplus countries are always preaching that deficit countries should contract, while deficit countries constantly urge those in surplus to expand. Deficit sharing has to be managed. The "iron law" of international economics is that of interdependence: deficits exactly match surpluses. Adjustment is ipso facto a problem of interdependence, just as exchange rate management is. It is the supervision and management of this interdependence which gives the Fund its fundamental and unique role.

The IMF in 1944 was given a certain set of functions and responsibilities. It has grown mightily since then. But it is still too small to cope with increasing responsibilities. In the new setting of managed flexible exchange rates it will, sooner or later, have to embark on the new career of Supreme Monetary Authority.